PASÓ POR AQUÍ SERIES ON THE
NUEVOMEXICANO LITERARY HERITAGE

SANTA FE NATIVA

A Collection of Nuevomexicano Writing

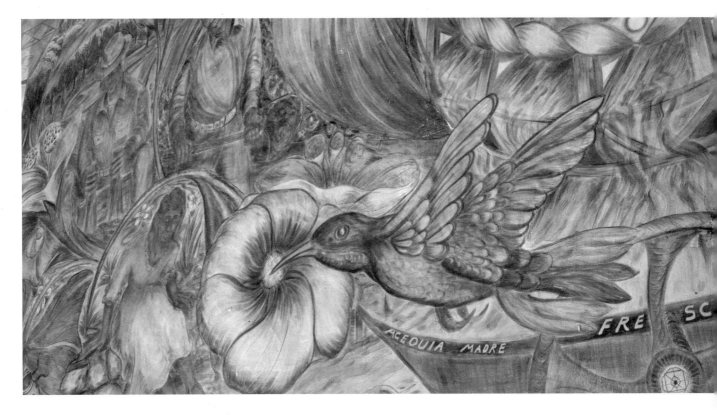

EDITED BY **Rosalie C. Otero**

A. Gabriel Meléndez AND

Enrique R. Lamadrid

PHOTOGRAPHS BY **Miguel A. Gandert**

UNIVERSITY OF NEW MEXICO PRESS • Albuquerque

15   14   13   12   11   10   09   1   2   3   4   5   6   7

Library of Congress Cataloging-in-Publication Data

Santa Fe nativa : a collection of Nuevomexicano writing / edited by
Rosalie C. Otero, A. Gabriel Meléndez, and Enrique R. Lamadrid ;
photographs by Miguel A. Gandert.
    p. cm. — (Pasó por aquí series on the Nuevomexicano
    literary heritage)
Some texts in Spanish, with English translations.

ISBN 978-0-8263-4818-0 (cloth : alk. paper)

  1. Santa Fe (N.M.)—Literary collections.
  2. American literature—New Mexico—Santa Fe.
  3. American literature—Mexican American authors.
  4. Hispanic American literature (Spanish)—New Mexico
    Translations into English.
  I. Otero, Rosalie C.
  II. Meléndez, A. Gabriel (Anthony Gabriel)
III. Lamadrid, Enrique R.

PS571.N6S36 2009
810.8'0978956—dc22

2009039087

THE UNIVERSITY OF NEW MEXICO PRESS

GRATEFULLY ACKNOWLEDGES THE GENEROUS

CONTRIBUTION OF ACADEMIA/EL NORTE

TOWARD THE PUBLICATION OF THIS BOOK.

Contents

Foreword   xi

Preface   xv

Acknowledgments   xxi

Introduction   xxiii

PART I

Homenajes: Praise for Our Villa

Villa de Santa Fe (1630)
Fray Alonso de Benavides   3

Villa of Santa Fe
Translation by Enrique R. Lamadrid   4

A Santa Fe (1924)
Felipe Maximiliano Chacón   4

To Santa Fe
Translation by A. Gabriel Meléndez   5

Ode to Santa Fe (2006)
Pat Mora   7

PART II

Querencia: The Root of Belonging

And They Called It Horizon (2009)
Valerie Martínez   11

¿Dónde Vivo Yo? (2006)
Tommy Archuleta   13

Where Do I Live?
Translation by A. Gabriel Meléndez   14

Santa Fe—Coplas Para El Tiempo Santo (1976)
Fr. Benedicto Cuesta   14

Santa Fe—Verses for the Lenten Season
Translation by Rosalie C. Otero   15

Bells (1989)
Jimmy Santiago Baca   16

PART III

Historias: Subjects of Two Empires

Leyendas Neo-Mexicanas: Popé (1896)
Episodios de la revolución de los indios en 1680
José Escobar   19

New Mexican Legends: Popé
Episodes from the Pueblo Revolt of 1680
Translation by A. Gabriel Meléndez   20

Once A Man Knew His Name (1987)
E. A. Mares   34

When Cultures Meet (1987)
Orlando Romero   37

La Invasión Americana (c. 1874)
Rafael Chacón   38

The American Invasion
Translation by Enrique R. Lamadrid   39

Doña Tules, Her Fame and Her Funeral (1950)
Fray Angélico Chávez   40

Tras la tormenta, la calma (1892)
Eusebio Chacón   45

The Calm after the Storm
Translation by A. Gabriel Meléndez   56

PART IV

Nuestra Cornucopia: Place, Water, Food

Oración al Río Grande/Prayer
to the Rio Grande (2009)
A. Gabriel Meléndez 69

El Río de Tesuque (1884)
Anónimo 70

Down by the Tesuque River
Synopsis by A. Gabriel Meléndez 70

Sum-Sum Summertime (2007)
Marie Romero Cash 70

Los duraznos de mi casa (1979)
Robert Lara Vialpando 72

Peaches at My Home
Synopsis by A. Gabriel Meléndez 73

Nuestra Cornucopia (2008)
Alfredo Celedón Luján 73

PART V

Los Barrios: Home Spaces

Barrio de Analco (1995)
Francisco X. Alarcón 79

The Neighborhood of Analco
Francisco X. Alarcón 80

De la capital (1892)
Bonafé 81

From the Capital
Translation by A. Gabriel Meléndez 83

Los Caminos del Barrio (1999)
J. Chris Abeyta 85

The Roads of the Neighborhood
Translation by Rosalie C. Otero 85

Corrido de la Prisión de Santa Fe (1980)
*Alberto "Al Hurricane," Amador "Tiny Morrie,"
and Gabriel "Baby Gaby" Sánchez* 86

Ballad of the Santa Fe Prison Riot
Translation by Enrique R. Lamadrid 88

Memories of el Camino del Cañón (1999)
Lydia Armenta Rivera 90

Shine Boys: A Story About Santa Fe (1995)
Vincent Younis 94

PART VI

Los Cambios: A Legacy of Change

Nuevo México en el año 1950 (1908)
Enrique H. Salazar 103

New Mexico in 1950
Translation by A. Gabriel Meléndez 105

El Idioma Español (1905)
Jesús María Hilario Alarid 107

The Spanish Language
Translation by A. Gabriel Meléndez 108

¡Viva la Fiesta! (1999)
Gloria Armenta Gonzales 110

The Spider & The Pants (2006)
G. Benito Córdova 111

Down and Out Along the Santa Fe Trail (2000)
Leo Romero 113

Juxtaposition (2009)
Levi Romero 119

Las dos Lloronas de Santa Fe (2008)
Enrique R. Lamadrid 120

PART VII

Aquel Entonces: Selected Memoirs

Before the War (2001)
Anita Gonzales Thomas 129

A Night of Horror (1955/2000)
Cleofas Jaramillo 144

What Goes Around Comes Around (1991)
Robert Himmerich y Valencia 150

PART VIII

Cuentos: Story Telling

Mi abuela cobraba interés (1988)
Sabine Ulibarrí 155

My Grandmother Charged Interest
Sabine Ulibarrí 157

The Colonel and the Santo (1957)
Fray Angélico Chávez 161

The Santa Fe Dress (2008)
Rosalie C. Otero 166

And One for John Coffee (2008)
E. A. Mares 174

Mrs. Rael (2000)
Demetria Martínez 178

PART IX

Arte y Tradición: Expressive Culture

Epilogue: Recapitulación Breve (1973)
Pedro Ribera Ortega 183

Bernardo Miera y Pacheco, Celso Gallegos, Eliseo
Rodríguez: Mystery, Mastery, and Identity in
Hispano Art in Santa Fe (2009)
Carmella Padilla 188

Credits 203

Contributors 205

About the Editors and Photographer 213

Santa Fe del Alma Mía:
A Personal Photo Essay (2009)
Miguel A. Gandert *Throughout the book*

COLOR PLATES

Murallas de lumbre: Photo Essay
on the Murals of Santa Fe
Miguel A. Gandert *Following page 66*

Recordando Santa Fe

A FOREWORD TO *SANTA FE NATIVA*

Estevan Rael-Gálvez

Pasó Por Aquí Board Member

RECENTLY, A REPORTER ASKED ME WHAT YEAR I WOULD ASCRIBE AS THE FOUNDING OF SANTA FE, SINCE IT HAD BECOME THE subject of considerable debate. My head filled with the events of recent years that seemed to underlie the question. For one, I had the privilege of being a party to a challenging, yet deeply meaningful consultation process over the question "Who owns the past?" This particular consultation had begun with an archaeological permit application and ended with a precedent-setting agreement between the Pueblo of Tesuque and the City of Santa Fe. With many difficult conversations in mind, I responded simply, noting that I would address the issue by standing at the site of the new convention center that had risen from the dust of the Sweeney Center, from the dust of a school and gym, from military barracks long since buried, and deeper still, from a place holding the memory of a great Pueblo village. This place we now call Santa Fe carries the spirit of antiquity and change, yet is a living force that is all around us. This spirit is, I think, like an old man

or old woman, who when asked their age does not answer directly but smiles knowingly, their eyes filling with memory and tears, telling of ages past. To be sure, we will commemorate this elder's birthday in 2009–10, yet it is important still to recognize that this elder, Santa Fe, is far older than a mere four centuries.

This focus on anniversaries is not anything new. Perhaps a part of the human condition, we often want to date things, to commemorate origins, and even when a date cannot be found, it can be imagined. The Tertio-Millennial Celebration, celebrating 333 years of Santa Fe's founding, was one such event. It was a grand, if not altogether imagined celebration. That year, Santa Fe leaders invited one of the nation's greatest poets to attend the events. The kind old man declined the invitation and instead wrote a letter:

Dear Sirs: Your kind invitation to visit
you and deliver a poem for the 333rd
Anniversary of the founding of Santa

Fe has reach'd me so late that I have to decline, with sincere regret. But I will say a few words off hand. We Americans have yet to really learn our own antecedents, and sort them, to unify them . . . we tacitly abandon ourselves to the notion that our United States have been fashion'd from the British Islands only, and essentially form a second England—which is a very great mistake. Many leading traits for our future national personality, and some of the best ones, will certainly prove to have originated from [something] other than British stock . . . To that composite American identity of the future, Spanish character will supply some of the most needed parts. No stock shows a grander historic retrospect—in religiousness and loyalty, or for patriotism, courage, decorum, gravity and honor . . . As to our aboriginal or Indian population—Aztec in the South, and many a tribe in the North and West—know it seems to be agreed that they must gradually dwindle as time rolls on, and in a few generations more leave only a reminiscence, a blank. But I am not at all clear about that. As America, from its many far-back sources and current supplies, develops, adapts, entwines, faithfully identifies its own— we to see it cheerfully accepting and using all the contributions of foreign lands from the whole outside.

Very respectfully, Walt Whitman

Whitman's astute observations about what will dwindle and what will develop are noteworthy. When Whitman spoke of the Spanish character of New Mexico, this sense of New Mexicans being solely connected to Spain was just beginning to take hold locally. Countless artists, writers, boosters of tourism, and politicians were just then beginning to construct this past, to whiten it, erasing its natural beauty and complexity. The reality, however, is that Spanish identity as it is thought about today is somewhat fabricated. We only need to glance at the 1790 census for Santa Fe, itself a fascinating narrative of identity, to know that the people here were deeply caste and irrevocably mixed within a mere two centuries of Spanish occupation. The roots are drawn from numerous indigenous nations and its taproots are multiple. Nevertheless, the engagement of such a prominent literary figure was as significant then as it remains today, and yet all of us, as Americans, remain still woefully reluctant to learn and know the full complexity of our antecedents.

This is why all the stories about Santa Fe are important. Stories from the past four hundred years, as well as the recovery of those not yet told, are critical to the understanding of its history locally, nationally, and globally. Indeed, this place, its people, the events and stories, are all worth remembering, but none of it can be relegated to a singular museum piece, an identity frozen into nostalgia, or even a simple binary. Recovering history requires the active process of memory, research, writing, and telling. It demands looking closely at what we see, listening intently to what we hear, distinguishing between the surface and the obscured, suppressed, and deeply contested layers. Sometimes it even requires getting close to the ground. In 2006, the Santa Fe Art Institute invited me to participate in a community performance piece, "Before You Can Walk: Crawl Santa Fe 2006." Participants (myself included) crawled around the plaza with narratives excerpts from Santa Fe's past (that I had scripted) pinned to their backs. It was humbling but immensely engaging and meaningful. It was a profound act of storytelling that I will not soon forget.

Santa Fe Nativa is also an act of storytelling, which invites its readers to pull back the layers, imagine people and places long since gone. In between its lines, the Old Paris Theater and Claude's Bar are lively locales, set against the privilege of Loretto Academy or the power of the capital. Here chapels became drugstores, and family homes, once turned into art galleries, become homes again filled with laughter and mourning. Here the names and deeds of Gertruditas Armijo de Gonzales, Bonafé, Tsianina, East and West Side Llorona, Popé, Felipe Maximilano Chacón, and Los Shine Boys all nuance a more interesting Santa Fe identity, perhaps unknown, save for this telling. Here, time moves at a different pace, as set by summertime, the sanctity of Lenten season, the movement of a revolt, an invasion, the annual fiestas, or with the grief of a mother who can only move through her pain by taking pen to hand and telling the story of tragedy on Griffin Street. Here too, Santa Fe is seen as a story of contradiction, if not division, or as a poet tells, of juxtaposition, where one's design and creativity are left for another to enjoy in the sun's last light. The creativity of words is not the only tradition accentuated within these pages. The work of an altar screen produced in the mid- to late eighteenth century as well as the many murals throughout the city photographed herein showcase expressive art as well.

On these pages, and amidst them as well, the reader is invited to revel in the glory and also feel the uncomfortable tensions its authors create, those whose pens and points of view have largely shaped the history of this place. Lew Wallace, New Mexico governor and storyteller, once wrote, "Every calculation based on experience elsewhere fails in New Mexico." True though this often-quoted phrase may be for some, it simply and erroneously presumes that one's experience is not based on being born and raised in New Mexico. *Santa Fe Nativa* is a volume born, it seems, in the process of crisis and change and the need at this time to provide a counterpoint, a counterstory to what is seen, known, and formerly understood.

Recovery is not simply about recovering what has been lost; it is about recovery from a history of colonization, racism, and detachment. Recovery in this sense is an active process of remembering, as the Spanish word *recordar* implies, to awaken, perhaps in this case from a dream. Each of the stories in this book, *Santa Fe Nativa*, demands vigilance, for as one layer of imperial gloss is pulled away, there may be one even deeper. Literature and testimony—and that which is born from collective memory, fragmented as it may be—provide a way to begin working through the myths, past the imagined communities, beyond the images and curios tourists always demand of a people who have been internally colonized. The work of this volume includes a body of critical fictions and present-tense testimonies, which constitute a genealogy of subjugated knowledge and provide a cultural location for the construction of alternative readings of history. Recovery is more process than product. In this way, this volume serves as an invitation. The editors are calling for more storytelling as a way to recover a consciousness of a shared, contested, and deeply layered past. ☼

Santa Fe Nativa

PREFACE

IN THE WINTER OF 1892, SANTA FE NATIVE
CAMILO PADILLA, WHO WOULD LATER PUBLISH
LA REVISTA ILUSTRADA, A SANTA FE LITERARY
and arts magazine, for more than twenty years,
expressed concern over the growing tendency in
some of his fellow Nuevomexicanos to acquiesce to
the economic pounding they were experiencing by
selling off their lands. Padilla admonished the readers of his newspaper, *El Mosquito*, that "if you sell
your lands, you are giving up what should be most
sacred to you. The New Mexican earth, bought and
paid for with the blood of our forebears, should be
as sacred to us as the ground of the nation is to the
good patriot and citizen." Padilla was echoing the
common sentiment among Hispanic New Mexicans
that the land was sacrosanct and selling it profaned
the memory and inheritance of those who had sacrificed so much to settle it in the first place. Padilla
was moved by the profound sense of *querencia*, or
attachment to place, that infused his community.
Querencia, writes Enrique R. Lamadrid, is "the
center space of desire, the root of belonging, that

vicinity where you first beheld the light" (Lamadrid
2000, 100). While this sentiment can be found in
communities across the Hispanic Southwest, our
work as the editors of this collection has been to
provide textual and visual evidence to show how
Santa Fe centers querencia in special ways for New
Mexico Hispanos. Even those who were not born
and raised in Santa Fe express special regard for the
place, the spirit, and the point on the map that the
city occupies, for they have long considered the city
to be their administrative, cultural, and religious
home. While this centering is both geographic and
symbolic, it is also the result of economic strife
and political machinations. Chris Wilson points
out how "the loss of land and water rights, com-
pounded by the agricultural depression of the early
1920s, forced many New Mexican villagers into the
migrant labor force and the working-class barrios
of Santa Fe" (Wilson 1997, 155). In the writings
gathered here one finds a special sense of attachment expressed in every possible manner. Most
often it is a welling up of sentiments related to the

cultural, political, and economic decentering that visited the residents of Santa Fe in the wake of the loss of land and a land-based livelihood. Time and again the contributors to this volume return to this theme in all manner of oral, visual, and published texts. So it is not surprising to find that the texts represented in this anthology lean on memory and faith to evoke "the root of belonging."

In 2010 Santa Fe will celebrate the four-hundredth anniversary of its founding, and thus, we might ask, is this time enough for the Hispanos of New Mexico to claim nativity and a birthright to this place? It is curious to discover that somewhere toward the end of the nineteenth century, Spanish-speaking Nuevomexicanos already thought of themselves as native to the region and proceeded to apply the term *nativo* quite liberally to their experience and condition. It must be understood that when earlier generations of Santa Fe residents took up the term they were not defining themselves against the Native Americans who as first peoples would surely beg to differ with this usage; rather they were defining themselves against the Anglo-American wave of immigrants who arrived on the scene in massive numbers in the 1890s. They were latecomers to a process of ethnic interaction among Spanish, Mexican, and Indian peoples that had been in motion in the New Mexican capital for a full two hundred years. More precisely, Nuevomexicanos were evoking the fuller terms *colono nativo* or *paisano nativo* (native settler or countryman) as a shield against the external, extraneous, foreign settler—the *extranjero* or inmigrante—those who, while newly arrived, were backed by enough political power and venture capital to set the terms and call the shots in New Mexico. Among the first things this new group did was to draw a stringent and cutting new racial boundary that placed them socially above Indians and Hispanics. First,

the Pueblos, but later the more mobile tribes, the Navajos, Apaches, and Utes, were cordoned off onto reservations at the close of the Indian Wars to become wards of the federal government. The close relationship that Hispanics had established with their nearest neighbors, the Pueblos, was severed quite abruptly in political terms, though there is evidence to suggest that cultural exchange between these two groups remained in place for many years. The Nuevomexicanos, 93 percent of the population of Santa Fe in 1850, became citizens of the United States by virtue of the Treaty of Guadalupe Hidalgo (1848), a status that on paper made them the equal of the newly arriving Anglo extranjeros. U.S. citizenship was enough of a new identity to estrange the Nuevomexicanos from their Indian neighbors, but it was not strong enough to overcome the de jure racism and discrimination that became an everyday occurrence in a newly racialized Santa Fe. Neither was it enough to guarantee that Spanish-speaking New Mexicans would be able to determine their future for themselves, or at least participate fully in major social decision making. De facto citizenship meant they could continue to live in Santa Fe provided they had the economic and political means to do so, but they were required to compete in a social order ruled by business, banking, and real-estate interests. In practice, the arrangement skewed social advantage in favor of the political and economic well-being of Anglo newcomers to the Southwest. The term nativo suggests that Nuevomexicanos sensed themselves to be locked in competitive struggle with their economic and political conquerors. Santa Fe, the locus of civil government and public life, became ever more important. Under American rule it became the site where the cultural and political survival of Hispanos was being determined on a daily basis.

Although not widely known, nativo Nuevo-mexicanos resolved to contribute to the new society and compete as best they could with their Anglo counterparts. Pulled along by stronger economic and political forces, they nonetheless scrutinized, weighed, judged, reasoned, amended, and challenged, and when their survival was endangered, they denounced the schemes of power brokers, water authorities, civic boosters, land speculators, missionaries, and carpetbaggers as these took root in Santa Fe and in the region. Many of the writings we include here perform their work through a distinctive venue that has been called *sentimiento*, a term that becomes the expressive pathway of *querencia*. In considering the popular modalities that Nuevomexicanos have drawn from to express themselves in oral and written texts, I argue that sentimiento is more a disposition than an emotional outburst:

> Sentimiento at once expresses the competency of the speaker to communicate both his disposition of mind (rationale) and his point of view (opinion) while disclosing an intimate view of self within communitarian life experience. At times of great joy or sorrow within the community, sentimiento is revealed in the externalization of deeply felt emotions, feeling and passions. Thus, sentimiento remains a particularly apt vehicle for relating a distillation of past experience to the present unfolding life-drama of community. (Meléndez 2005, 38)

Judging by the writings herein, Santa Fe residents have been most troubled and vexed by the threat of being erased from history and snubbed by the elitism they see as dominating civic and public life in their capital city. Our desire to bring their words forth in this volume is meant to reverse their exclusion from the very story of what Santa Fe is.

The displacement of the native New Mexicans from certain zip codes in Old Santa Fe is now all but complete. They have been priced and taxed out of real property at the same time that the "Santa Fe Style" and the trendy accoutrements (Starbucks to Wild Oats) of amenity migrants and tourists who have outflanked them. Santa Fe's makeover from a hometown to a tourist and art mecca has not been kind to old-time residents. Walk down any of Santa Fe's downtown streets or older residential areas and you would be lucky if you ran into one or two longtime residents. Spanish is no longer naturally and regularly spoken on the plaza as it once was, and local family-run markets, pharmacies, bars, and restaurants have all been expelled from the city's core historic district. It is as if the nativos have all been disappeared, as happens to California's Latino community in the 2004 film by Sergio Arau, *A Day Without A Mexican*. Unlike the movie, however, no one seems to be concerned about getting nativos back to Santa Fe. The old neighborhoods, Canyon Road, the Plaza, Analco, Acequia Madre, and the east-side foothills have also been transformed. Even as the economic displacement imposes greater pressures on the working poor who still have a connection to Santa Fe, their battle is less about acquiring certain swank addresses or hilltops and more about refusing to be snubbed out of the foundational story of their town or what's worse, to be "white-faced" into the marketing story of Santa Fe at fiesta time or when the New Mexico National Guard is called upon to do multiple tours of duty in the endless global war on terrorism. They are determined not to be erased from public life in the city they organized and founded four hundred years ago. At certain times of the year they come back like swallows rebuilding old nests. Two or three times a year, during Spanish Market or for the public reveling that follows the yearly burning of Zozobra at fiesta, *familias, plebe,* lowriders, and fiesta queens make the plaza comes alive with brown joyful faces.

In addition to exploring the idea of nativity and examining the question of how longtime Santa Fe residents have been bold enough to claim a native status in and around Santa Fe, this anthology is also concerned with other aspects of place-making identity. It is concerned with how memory becomes the key to recovering a hidden or suppressed past, in particular with how the telling and retelling of stories is the cornerstone for unearthing new knowledge of Santa Fe's mestizo or hybrid past. The Spanish-speaking founders of Santa Fe did not come into a place barren of people. Several Pueblo villages with a population of a several hundred families existed at Ogaponge, the place "at the shells by the water," although most had been abandoned nearly a century before Pedro de Peralta set in motion a plan for a Spanish/European plaza to be built north of what is today the Santa Fe River. The Spanish-Mexican soldiers, colonists, and clerics then organized the existing Pueblo settlements into an urban cluster of satellite communities (complete with "green space") tethered by a grid of streets to the central plaza. Community building was not just the doing of colonial administrators; the Spaniards, it should be remembered, were already in profound ways very Mexican. They entered history as creoles, mestizos, mulattoes, and Indians who, as part of a process under way across the southern half of the Americas, saw themselves as participating in change on a hemispheric scale. Several hundred Tlaxcalans, most simply described in documents as "Mexican Indians," joined with the Spaniards to assist in the founding of colonial

Santa Fe. Over the course of Santa Fe's history other Indian groups, the Navajo, Apache, Comanche, and Ute, would provide major infusions to Santa Fe's resident population, which already included a number of *genízaros.* Thus, from its very origins Santa Fe was a hybrid community.

Santa Fe's peculiar brand of *mestizaje,* or cultural pluralism, is expressed throughout this collection. As editors it is our hope that the writings herein, some which are as old as Santa Fe itself and some, newly created, directing our thoughts to the future, will bring readers to a fuller appreciation of the power of this place. We believe that an acknowledgment of this particular history is in order and so too the need to raise up the voices of those who have known and lived Santa Fe's story in the intimate way of respect and querencia. This must become Santa Fe's future and not its past. It is our view that Santa Fe has gone too many days without the nativo being seen or heard on its streets. Santa Fe is in need of some social readjustment that will return it to the place where nativos and everyone else can feel comfortable, included, and respected when they walk its streets or stop midstride to call out without shame, "Hey *paisano, paisana,* how are you doing?" The Borderlands writer Gloria Anzaldúa wrote that "nothing truly happens in the real world unless it is first happens in your head." Changing this view slightly, we would add that as a modern multicultural city Santa Fe will only change and heal itself when the voices of past and present are fully accounted for and when these concerns are represented in bookstores, libraries, university courses, and in high school classes. It is our hope that the works we include here will find their way into all these settings and more, for we believe that the stories and reports from those who have made and remade Santa Fe over time are indeed crucial to our future. We hope that ours will be the first in a long line of books and scholarship that will bring the laughter and spirit of the nativo back to the plaza, to what is the public face of the civic, cultural, artistic, and religious life of Santa Fe.

For the editors, A. Gabriel Meléndez ☼

References

Lamadrid, Enrique R., with Miguel A. Gandert. 2000. *Nuevo México Profundo*. Santa Fe: Museum of New Mexico Press.

Meléndez, A. Gabriel. 2005. *Spanish-language Newspapers in New Mexico, 1834–1958*. Tucson: University of Arizona Press.

Noble, David Grant. 1989. *Santa Fe: History of an Ancient City*. Santa Fe: School of American Research.

Sánchez, Joseph P. 1989. "The Peralta-Ordóñez Affair and the Founding of Santa Fe." In *Santa Fe: History of an Ancient City,* ed. David G. Noble, 27–38. Santa Fe: School of American Research.

Wilson, Chris. 1997. *The Myth of Santa Fe: Creating a Modern Regional Tradition*. Albuquerque: University of New Mexico Press.

Acknowledgments

Santa Fe has special significance for everyone. It is a name that belongs with other picturesque, alluring, and historic places. In writing such a broad-ranged volume, we have many people to thank. We wish to thank the contributors who so generously gave of their talents and whose eloquence made this book possible. To Academia El Norte, for its financial backing. To Anselmo Arellano, for his generous loan of an original typescript copy of the chapter, "La Invasión Americana/The American Invasion," by Rafael Chacón. To Jerry Gurulé for his assistance with cartography. To W. Clark Whitehorn, senior acquisitions editor at the University of New Mexico Press, who originally encouraged us to submit the manuscript for publication. To Lisa Pacheco, for her professional advice, and the editorial staff at the UNM Press, especially Meredith D. Dodge and the designers, Mina Yamashita and Cheryl Carrington. To Jennifer Mason and Marcia Glenn, staff in the University Honors Program, for their assistance with such things as scanning, restoring lost files, and making sure the computer functioned properly. Finally, we offer special thanks to our families for all their support over many years. ☼

Santa Fe Nativa

INTRODUCTION

La Villa Real de la Santa Fe de San Francisco de Asís was built at the foot of
the Sangre de Cristo Mountains on
the north bank of the Santa Fe River in a sheltered
area that had been previously occupied for centuries. After the departure and exile of Governor
don Juan de Oñate, don Pedro de Peralta assumed
the office and made the town the new capital of La
Nueva México in 1610. In the Pueblo Revolt of 1680
Santa Fe was abandoned, then reestablished as the
capital in 1692. In early Spanish colonial times, New
Mexico was actually a *reino*, or kingdom, whose
legitimacy was attributed to both Spanish as well
as indigenous roots, since Oñate's son Cristóbal
descended from both Cortés and Moctezuma. The
founding families came from all over Spain and
New Spain, including peninsulares, criollos, mestizos of different castes, and Tlaxcaltecan Indians.
One of the reasons the settlers came was the promise of land grants and hidalgo status. Everyone was
to be an *hijo de algo*, son of great worth, the entry-
level rank of nobility.

The south side of the Santa Fe River had already been settled by the Tlaxcaltecans, who called it
Analco, Nahuatl for "Across the River." They founded
their community according to their own mestizo cos-
mology, where the first emergence of the people from
the Seven Caves of Chicomostoc is just as important
as their favorite Christian saints like the archangel
San Miguel. They were not servants but full partners in the settlement of northern New Spain. The
Spanish crown had granted them their own *capitu-
laciones* recognizing and perpetuating their royalty
and nobility, thanks to their key alliance with the
Spaniards in the conquest of the Aztecs. While the
Spaniards were interested in mining, the Tlaxcalans
exercised their own expertise—desert agriculture.
They were the ones who brought in chile and other
new crops and they were the ones who expanded the
existing acequia systems. Acequias played a critical
role in the early history of Santa Fe. Both the Pueblo
Indians and then later the Spaniards gained control
of the city by cutting off the water supply from the
Acequia de la Muralla. Although little remains of the

acequia system, the Acequia Madre, on the south side of the Río de Santa Fe, still flows when the irrigation gates are open.

While Santa Fe was inhabited on a very small scale in 1607, it was truly settled by don Pedro de Peralta in 1609. For a period of seventy years beginning in the early seventeenth century, Spanish soldiers and officials, as well as Franciscan missionaries, sought to subjugate and convert the Pueblo Indians of the region. In 1680, Pueblo Indians revolted against the estimated twenty-five hundred Spanish colonists, killing many of them and twenty-one Franciscan missionaries, and driving the remaining refugees into Mexico. The conquering Pueblos sacked Santa Fe and burned most of the buildings. The Pueblo people occupied Santa Fe until 1692, when don Diego de Vargas reconquered the region and entered the capital city. The success of De Vargas in retaking and reestablishing Santa Fe is within the spirit of the reconquest of Spain two centuries earlier, where the namesake city, Santa Fe de Granada, was the camp from which the siege of Granada was conducted. The new Hispano settlers of Santa Fe knew that it was the bicentennial of the other reconquest and took pride in the similarities.

After Mexico became an independent republic in 1821, the Department of New Mexico developed a strong sense of regional identity in exactly the same way as happened in other areas of Spain's former colonies. Administrative and regional centers began emerging as nations. The new identity was negotiated in two venues: newspapers and foundational fiction. People got a sense of the group by reading both. *Santa Fe Nativa* represents the cultural journalism that was so important, especially after the American invasion.

When New Mexico gained statehood in 1912, many people were drawn to Santa Fe's dry climate and unique culture. Throughout Santa Fe's long and varied history, the city has been the region's seat of culture and civilization. Regardless of whether one is a resident Santa Fean, a native of another New Mexico town, or a visitor, everyone has a sense of Santa Fe as a center—of government, culture, tradition, and history.

For Hispanos, this New Mexican capital holds, and has held, great significance throughout its history. We consider Santa Fe our own, having lived in the city for almost four hundred years. It is fitting, therefore, that this collection of poetry, short fiction, and essays focuses on works written by Hispanos. The anthology expresses *arraigo* and querencia, or the sense of rootedness and belonging to place and region. Santa Fe is thus perceived as the origin, core, and foundation of New Mexico Hispanic culture, more eloquently discussed in the preface written by A. Gabriel Meléndez. The literature in this anthology includes published and unpublished manuscripts. Some of the work appears in its original Spanish as well as in translation, and some of the writings include a mix of English and Spanish or code-switching, which is a common phenomenon among Hispanos. The result is an intrinsically fused third language that increases both the associative and expressive range of words in both languages.

Santa Fe Nativa is divided into nine parts that encompass poetic homage to the city (part 1), foundational and historical pieces (parts 2 and 3), writings about *la región* and *costumbres* (part 4), the barrios (part 5), conflict and change (part 6), memoirs (part 7), fiction (part 8), art and traditions (part 9), and a personal photo essay by Miguel A. Gandert distributed throughout the manuscript as well as photos of Santa Fe murals and historic maps.

Part 1, "Homenajes: Praise for our Villa," consists of a 1630 excerpt from fray Alonso de Benavides's *Memorial*, which describes Santa Fe. Benavides was assigned as custos, the supervisor of New Mexico missions, from 1626 to 1629. Benavides wrote his memorial for King Philip IV of Spain and Pope Urban VIII. He documented his experiences in New Mexico, partially exaggerating his account because it was written primarily to induce the king to send more missionaries to New Mexico. Benavides claimed the conversion to Christianity of thousands of indigenous people, describing the toils of setting up ministries in the region and providing descriptions of the mineral resources widely available in New Mexico. This piece is followed by a nostalgic poem Felipe Maximiliano Chacón (1873–1948) wrote that expresses the affection and attachment he felt for Santa Fe. Chacón's writings were collected under the title *Obras de Felipe Maximiliano Chacón, El Cantor Neomexicano, Poesía y Prosa*, published in 1924. His writings come from a man with a sharp sense of the past and its relation to his time. In "To Santa Fe," Chacón refers to Santa Fe as holy and beautiful. He writes expressively and passionately about the flowers in the gardens and the vibrant songs of birds. He also speaks, though, of the sadness at the subtle changes that are beginning to take place in the city and among the people. Part 1 concludes with Pat Mora's "Ode to Santa Fe." Mora is an award-winning author and a leading figure in contemporary Hispano poetry. She resides in Santa Fe and Cincinnati. "Ode to Santa Fe" expresses her affection for the city. She cherishes the landscape and is deeply inspired by it.

Part 2, "Querencia: The Root of Belonging," expresses the ardor and sentiment that Hispano writers have for Santa Fe. Valerie Martínez's poem "And They Called It Horizon" resounds with a fervent appreciation for the city. Martínez, poet laureate of Santa Fe in 2008, draws on her Hispanic language and heritage as well as those of the early people to trace the origin of the city from before

time began. Tommy Archuleta's poem "¿Dónde Vivo Yo?" parallels Francisco X. Alarcón's sense of place. He describes various aspects of Santa Fe that make it unique. Fr. Benedicto Cuesta extols the ambience of Santa Fe during Holy Week in his poem. He writes of Santa Fe as being in mourning and shrouded by a mantilla of sadness. This is a romantic rendition that evokes the strong Roman Catholic milieu still present in the city. Jimmy Santiago Baca's poem describes the varied features of the city in which he was born, including the lore associated with the famous miraculous staircase in the Loretto Chapel.

Part 3, "Historias: Subjects of Two Empires," chronicles historical accounts and narratives of Santa Fe's history. An exceptional document in this section is José Escobar's "Leyendas Neo-Mexicanas" in which he describes the Pueblo Revolt. This major narrative poem is truly a unique piece in the anthology. Escobar was writing at the same time that Mexico, Ecuador, Peru, and other mestizo republics were choosing their national heroes. In each case a native hero was chosen to fill out the pantheon of fathers of the country. When Mexico rehabilitated and elevated Cuauhtémoc as the indigenous father of his country was when Popé was chosen here. He represents resistance to all tyranny and colonial rule, whether it be Spain or the United States. "Leyendas" appeared in print in ten parts or cantos in *Las Dos Repúblicas* in Denver, Colorado, in 1896. Seven of the original ten cantos are extant and reproduced here. Some parts are not extant; the cantos that survive, however, provide a detailed account of the destruction and reestablishment of Santa Fe.

E. A. Mares, Orlando Romero, Rafael Chacón, and Fray Angélico Chávez allow the reader to relive various historical elements of Santa Fe life. Mares's poem traces the place that became Santa Fe from its early history of native people, the coming of the Spaniards followed by the Pueblo Revolt, and then the peaceful fusion of both cultures. Romero addresses intermarriage and peaceful coexistence that forged a unique Indo-Hispano character and culture that defines Santa Fe today. His essay describes the daily struggles for existence of the countless men and women who came to this isolated frontier and clung tenaciously to it for four centuries. Chacón describes Santa Fe in 1846, when the American troops overthrew the Hispano leaders and took control of the city. It was at this time, the 1840s, that the famous woman, Gertrudis de Barceló, known as doña Tules, ran a gambling hall. Fray Angélico Chávez's essay brings to life this interesting historical figure who shocked some people but gave some women satisfaction, and often secret delight, that a woman could run a successful business.

Our nation-building project was complicated by the "Storm" of the endless American occupation. We are children of the storm, now children of two empires. Part 3 also celebrates Eusebio Chacón, who is considered to be one of the first New Mexican novelists with his two short allegorical novels, *El hijo de la tempestad* (*Son of the Storm*) and *Tras la tormenta, la calma* (*The Calm after the Storm*), the second of which is included in this anthology. Chacón's novels establish a new genre for the region and serve to disclose political, cultural, and behavioral dilemmas of his people. *Tras la tormenta, la calma* is a romance, an allegorical novel where the characters represent social types. The sense of nation is symbolized by women— *Doña Bárbara* for Venezuela, *María* for Colombia, *Amalia* for Argentina, and so on. These are all titles of novels. In *Tras la tormenta, la calma*, New Mexico is embodied by Dolores (Lola) in Chacón's novel. She is a beautiful mestiza who is in the middle

of a love triangle. The two men are students at St. Michael's School. Her seducer is a *rico*. Her redeemer is his best friend, a humble but virtuous mestizo like Dolores. This is not a novel about local color; it is working out the history and future of New Mexico in allegorical form. The novel examines the concept of honor while also giving readers a glimpse into local gossip and amorous affectations. The narrator-character frequently interrupts the action to divulge information about his native Santa Fe. He contributes to the narrative by manipulating and observing his surroundings.

Part 4, "Nuestra Cornucopia: Place, Water, Food," includes writings that give us a historical map to the places that have been reconstructed or obliterated by commerce and development. They speak of those resources that people value—place, food, and water. A. Gabriel Meléndez's poem, "Oración al Río Grande/Prayer to the Rio Grande," is an ode to the river that stretches the length of the state and on whose boundaries villages, towns, and cities were built. The poem traces geologic, historic, generational, and cultural landmarks that flow from the bloodline of this river. The river is a birthplace, healing site, purifying tributary, and the metaphysical continuity from life to afterlife. The river, like the capital, serves to preserve and conserve the heritage and culture of the state. "El Río de Tesuque" speaks of stillness and peace. It harks back to a time when Santa Fe was a small town and not yet caught up in the activity of a modern city. Marie Romero Cash writes a very personal narrative about growing up in Santa Fe in *Tortilla Chronicles: Growing Up in Santa Fe*. "Sum-Sum-Summertime," the excerpt included in this anthology, describes the acequias and their importance in the lives of the people, including the children who dammed the culverts into ponds that served as swimming holes, a cultural inheritance bequeathed to the people of Santa Fe by Tlaxcalans and Spanish colonists. Robert Lara Vialpando's *octavilla* (each stanza divided into eight lines) extols the beauty of the fields in Chinguayé in spring. "Nuestra Cornucopia" by Alfredo Celedón Luján is a remarkable piece describing, with good humor, the enduring traditions such as peeling chile and the shifting traditions and customs of the people, including the changing shopping habits and tastes.

Part 5, "Los Barrios: Home Spaces," refers to the distinctive neighborhoods of the city. The contemporary Chicano poet Francisco X. Alarcón pays respect to the Barrio de Analco, a historic neighborhood in Santa Fe. This barrio was located on the south side of the Santa Fe River in a place that was first inhabited by Tlaxcalan Indians. It remains as a reminder of Santa Fe's multiethnic and intracultural origins and a symbol of indigenous resistance. Bonafé, a pseudonym for the Santa Fe correspondent to the Las Vegas, New Mexico, newspaper *El Independiente*, often wrote pieces informing his readers of the comings and goings in the New Mexican capital. Acting as a kind of cultural reporter, Bonafé reports on the details of social events and public meetings. His writing is unsophisticated and folksy. J. Chris Abeyta, Lydia Armenta Rivera, and Vincent Younis reminisce about their barrios, including Canyon Road, which has seen many changes over the years primarily because of the influx of artists. Cristo Rey is another neighborhood at the point where Canyon Road becomes Upper Canyon Road. Abeyta is presumably referring to the Patrick Smith Park area on which a traditional mission-style church was built in 1939, designed by the influential Santa Fe architect John Gaw Meem. The church houses a notable eighteenth-century Spanish colonial carved stone reredos (altar screen). Abeyta's poem speaks with nostalgia and longing for Santa Fe in a bygone era.

The excerpt from Vincent Younis's short novel, *Shine Boys: A Story About Santa Fe*, gives the reader a look at Santa Fe through the eyes of two young boys as they meander on their daily odyssey, shining shoes and selling newspapers. The reader has the opportunity to visit many of the recognizable haunts of Santa Fe, including the Loretto Chapel, the plaza, downtown bars, and pool halls.

In part 6, "Los Cambios: A Legacy of Change," the writers describe the changes that have taken place in Santa Fe over the years. Enrique H. Salazar's reflections on Santa Fe in 1950 are a critical and unusual way of looking back. The protagonist is dead and has been allowed to return to the city where he had lived to see and chronicle the changes since his death. Santa Fe is no longer the capital. The new capital was named Pujancante because the people admired everything concerning Indian tribes. The protagonist is disheartened by the changes he sees in his dystopia and vows never to return. Gloria Armenta Gonzales writes about the Santa Fe Fiestas, an annual event since 1625, with special emphasis on Zozobra, an enormous monster that represents Old Man Gloom. Zozobra is burned as a symbolic purging of the city from the troubles and evils of the previous year. Gonzales, however, criticizes the festivities. They have lost their meaning. Instead of a religious and community activity, Zozobra has become a "sacred cow" used by promoters and developers to make money. The excerpt from G. Benito Córdova's novel, *Big Dreams and Dark Secrets in Chimayó*, published in 2006 by the University of New Mexico Press, gives the reader an account of superstitions and rituals associated with *curanderas* (healers) and brujas (witches) and wonders about the mystery of Santa Fe's disappearing doors. Leo Romero's piece, "Down and Out Along the Santa Fe Trail," expresses the tenuous thread between native peoples and their conquerors. Two friends, one Indian, one Hispano, have collective experiences from Vietnam to bar brawls. The Chicano has attended dances at the pueblo, and they both hang out in cantinas, but their friendship is uneasy because their legacies are disparate. Levi Romero's poem "Juxtapostion" illustrates the variety of attitudes of the people living in Santa Fe. In some of the historical pieces, people are welcoming and benevolent, but Romero's poem addresses the stark contrast between family and *vecinos* and the strangers who live in the Santa Fe–style homes he built. Enrique R. Lamadrid's essay "Las dos Lloronas de Santa Fe" explains the renowned legend of the weeping woman who appears near rivers and abducts children on both sides of town.

Part 7, "Aquel Entonces: Selected Memoirs," begins with Anita Gonzales Thomas's essay "Before the War," an account based on a series of interviews in Santa Fe before World War II. She describes *la cosecha* (crops), piñon, music, religion, ethnicity, and social mores, all with good humor and homey appreciation of her life in Santa Fe. Cleofas Jaramillo also used autobiography. Her point of view, however, renders memories of a way of life that were rapidly changing. Here, sense of loss is authentically felt in her glimpses of a world grounded more in contradiction and conflict than in the pastoral setting of Thomas. "A Night of Horror" is a story from Cleofas's *Romance of a Little Village Girl*, published in 1939. In ballad form, she narrates the descent from Edenic girlhood to a more ambivalent present where she feels the loss of tradition. The ambience of Santa Fe is felt through the narrative about a famous murder that took place in Santa Fe in 1931. Robert Himmerich y Valencia's essay was published in 1991 in *A New Mexico Scrapbook*, edited by Michael Miller. This short piece traces a personal history in which Hispanic traditions that respect the earth and culture are praised. Having left the region, he returns to a place he has always thought of as home.

Part 8, "Cuentos: Story Telling," contains a group of short stories that reveal various characteristics and facets of the capital. Sabine Ulibarrí's "Mi abuela cobraba interés" is a humorous and poignant story of his grandmother, an emancipated woman who lived in Santa Fe. Ulibarrí's writing is steeped in traditional life. He draws upon Spanish belles letters and the bucolic life-style of his youth to give us stories tinged with the same nostalgia that appears in the work of early writers. His use of Spanish links him to the contemporary Hispano because language is central to his discourse of cultural identity, affirmation, and self-determination. Fray Angélico Chávez began writing in the thirties. Behind his idyllic religious vision lie hidden allegories of class conflict and indictments of the aggressive *americanos*. It should be remembered that Chávez wrote in a period in which the pressure to adapt to "the ways of the Americans," to pay proof to patriotism, left little room for public expression of discontent with their subordinate social position. "The Colonel and the Santo" pits an arrogant stranger, an American officer, against simple villagers. It is a story set after World War II that dramatizes some of the cultural misunderstandings that continue to strain Hispano and Anglo relations.

People from other towns and villages in New Mexico see Santa Fe as the center of the state, as the place to shop, participate in annual festivals and events, attend the opera, and visit museums. Rosalie Otero's narrative "The Santa Fe Dress" is an account of a young woman's shopping trip to the capital. E. A. Mares, a renowned poet, essayist, playwright, and historian, addresses significant Chicano issues in his writings. "And One for John Coffee" is an excerpt from a novel in progress. The novel is set in the Southwest and the South, although it sprawls all over the United States and Mexico. It is a work concerned, in the narrow sense, with the civil rights and antiwar movements of the sixties, the Chicano movement, and other issues. The excerpt included in this anthology is set in Santa Fe in the early 1970s. Roque Smith is a veteran student organizer and political revolutionary who has become disillusioned with everything in his life. He has reached a point where it is possible for wisdom to begin to develop. "Mrs. Rael," by Demetria Martínez, is an excerpt from her novel *Mexican Rubies*. Mrs. Rael, the protagonist, is the owner of Rael's Remedios on the Santa Fe Plaza. In a literary tour through her house, the reader traces a poignant personal history. The adobe home, very different from the gated communities built à la "Santa Fe–style," has character and stories of lives of many who have inhabited or passed through the portals of Mrs. Rael's home.

Part 9, "Arte y Tradición: Expressive Culture," encapsulates many of the traditions still occurring in Santa Fe. The "Epilogue: Recapitulación Breve" by Pedro Ribera Ortega is taken from his book *Christmas in Old Santa Fe*. It describes a historic account of the various Christmas traditions that happen in the city in the Christmas season, including an account of luminarias and *farolitos*, the Feast of Our Lady of Guadalupe, and Las Posadas. Art critic Carmella Padilla recapitulates two centuries of Hispano art in Santa Fe, beginning with Bernardo Miera y Pacheco, the famous eighteenth-century cartographer and sculptor, and ending with the great contemporary artistic dilemma of what is fine art and what is folk art in the work of Celso Gallegos, the Agua Fría *santero*, and WPA painter and straw appliqué master Eliseo Rodríguez.

"Santa Fe del Alma Mía: A Personal Photo Essay" by award-winning photographer Miguel A. Gandert is distributed throughout the anthology. The book includes Santa Fe murals photographed by Miguel A. Gandert. These murals were painted on neighborhood buildings, schools, and churches. They revealed cultural identity and supported social and political movements. The book also includes historical maps of Santa Fe.

We are indebted to the many authors, both living and some who no longer are, who have contributed to this project. These writers wrote from their hearts, and their works reveal the humorous and the serious, the picturesque and the ordinary, and the wide range of cultural diversity and history that reflect and reinforce the very essence of Santa Fe. Notes on contributors can be found at the end of the book. We have made an effort to be inclusive in the subjects and principles upon which we focused here. It is the intent of this book to bring the work of New Mexican Hispano writers to the attention of a broad reading public and illuminate Hispano writers' interpretation of the social and historical events that have shaped Santa Fe.

For the editors, Rosalie C. Otero and Enrique R. Lamadrid. ☼

PART I

Homenajes

PRAISE FOR OUR VILLA

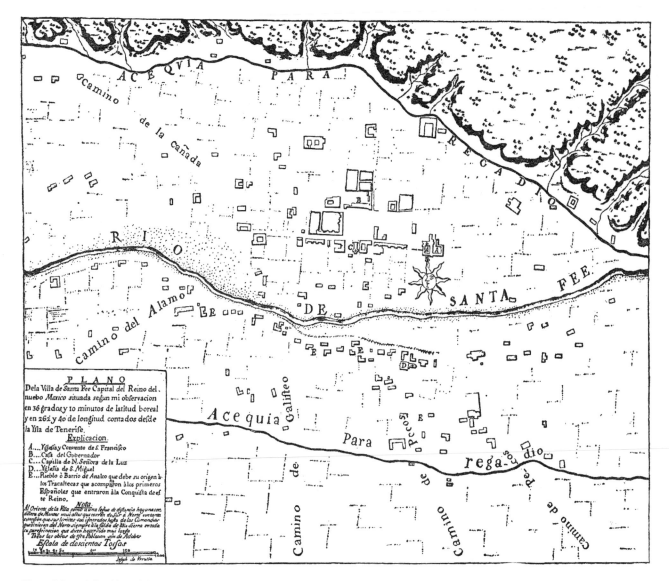

Plan of Santa Fe, New Mexico, 1766, by José de Urrutia, British Library Add. Ms 17662 M.

Villa de Santa Fe

Fray Alonso de Benavides
(Memorial, 1630)

Volviendo del pueblo antecendente ázia el Ocidente siete leguas, está la villa de Santa Fe, cabeca deste Reino, adonde residen los Gouernadores, y Españoles, que serán hasta dozientos y cincuenta, aunque solos los cincuenta se podrán armár por falta de armas, y aunque pocos y mal auiados, ha permitido Dios, que siempre salgán con vitoria, y causado en los Indios tan grande miedo dellos, y de sus arcabuzes, que de solo oír dezír, que va vn Español a sus pueblos huyen, para conseruar este miedo, quando se ofrece castigar algun pueblo reuelde, vsan con ellos de grandes rigores, que sino fuera esto, muchas vezes huuieran intentado matar a los Españoles, viendolos tan lexos de la Nueua-España, de donde les podría venir algún socorro: son todos soldados bien dotrinados y humildes, y de buen exemplo, por la mayor parte a los Indios. A este presidio sustenta V. M. no con pagas de su caxa Real, sino haziendolos encomenderos de aquellos pueblos, por mano del Gouernador; el tributo que les dan los Indios, es cada casa vna manta, que es vna vara de lienço de algodon, y vna fanega de maiz cada año, con que se sustentan los pobres Españoles; tendrán de seruicio setecientas almas, de suerte, que entre Españoles mestizos, y Indios aura mil almas, y gente tan puntual en la obediencia de sus Gouernadores, que a qualquiera facíon que se ofrezca, salen con sus armas, y a su costa, y hazen valerosos hechos: solo le faltaua lo principal, que era la Iglesia, y la que tenían era vn jacal malo, porque los Religiosos acudian primero a fabricar las Iglesias de los Indios que convertian, y con queines asistian y viuian: y asi luego que entre por Custodio, comence a fabricar la Iglesia, y Conuento, y a honra y Gloria de Dios nuestro Señor, puede luzir en qualquiera parte, adonde ya los Religiosos, enseñan a Españoles, y a Indios a leer, y escriuir, tañer, y cantar, y todas artes de pulicia: es puesto, aunque frío, el más fertil de todo el Nueuo-Mexico.

Facsimile from Alonso de Benavides, *Memorial que fray Ivan de Santander de la orden de San Francisco comissario general de Indias, presenta a la magestad catolica del rey Don Felipe Quarto nuestro señor.* Madrid: Imprenta Real, 1630.

Villa of Santa Fe

Fray Alonso de Benavides

Translation by Enrique R. Lamadrid

Returning from the previous pueblo [of Jémez], toward the west some seven leagues lies the Villa of Santa Fe, the head of this kingdom, where the governors reside, and the Spaniards, who are probably up to 250 in number, although only 50 are armed for lack of weapons. Although few and poorly equipped, God has permitted that they always reign victorious, which has caused among the Indians such great fear of them and their harquebuses that on hearing it said that a Spaniard goes to their pueblos, they flee. To maintain this fear, when they must punish some rebel pueblo, they employ great rigor against them, and were it not for this, many times they would have tried to kill the Spaniards, seeing them so far from New Spain, whence some help might come to them. All the soldiers are well versed and humble and of good example, for the most part, to the Indians. Your Majesty sustains this presidio not with payments from the royal treasury but with making them encomenderos over those pueblos, by the hand of the governor. The tribute the Indians give them is from each house a manta, which is a vara of cotton cloth, and a fanega of corn each year, with which the poor Spaniards sustain themselves. They must have under service some seven hundred souls, such that among Spaniards, mestizos, and Indians, there are probably a thousand souls, a people so prompt in obedience to their governors that whatever problem that happens, they come forth with their weapons and horses and at their own expense and do valorous deeds. They lack only the principal thing, which was the church, and that which they had was but a poor hut, because the missionaries went first to build the churches for the Indians they were converting, with whom they served and lived. So after I entered as custos, I began to build the church and residence, and to the honor and glory of God our Lord, they would shine in any place, where the missionaries teach the Spaniards, and the Indians to read, and write, play instruments, and sing, and all the appropriate arts. Although cold, the place is the most fertile of all New Mexico.

A Santa Fe

Felipe Maximiliano Chacón

(*Poesía y Prosa*, 1924)

Suelo bendito de la antigua villa,
Histórico vergel donde las flores
Abren gustosas ante el sol que brilla
Sus broches de perfumes y colores;
Allí donde florecen de tu arcilla
Frutas y mieses, entre mil amores,
Bajo tu azul repleto de fragancia
Se ha mecido la cuna de mi infancia.

Bendito es para mí tu suelo hermoso
Como es bella la flor de tus pensiles
Bendito por el ósculo afectuoso
Que ha brindado a mis labios infantiles
El amor maternal que cariñoso
Mi ser alimentó en otros abriles,
Que allí sufrió sobre amoroso lecho
Por darme vida de su noble pecho.

Bendito porque abrigas en tu seno
Del autor de mi tiempo la ceniza,
Y porque tú eres relicario ameno
De hermanos que la muerte arrojadiza
Arrebató, como la voz del trueno
Arrebata la calma; y tu inverniza
Escarcha, ya mi madre ha bendecido

Todo un caballero: Nostalgia for a Center Space, 1976.

Con lágrimas que viuda allí ha vertido.
Y aunque tristes memorias aparecen
Cuando van mis recuerdos al pasado
Y forman una escena en que me ofrecen
Mil dolores que mi alma han penetrado,
Al mirar tus espinas que adolecen
También miro el arbusto perfumado
Della rosa halagüeña del cariño
Que me dieron mis padres cuando niño.
Nunca olvido esos toques peregrinos
Que manan de tus regios campanarios
Ni de tus aves los vibrantes trinos
Que anuncian dulces tus albores diarios;
Lo mismo tus arrullos vespertinos,
Susurro de tus árboles agrarios
Que me arrebatan con deseo ardiente.

Mas si la suerte inevitable mía
Quiere llevar a mi bajel bogando
Lejos de tí con gélida apatía,
Y nunca llegan a tu ambiente blando

Los tristes ecos de mi nostalgia,
Mira en el éter y verás brillando
De mis recuerdos la constante estrella,
Que tú, entre halagos estarás con ella . . .

To Santa Fe

Felipe Maximiliano Chacón
Translation by A. Gabriel Meléndez

Holy earth of the ancient city,
History-filled garden where flowers gladly
        open to the bright sun
in swatches of fragrance and color.
From earthen pots
grains and fruits grow with great love.
There under your blue aroma-filled sky,
the bed of my childhood is cradled.
Your lovely earth is holy for me,
just as beautiful as the flower of your gardens,

holy for the loving kiss upon my lips, a child
      of maternal love nourished
in times when she suffered in her loving bed
to give me life from her noble breast.
Holy because you hold in your bosom
the dust of he who gave me life, and
because you are the sweet reliquary of my
      dead brothers,
inflamed, torn, as the voice of thunder
      snatches away the calm,
and your winters have frosted the tears
blessed by my mother which she has shed
      there.

And even though sad memories come back
      to me
when my thoughts return to the past
and form a scene that offers me
a thousand heartaches that pierce my heart,
upon seeing the thorns that pain me,
I also see the fragrant rosebush filled with
      the joy
that my parents gave me as a child.
I never forget the fleeting tolling
sent from your regal bell towers,
Nor the birds in vibrant song
that sweetly greet the first light of each new day
and the evening lullabies in the soft whisper
      of your orchards
that fill me with burning desire.
But if my unavoidable fate
sends my ship sailing from you
with indifference, and though the sad echoes
      of my nostalgia
never again reach your soft embrace,
look to the sky and you shall see the constant
      star of memory
shining and you, among that delight, will
      be there.

Synopsis

Chacón speaks of Santa Fe as holy earth and an ancient city. He describes it as a garden filled with swatches of aroma and color. The poet says that in this garden where fruits, grains, and flowers grow from earthen pots, his childhood was nurtured. A time, he describes, as one when the crib of his childhood was gently rocked. Chacón regards Santa Fe as holy for it is the place where he received the love of his mother in affectionate kisses. He speaks of his mother's sacrifice and of her selflessness in giving him life by suckling him at her bosom. Santa Fe is also holy because it is the place where the dust or ashes of his father's remains lie. The city, says Chacón, is a reliquary that holds brothers taken by death, when death, enraged, like violent thunder breaks the calm of life. The city is also holy because the tears of the poet's widowed mother cover it like the frost of winter. Using the metaphor of home and roses, Chacón shares two recollections of Santa Fe. The first evocation is of the loss of family members and friends, and the second is of his childhood, which he names as the pleasing rose of love given to him by his parents.

Chacón says he is unable to forget the regal-sounding tolling of Santa Fe's bell towers, the vibrant song of the birds that greet each new day, or the soft whisper of the city's orchards each evening. These are like lullabies that evoke strong desire in him. In the final stanza Chacón speaks of the course of his life, comparing his wanderings to the movements of a sailing ship pulled by cold, indifferent winds. He conjectures that the sad echoes of his nostalgia may never reach the city from the far-off places where he may be, yet he affirms that if the reader looks to the sky he will see the constant star of his memories, and among the delights of the sky will be the city of his birth: Santa Fe.

Ode to Santa Fe

Pat Mora

(2006)

      Like a pilgrim, I journey
anxious for the sight and scent
      of your brown garment.
I find you in the hills,
      Old Spirit,
trudging along, exploring
      a duet with a raven,
shaking your head at skittish quail
      that scurry
under the folds of your long, patched skirt.

You open your arms wide
      when you see me and lift me
        from all I carry, swoop me up
into your glorious light.
      You take my hand,
pull me along
      accompanied by your old love,
        the wind, tu músico,
          who strums wild grasses

With his long, bony fingers,
      serenades us
by fiddling on dry cholla stems,
      whistles through yucca pods,
        drums an old aspen
and for a grand finale
      conducts cottonwoods' hushed carols.
We study the mountains, meditating
      in their cloud shawls,
        rising,
their stern habit, undaunted
      even by the bravado of thunderstorms.

From your deep pockets,
      you offer handfuls of seeds, fling
them out with a wide arc,
      teach me to stretch my arm for miles,
hoarding nothing.

      You kneel,
put your ear low
      to hear the arroyo's newest
composition, the daily incorporation
      of sky, eaves, the murmurings
of minnows and tadpoles
      the liquid lyric.

You shape new hills,
      hollow a small cave,
furnish it with dry branches
      and pink plumes for a fox hunting
a new home, a quiet place to curl
      into the extravagance of his tail.

Ignoring my subtle suggestions
      that we rest, on you stride,
        deeper into the earth's old story,
fingering fossils and myths,
      in the pine's perfume.

      Solitary woman, philosopher of silence,
brown caress,
      vessel of light,
      after sunset, you point to the stars
I haven't seen in months,
and to los espíritus
      who wander a land they refuse to leave.

PART II

Querencia

THE ROOT OF BELONGING

And They Called It Horizon

Valerie Martínez

(excerpt, 2009)

I.

Today we say Santa Fe, our Santa Fé
in the Sierra Madre, in the cradle between
the Pecos Mountains, Cerro Piñón,
Tano Point, Caja del Río, Tetilla Peak.

But there was a time, long ago,
before names, dream before dream.
Aho niishnee, principio, the beginning.

It was a seed, imagine it,
smaller than the eye's dark pupil,
smaller than the tiniest yellow idea of seed,
and tinier. Inside, the dream
of something blue and unbelievably wide,
something rising to blue, algún encuentro
magnífico de marrón y azul.
And the seed, there buried.
Perhaps it was the eye behind the eye
of some great Being, or the eye
of a fantastic explosion, or the spot
on the tail-flick of a lizard
with red and black ridges on his back.
The seed nestled in what became an orb,
an orb hurtling through indigo space,
then a spinning, whirling mass of blue
become this planet we call Mother Earth.

And it hung there, inside,
weaving a garment of brightness.

And the warp was the white light of morning;
and the weft was the red light of evening;
and the fringes were sky-water falling;

and the borders the dewy rainbows of afternoons.
Cielo-agua que cae,
arco iris arqueando.

The seed, buried in the earth
we later called Pangaea,
Laurasia, Gondwanaland,
the earth's first continents.

And the sea floor moved and kept moving
under magnetic waves, tectonic shifts,
plates going up and over and under.
The land rising up, volcanic,
to the east and to the north,
and to the northwest and the southwest.

The seed, the Being's eye, finally opening
its lid, or the explosion bursting forth,
or the black spot moving back and forth
on the tail of this earth. Here, in this place,
ghe, ghe, ghe, ghe,
warp, weft, sky-water,
than pi, thamu tsan,
arco iris.

What came from the seed emerged
into some unbelievable expanse of sky
tempered only by mountains above
and right and left, then a blanket
of brown and green and gold
unfolding to the south.

The line of the horizon, the sky-vault
resting like an ocean in the cradle of this place.

Before time, before memory.

Así comenzó esto, antes que naciéramos
antes de que alguién llamara cualquier cosa, hogar.

antes cualquiera llamó algo hogar.
This is how it began, before we were born,
before anyone called anything tierra,
ghe, madre, ashéé, Santa Fe, home.

II.

Millipede, darkling beetle, picture-winged fly.

The stink bug finds its likeness
in the shadows of windblown welchii,
winterfat, bristlecone pine, bigleaf sage.

Psorothamus scoparius, erioganum
umbellatum, sulfur buckwheat.
This is their sound, a quarry of names.

And here the small thunder of creature-feet:
dwarf shrew, western pipistrelle,
mogollon vole, rock pocket mouse.

The Zuni prairie dog and family clan
abandon their burrow, climb up
into the spring sun, lean and hungry.

The feed and starve, feed and starve,
of the tassel-eared squirrel
and ponderosa pine,
their symbiotic hum.

Then a larger thunder: elk, mountain lion, coyote.
The wapiti's resounding call, antlers clacking
in the sunset wings-sound of pygmy nuthatch,
brown creeper, mountain chickadee, dark-eyed
        junco.

Eye-spot, explosion, the creatures of shadow
        and air.
Cellular, ancestral—bridging now and there.

III.

In the beginning
the People lived in the darkness of underground.
One day the Mole came to visit them.
The People asked if there was another world
beside the one they lived in.
The Mole told them to follow him.
The People formed a line behind the Mole
as he began to dig his way up.
Each took the soil he loosened
and passed it back to the next,
and to the next, to the back of the line.
This is why the tunnel closed behind them
and they could never go back.
The Mole led them to a place of sunlight and
        blue sky.
This is the end; this is the beginning of their story.

IV.

They stood, dizzy with light, the blue
an enormous bowl inverted above them.
And there was a seam that sewed together
the earth and sky, and they called it
horizon, and they traced it with pointed fingers,
turning in place, all the way around.
After a while they sang.
They moved their feet.

After a while their tongues, their ribcages,
their knees and ankles and toes stilled
to the crawl of thunderclouds
and mountains song.

They slept.

And then, they got to work.

Santa Fe para Santafeños:
Mayor Jaramillo's Victory, 1994.

¿Dónde Vivo Yo?

Tommy Archuleta

(2006)

Yo vivo donde
la sangre de millares de
indígenas
se ha cambiado en polvo
como si nada—
abajo las botas
de millares de soldados españoles,
mis antepasados;
donde cada estación
se muda con la airosidad
de antílope al alba
mientras puestas del sol
queman cada nube
hechas de algodón
en un estallido
de morado y oro

Así búscame
entre los árboles
de hoja perene
y los álamos temblones
que armentan
en la sangre de Cristo;
búscame en el ladrillo
de las calles de la plaza
y en las piedras
de la casa
de San Francisco;
y búscame en el interior
de las manos
de mujeres sabias
en chales viejas
rezando sus rosarios
encima de portales calmados;
y búscame entre las risas
de los niños
corriendo en cualquier parque,

y en cada sonrisa
de cada perro,
en cada pedazo de sombra;

y si quieres,
búscame en cada girasol
creciendo en cada lado
de cada camino,
y adentro de cada prado
desocupado ya no desocupado,
aquí en la ciudad
de Santa Fe, Nuevo México
donde yo vivo.

Where Do I Live?

Tommy Archueleta

Translation by A. Gabriel Meléndez

I live where the blood of thousands of Indians
Has become earth, just like that,
As it if disappeared
beneath the boot heels of thousands of Spanish
    soldiers
—My ancestors;

Where each season changes
Like the wispy stride of antelope at dawn
And where dusk burns each cotton cloud
with shimmering purple-gold light.

So, look to find me
Among the pine trees
And quaking aspens
That grow high in the Sangre de Cristo
    Mountains.
Look for me on the brick streets of the plaza,
In the rocks that surround San Francisco's
    home
And look for me in the hands of the wise women

Covered in old shawls as they pray their rosaries
above the quiet portales
And look for me in the smile of the children
Running in any park
In each broad smile
And in each dog hiding in the cool shadows;
And, if you care,
Look for me in each sunflower
Growing by the side of every lane and
Across every meadow,
Left fallow, but still not fallow,
Here in Santa Fe, Nuevo México,
The place where I live.

Santa Fe—Coplas Para El Tiempo Santo

Fr. Benedicto Cuesta
(1976)

Santa Fe, dolor y encanto,
Corazón, punto y destino,
Cuando me alejo de ti
Se me borran los caminos.

Santa Fe estaba de duelo
En mantilla de tristeza,
Y par las penas del río
Lágrimas de hierbabuena.

Santa Fe estaba sin luna
La noche del Viernes Santo,
Desde la Sangre de Cristo
Ángeles la están velando.

Solita con su rosario
La Virgen va entre los pinos
Katchinas y niños juegan
Por el chamizal florido.
La Virgen de Guadalupe

Conquistadora de la Paz:
Our Lady of Santa Fe, 2005.

De luto se está vistiendo,
Por Agua Fría los pájaros
Lloran lirios de silencio.

San Miguel junto a la Cruz
Montaba guardia de honor,
San Francisco deshojaba
Cinco genarios en flor.
Santa Fe, dolor y encanto,
Corazón, punto y destino
Cuando me alejo de ti
Se me borran los caminos.

Santa Fe: Verses for the Lenten Season

Fr. Benedicto Cuesta
Translation by Rosalie C. Otero

Santa Fe, city of sorrow and joy
Heart of my destiny
When I am far from thee

All paths are veiled to me
Santa Fe was mourning
in a shroud of sadness
and like the river
weeps tears of Yerba Buena

Santa Fe was without a moon
the night of Good Friday
From the top of the Sangre de Cristo
        Mountains
angels are keeping vigil

Alone with her rosary
The Virgin walks among the pines
Katchinas and children play
Among the flowering sagebrush

The Virgin of Guadalupe
dressed in mourning
by the street of Agua Fría
The birds cry litanies of silence

Saint Michael, near the cross
kept a guard of honor
Saint Francis plucks petals
From five geraniums in bloom
Santa Fe, city of sorrow and joy
Heart of my destiny
When I am far from you
The paths are hidden from my view

Bells

Jimmy Santiago Baca
(1989)

Bells. The word gongs my skull bone . . .
Mamá carried me out, just born,
swaddled in hospital blankets,
from St. Vincent's in Santa Fe.
Into the evening, still drowsed
with uterine darkness,
my fingertips purple with new life,
cathedral bells splashed
into my blood, plunging iron hulls
into my pulse waves. Cathedral steeples,
amplified brooding, sonorous bells,
through narrow cobbled streets, bricked patios,
rose-trellised windows,
red-tiled Spanish rooftops, bells
beat my name, "Santiago! Santiago!"
Burning my name in black-frosted streets,
bell sounds curved and gonged deep,
ungiving, full-bellowed beats of iron on iron,
shuddering pavement. Mamá walked,
quivering thick stainless panes, creaking
plaza shop doors, beating its gruff thuds
down alleys and dirt
passageways, past men waiting in doorways
of strange houses. Mamá carried me, past

peacocks and chickens, past the miraculous
stairwell winding into the choir loft, touted
in tourist brochures, "Not one nail was used
to build this, it clings tenaciously
together by pure prayer power, a spiraling
pinnacle of faith. . . ." And years later,
when I would do something wrong,
in kind reprimand Mamá would say,
"You were born of bells, more than my womb,
they speak to you in dreams.
Ay, Mejito,
you are such a dreamer!"

Lamy y su media torre: Mission Accomplished, 1998.

PART III

Historias

SUBJECTS OF TWO EMPIRES

Plano de la Provincia interna de el Nuevo México, 1779, Bernardo
Miera y Pacheco. (An image of this map can be found in the Fray
Angélico History Library at the Palace of the Governors New Mexico
History Museum, Santa Fe New Mexico.)

Leyendas Neo-Mexicanas: Popé

Episodios de la revolución
de los indios en 1680

José Escobar

(Las Dos Repúblicas, Denver, Colorado, 1896)

Cantos I–II

Cantos I and II of "Leyendas Neo-Mexicanas: Popé" are not extant. The poem appeared in print in *Las Dos Republicas*, Denver, Colorado, on March 21, 1896. *Las Dos Repúblicas*, a weekly edited by José Escobar, ran Cantos III and IV as the second installment of the Popé series a week later on March 28, 1896. The entire poem consisting of ten Cantos was published between March 21 and April 18, 1896.

Canto III

Ven, con júbilo contempla
esa luz bendita y santa,
pues, que es la luz redentora
que la libertad encarna,
y como yo, conmovido
esa luz admira y ama
pues ella es la tez sublime
que alumbra al fin la venganza
y la reinvindicación de nuestra patria.
Mañana cuando la aurora
con sus nubes de escarlata
y sus celajes de oro
rompa la azulada gasa
que ayer encubrió todavía
el dolor de las esclavas,
alumbrará un pueblo libre
que llena de gozo su alma
cantará sublimes himnos
de sus dioses ante el ara.

Maquette of Popé statue in the U.S. Capitol Rotunda, Washington, DC. Photo by Cliff Fragua.

Nuestras más lindas doncellas
con húmedas rosas blancas
coronarán a los héroes
que con sus flechas y lanzas
tintas aun de roja sangre
en las estufas sagradas,
formarán el bello emblema
¡de nuestra justa venganza!
Escucha el tombé de guerra

sus marciales sones manda
y estarás pues, convencido,
que Popé, no te engañaba.
Apresurémonos, pues,
continuemos nuestra marcha,
y al frente de esos guerreros
que su vida venden cara
por rescatar sus derechos
y sus libertades santas.

Luchemos los dos también
contras las huestas hispanas
para que sepan que aún somos
en campo de batalla,
dignos hijos de esa altiva
y gloriosa raza indiana . . .

La voz del jefe Popé
dejó de sonar airada.
Lentamente prosiguieron
los dos caciques su marcha,
y continuó la tormenta;
y allá, sobre la montaña,
con sus rojos resplandores
y fosforesencias blancas,
como una gigante antorcha,
como un faro de esperanza,
siguió su brillo la luz,
la luz de aquella fogata.

New Mexico Legends: Popé
Episodes from the Pueblo Revolt of 1680

José Escobar

Translation by A. Gabriel Meléndez

Canto III

Come and with joy observe
that blessed and holy light
the redeeming light
that liberty embodies,
and, like me, you shall be moved to
admire, to love that light
for she is the sublime incarnation
that fires the vengeance
and the vindication of our homeland.

Tomorrow when dawn
with its scarlet clouds
rips open the blue gauze
that only yesterday covered
the pain of the women slaves,
its golden skylight
will fall upon a free people
who, filled with joy in their soul,
will sing sublime hymns of their gods before
        the altars.
Our loveliest maidens
with moist white roses
will crown the heroes,
their bows and arrows
tinged with red blood
a fitting sign
for our just vengeance
above the sacred fires of the kiva!

Listen, the war drum
sends forth its call,
be assured that Popé,
does not deceive you.
Let us hurry then, continue
our advance at the head
of those warriors.
Let them set a high price
In return for their lives
that will rescue our rights and sacred liberties.
Let us together struggle against the Spanish forces
        so they will know on the

field of battle that we are the noble sons
of a proud and glorious
Indian race.

The voice of the chief, Popé,
lets off its highborn sound:
Slowly the two leaders resumed their march amid
    the storm
while, there, above the mountain
with its red splendor
and its phosphorescent snows,
like a giant torch
like a lighthouse of hope,
the glare of that fire is amplified.

Synopsis of Canto III

The Taos Pueblo leader Popé sits with Jaca at a campfire. In a soliloquy Popé invites Jaca to reflect on the idea that the light of the bonfire symbolizes the freedom and spirit of reprisal that will free the Indian people from the tyranny of Spanish rule. Popé tells Jaca that the next day will dawn on a free people. The coming sacrifice of the warriors will become legendary among the people, and the most beautiful Indian maidens will crown the heroes of the battle. Their bows and arrows, still tinged with blood, will become fitting emblems next to the fires of the kivas. Popé asks Jaca to take heart in the sound of the war drum and be assured that what Popé tells him will come to pass. Popé makes a plea for both leaders to join forces and lead the warriors as they struggle to win their liberty and prove that they are the noble sons of a proud people. The poet tells of Popé's words dropping off as both men return to lead the march of warriors. On a distant mountaintop a storm rages, and the red splendor of the mountain at sunset and its snowcapped peaks resemble a giant torch or a lighthouse symbolizing hope, which like the fire of the bonfire grows larger.

Canto IV

Brillaba indecisa apenas
la naciente luz del alba
del día décimo de agosto.
A toda rienda cruzaba
sobre el soberbio corcel
cubierto de espuma blanca
las calles de Santa Fe
el capitán Gómez Prada
que del Alcalde de Taos
llevaba importantes cartas
a Don Antonio Otermín
general que gobernaba
esta lejana provincia,
la última de Nueva España.

El caballero español,
cruzando calles y plazas,
llegó al fin hasta la puerta
de la señorial morada.
Desmontó con ligereza
del alazán que montaba,
arrojó sobre el galápago
la polvorosa y negra capa,
y con el puño acerado
de su damasquina daga
golpeó con mano insegura,
por el dolor y la rabia,
el hierro y el maderamen
de aquella puerta cerrada:
¡Quién Vive!, gritó un soldado
que de centinela estaba.
Y el capitán respondió:
Otermín y el rey de España.
Giró la puerta en sus goznes
y quedó franca la entrada.

El capitán español,
sin ceremonia ni traba,
cruzó los amplios salones

de aquella suntuosa casa
y poco después, llegando
hasta la soberana cámara
de don Antonio Otermín
entrególe aquellas cartas
en las que el Padre Velasco
relación sucinta daba
del complot que Tupatú,
Catiti, Francisco y Jaca,
teniendo a Popé por jefe
en silencio preparaban
para expulsar de esa rica
y subyugada comarca
a los pocos españoles
que por fuerza escaparan
de la cólera y el odio
de aquella nación esclava
que abruma de dolores
y sediente de venganza,
iban de nuevo a luchar
frente a frente y cara a cara
con el despótico ibero
que en época no lejana
con la humillante cadena
de la esclavitud amarga
había mantenido cruel
a toda esa noble raza
que por único delito
y por vergonzosa mancha
tenía la de haber nacido
en la cuna libre y santa
de los bosques tropicales
de la tierra americana.

Canto IV

The nascent light of dawn
had just broken on the tenth
day of August:

Captain Gómez Prada cut across
the streets of Santa Fe at full gallop
on his proud steed covered with
the foam of sweat.

He brings news from the alcalde of Taos
for don Antonio Otermín,
the general in command of
this distant province,
at the furthest reaches of New Spain.
The Spanish horseman
crossing plazas and streets,
at last, arrived at the door
of the regal dwelling.
He dismounts
from the roan he rode quickly,
and throws over the saddle
his dusty, black cape
and with the steel handle
of his Moorish dagger
he knocks with an unsteady hand,
full pain and anger,
the iron and timbers.

Arriving at the august chamber
of don Antonio Otermín
he turns over the letters
in which Padre Velasco
gives a precise account
of the plot prepared in secret
by Tupatú, Catití,
Francisco and Jaca,
who, with Popé to lead them,
would push the few Spaniards
that might be spared its rage and anger
out of that rich and subjugated province
belonging to an enslaved nation,
filled with suffering,
and thirsting for vengeance.

It would fight face to face
against the despotic Iberian
who in the recent past
had humbled that noble race
with the chain of bitter slavery
and whose only crime,
whose only shameful sin,
had been to have been born
at the free and sacred site
of the tropical forests
of the Americas.

Synopsis of Canto IV

The canto shifts the scene from the Indian camp
to Santa Fe as dawn breaks the following morning.
A Spanish solider, Captain Gómez Prada, rides at
breakneck speed through the streets of Santa Fe to
reach the home of the governor of the province,
Antonio de Otermín. Gómez Prada brings news
from the alcalde (magistrate) of Taos that details the
conspiracy of the Indian leaders to revolt against
the Spaniards. The canto describes the reasons the
Indians have to break the chains of subordination
and speaks of the unjustness of the Spanish domi-
nation of the Indians, whose only crime was to
have been born a free people in the Americas.

Canto V

Al terminar la lectura
De aquellas funestas cartas,
El General Otermín
Exclamó con voz airada:
Nunca creí, ¡voto a Cristo!
Que esa miserable raza
contra el rey nuestro señor
en armas se levantara;
y ya que lo quiere, que sea;

de nuevo nuestras espadas
domarán orgullo tanto,
contendrán audacia tanta.
Capitán, mandad al punto
Que el clarín toque ¡a las armas!

Despachad noticia pronta
a las villas comarcanas.
Haced que mi brava escolta
Se destaque en avanzadas,
Y que los roncos tambores
rompan su toque de alarma.
Marchad, pues, pero seguro
que si triunfan nuestras armas,
por servicio que hacéis
hoy a la nación de España,
ella os dará en recompense
gratificación bien amplia . . .

El capitán español
Abandonó aquella estancia
Y cuando solo quedó
Otermín, en voz muy baja,
Cual si temiera, quizá,
Al oir sus palabras,
exclamó quedo, muy quedo,
y llena de angustia el alma:

Un triste presentimiento
a mi corazón embargo
y no sé, por qué, Dios mío,
la tenaz ruda batalla
entre mi orgullo de ibero
y lo justo de esa causa,
por la que hoy los bravos indios
de nuevo a luchar se lanzan.
Ojalá que me equivoque,
pero preveo que esa raza
por tanto tiempo abatida,

por tanto tiempo humillada,
romperá al fin el grillete
que sobre ella puso España.

Calló el noble castellano:
y en esa suntuosa cámara
volvió a reinar el silencio
con su fatídica calma.
Y solo, con sus dolores
y con sus dudas amargas
que como garños de acero
su corazón desgarraban.
Quedó el general ibero
En su magnífico alcázar.

Canto V

Upon reading those
fateful letters
General Otermín
exclaimed in a haughty voice:

Never did I think, Christ!
that wretched race would
rise up in arms
against our king and lord.
But if this is what they want,
so be it, again our swords
will tame such pride and
contain such boldness.

Captain, order that the trumpets
sound the call to arms at once!
Send news to all the villas
of the province, prepare my
brave troops to lead the advance
and let the gruff drumbeat
sound out the alarm.

Go forth, assured that if our
arms triumph
for the service you render to Spain this day,
she will give you grateful payment.

The Spanish captain
left that dwelling
and left alone,
Otermín, in a low voice,
as if fearing the sound of
his own words,
exclaimed quietly, very quietly,
his spirit filled with anguish:

My God, I don't know why,
this sad premonition
sweeps over my heart,
nor why this fierce,
crude battle grows
between my Iberian pride
and the justness of the cause
for which Indian braves
rise up against me today.

I hope to God I am wrong,
but I foresee that that race,
downtrodden for so long,
humiliated for so long,
will finally break the shackle
that Spain has placed upon it.

The noble Castilian was silent
in the sumptuous chamber
silence reigned with deathly
calm and alone with his
pain and bitter doubt
that were like chains of steel,
that tore at his heart
the Iberian general was alone
in his magnificent fortress.

Synopsis of Canto V

Otermín pronounces a speech in which he expresses his disbelief after reading the letter sent to him of the uprising in the north. He orders that the news be sent to the outlying towns of the province and his troop to sound a general alarm. He speaks of the gratitude the mother country, Spain, will show the valor of the Spanish soldiers when they triumph over the Indians. Gómez Prada takes his leave, and once alone, Otermín's speech turns to doubt and fear. He is perplexed by the battle that rages within his thoughts that pits his self-concept as a proud Spaniard against the justness of the Indian struggle. Otermín hopes that he is mistaken but cannot rid himself of the premonition that the hour has come when the Indians will break the shackles Spanish rule has placed on them.

Canto VI

La noticia aterradora
de la insurreción indiana
se propaló como un rayo
en toda aquella comarca,
y los frailes y colonos
de las villas comarcanas
abandonando sus templos,
sus intereses y casas
llegaban a Santa Fe
donde las tropas hispanas,
sin darse tregua un momento,
con empeño levantaban,
en calles y callejuelas,
en avenidas y plazas,
altos y gruesos fortines,
trincheras y barricadas.

Como en la misma ciudad
los colonias castellanas
seguras y altas defensas
con prontitud fabricaban
en la Isleta, San Felipe,
Santa Cruz de la Cañada,
Santo Domingo, Sandía,
Cochití, Pojoaque, Puara,
San Lázaro, San Cristóbal,
Taos, Tesuque y Santa Clara.

Pasaron algunos días
de incertidumbre y de calma;
y por fin, el día catorce
al despuntar la alborada
a todo escape llegaron
cuatro de los avanzadas
diciendo: Que por el norte,
con banderas desplegadas;
al son de roncos tombes
y armados con fuertes lanzas,
quinientos indios de Pecos
venían como vanguardia
del ejército insurrecto
que a Santa Fe se acercaba. . . .

Un grupo de guerrilleros
capitaneados por Jaca,
llevando gigantes cruces,
unas rojas y otras blancas;
simbolizando las unas
destrucción, guerra, matanza;
y las otras, garantías,
amistad sincera y gracia;
sin aparente temor,
en actitud noble y franca;
sin escudos, ni carcajes,
y llevando por toda arma
un indiano pabellón
y de encino verdes ramas,
se acercaron hasta el pie

de la trinchera artillada
donde el general hispano
con sus tropas se encontraba.

Del grupo de guerrilleros
se adelantó el indio Jaca;
y con aspecto tranquilo
y con voz robusta y clara
dirigiéndose a Otermín
y a las filas castellanas,
dijo en lengua española
que el cacique bien la hablaba.

Canto VI

The terrifying news
of the Indian insurrection,
like lighting, raced
throughout those regions
and the friars and the settlers
of the neighboring villages
abandoning their churches,
their interests, and their homes
converged on Santa Fe
where the Spanish troops
without a moment's rest,
and with great effort put up high
fortifications in the streets and
alleyways, and laid trenches
and barricades along the avenues
and in the plazas.

And, as had happened in the city,
the villagers of the surrounding
Spanish hamlets quickly built
secure and high defenses at
Isleta, San Felipe, Santa Cruz
de la Cañada, Santo Domingo,
Sandía, Cochití, Pojoaque, Puara,
San Lázaro, San Cristóbal, Taos,

Tesuque, and Santa Clara.
Several quiet days of uncertainty
Passed, and finally on the fourteenth,
at the break of dawn
four scouts arrived at
breakneck speed, saying:

"From the north, with flags
unfurled and marching to the
sound of the raspy war drum
five hundred Pecos Indians,
armed with strong lances,
are advancing in the vanguard
of the army of insurrection
that nears Santa Fe."

A group of warriors
captained by Jaca,
and carrying large crosses
some are white and some are red
some symbolize destruction,
war, and death,
the others appeasement,
true friendship, and grace,
march forth without apparent
fear in a noble and honest manner
without shields or quivers,
unarmed, they carry only
a canopy, and green boughs
of scrub oak, as they approach
the defensive trench
where the Spanish general
is stationed with his troops.
Jaca, emerged from out of a group
of warriors and with a calm demeanor
and in a robust and clear voice
spoke to Otermín and to
the ranks of the Spaniards,
in Spanish, a language the
cacique spoke well.

Synopsis of Canto VI

News of the uprising spreads through the Spanish hamlets like wildfire. The settlers of the neighboring towns are forced to leave their homes and farms and begin to converge on Santa Fe. The soldiers in Santa Fe prepare for the defense of the city by setting up barricades, digging trenches, and raising fortifications. Canto VI tells of similar preparations at settlements in the Río Arriba and Río Abajo. Several calm but anxious days pass, and on the fourteenth of August four scouts arrive in Santa Fe with a report of having seen five hundred Pecos Indians at the vanguard of an army of Indians descending on the city from the north. A group of warriors commanded by Jaca near the city. They are carrying red and white crosses. The red crosses symbolize destruction and war and the white one friendship and the promise of peace. The group also carries a canopy and freshly cut green boughs of scrub oak. Arriving at the walls of Santa Fe, Jaca emerges from the group and directs himself to Otermín in Spanish, a language the poet says, Jaca knows well.

Canto VII

"General: Popé me envía
en nombre de nuestra raza
a decirte que si quieres
escapar de la venganza
de la nación que hasta hoy
quiso ser tu humilde esclava,
abandones al instante
y para siempre la patria
que sin derecho ninguno
y sin más ley que la espada,
conquistó no por bravura
de los huestes castellanos,
sino la negra traición
de algunos indianos sátrapas,

que manchando nuestro nombre
y nuestras glorias pasadas
prefirieron a la muerte
gloriosa, bendita y santa
de los héroes venturosos,
llenarse de negra infamia
presentándose a ser esclavos
del soberbio rey de España.

Esto te dice Popé
en nombre de nuestra raza.
Conque elige: Sangre y fuego
o la entrega de la plaza
que fue ayer dichosa y libre
la cuna gloriosa y santa
de los indios que ahora vienen
con su sangre a rescatarla."

El General Otermín
lleno de asombro y rabia
mirando de aquel cacique
el valor y la arrogancia
le dijo con voz de trueno:
"Dile al jefe que te manda
que el ejército español
jamás cedió a la amenaza
que antes que captitular.
que antes que entregar la plaza,
entre sus sangrientas ruinas
y entre sus ardientes escombros
sabrán morir como buenos,
sin volver jamás la espalda,
en defensa de su rey,
los nobles hijos de España."
"Marcha, pues; dile a Popé
que al rayar la luz del alba
el ejército español
en el campo de batalla
sabrá como en otro día

castigar audacia tanta;
y que si tanto confía
en su estrella y en sus armas
y quiere reconquistar
a la Tigua y sus comarcas,
que venga con sus guerreros
sin más demora a tomarla.

Regrese a tu campamento:
y en tu ruin memoria graba
lo que acabo de decirte
para que al llegar, ¡oh Jaca!
a Popé puedas decir
lo que le contesto . . . ¡Marcha!"

Los indígenas quebaron
sus gigantes cruces blancas
en señal de reto a muerte
frente a las filas hispanas,
y después a paso lento
siguieron su contramarcha
en tanto que el español,
de pie, sobre la muralla,
en actitud de desprecio
y con altiva mirada
contempla a los guerreros
y su jefe, el bravo Jaca,
que por la extensa llanura
poco a poco se alejaban.

Canto VII

"General, Popé has sent me
in the name of our people
to tell you that if you wish
to escape the vengeance of a nation
that up to now has sought to be
your humble servant,
that you must at once
and for all time abandon this country,

which, with no right other
than that of the might of the sword,
has been conquered,
and not by the bravery of Spanish soldiers,
but by evil treachery of some Indian
satraps who besmirched our name
and our past glories
and elected black infamy over
a death that would have been
glorious, holy, and blessed
by abasing themselves as
slaves to the arrogant king of Spain.

This is what Popé says to you in the
name of our people. So
choose blood and fire,
or surrender the plaza
that yesterday was
the birthplace of free
and bountiful Indians
who now come to take it back."

General Otermín,
filled with awe and hate,
seeing valor and pride in that cacique,
responded with the voice of thunder:
"Tell the leader who
sends you, that the Spanish army
has never given in to threats,
before it capitulates,
before it surrenders the plaza,
it will first die among its bloodied ruins
and in burning homes,
these noble sons of Spain will
die nobly and they will never turn
their swords away from the defense of their king.

Go back and tell Popé
that when the light of dawn breaks

the Spanish army will be on the field of battle,
and it will know how to punish,
as it has done before,
boldness so great,
and if he has such confidence
in his fate and his arms
and he wishes to retake
Tiguex and the surrounding lands,
let him come with his warriors
and not hesitate to retake it.
Go back to your camp
and etch into your miserable memory
what I have told you
so that upon your return, Oh, Jaca,
you can relay my answer to Popé
Leave now!"

The Indians broke their
white crosses as a sign
and challenge of death
in front of the Spanish ranks,
and then, slowly,
they took up their march back
while the Spaniard atop the wall
with a gestures of disrespect
and with haughty looks
looked over the warriors
and their chief, the brave Jaca,
who drew away little by little
over the expansive plain.

Synopsis of Canto VII

Addressing Otermín as General, Jaca informs him that Popé has sent him in the name of their race to tell Otermín that if he wishes to escape the reprisal of a people who have tried to serve him humbly, he must abandon Santa Fe immediately and for all time. Jaca adds that the Spanish victory over the people of the region was never the result of Spanish daring and bravery; rather Jaca says it resulted because a certain band of sly Indians who brought dishonor to all when they willingly abased themselves before the first Spaniards who came into New Mexico and became their willing slaves. Jaca reiterates Popé's demand, saying that the Spaniards must surrender the site that was the once the birthplace of the Indians when they were free. Filled with awe and rage at Jaca's insolence, Otermín responds in a booming voice. He tells Jaca to go back to his leader and tell him that the Spanish soldiers will never surrender the town nor turn away from defending the Spanish crown. Otermín throws back a challenge to Popé, saying that if Popé is sure of his fate and his arms, he should come and take Tiguex. The Spaniards, Otermín notes, will meet the Indians on the field of battle at the break of day. Hearing Otermín's response, the Indians break the red crosses in front of the Spanish soldiers and return across the wide plain to their camp.

Canto VIII

El genio de las tinieblas
con sus negrísimas alas
había cubierto a la tierra:
las estrellas alumbraban
con sus diamantinos rayos
de Dios el azul alcazar,
cuando el campamento
indiano donde Popé se encontraba
con sus tres mil guerrilleros.

Llegó el mensajero Jaca.
Los rojizos resplandores
de las ardientes fogatas
daban un tinte sangriento
a las tiendas de campaña

hechas de pieles de cíbolo
donde a esa hora descansaban
los indígenas guerreros
de su fatigosa marcha,
mientras al dulce reposo
los soldados se entregaban,
Popé, y los caciques todos,
con impaciencia marcada,
oían la relación
de las altivas palabras
que el general Otermín
dio como respuesta franca
al enviado de Popé.

De Popé, que con voz clara,
dijo cuando terminó
de hablar al guerrero Jaca:

"Está bien: los españoles
para castigar mi audacia
esperan, según dijeron,
que alumbre el sol de mañana:
en cambio Popé y sus bravos
caerán como una avalancha
sobre la española villa
esta noche, y cuando el alba
de nuevo alumbre la tierra,
Tigua y sus bellas comarcas
otra vez, pese a Otermín
ya las hordas castellanas,
estarán en nuestras manos
libres del yugo de España."

Canto VIII

The architect of darkness
covered the earth
with his black wings.
The stars like the diamond rays

of God lit the blue palace,
when Jaca, the envoy, arrived
at the Indian encampment
where Popé and
three thousand warriors stood.

The red splendor of the burning fires
cast a bloody tint
on the war tents made of buffalo
hides where the indigenous warriors
rested at that hour from their rigorous march.

While at the same hour the soldiers
gave themselves to a delicious sleep.
Popé and all his caciques
with impatience listened to
the retelling of the harsh words
that General Otermín gave
as a clear response to Popé's envoy.
"So be it. To punish my boldness
the Spaniards await as they have said that the
sun will light the way tomorrow,
but Popé and his warriors will
fall like an avalanche upon the
Spanish town tonight, and
when the dawn again lights up the earth
Tiguex and its beautiful lands
will once more, despite Otermín
and the Castilian hordes,
be in our hands and
free from the Spanish yoke."

Synopsis of Canto VIII

The poet describes night falling as a struggle between good and evil forces. Darkness comes from
the hand of the devil, but the starlight in the sky
lights up God's blue place. When Jaca returns, the
fire of the Indian camps cast a red tint on the tepees

made of buffalo hide. Some of the Indian warriors are resting in the tents after their long march, while at the same time the Spanish soldiers have given in to a deep sleep. Jaca relates Otermín's harsh and arrogant words. Popé listens and accepts the challenge saying that while the Spaniards expect the Indians to meet them on the field of battle at daybreak, they will fall upon the city like an avalanche that same night. By the new day, Popé adds, Tiguex will be free from the Spanish yoke.

Canto IX

Y sus templos y palacios,
y sus cuarteles y casas,
presas del voraz incendio
en las destructoras llamas,
como dijo ese español,
ante tus guerreros, Jaca,
serán las humeantes tumbas
y las luces temerarias
que alumbren la inmensa pena,
la derrota y la desgracia
de los que no mucho hicieron
una vergonzosa esclava
de la poderosa Tigua,
y con ella, a nuestra raza.

Haced que el tombé de guerra
rompa la fúnebre calma
para que al llegar al frente
de la ciudad castellana,
los que la defiendan, sepan,
que esta altiva raza indiana
va a reconquistar luchando
esa ciudad y esa patria
que como dijiste ha poco,
mi valiente hermano Jaca,
hasta hoy quiso ser sierva
de la corona de España.

Marchemos, pues,
ha sonado para la nación esclava
la hora de la libertad
y la hora de la venganza:
y si la mudable suerte
es adversa a nuestra causa;
si nos venciera Otermín;
y si nuestra sangre indiana
para romper el grillete
que nos oprime, no basta,
siempre tendremos la gloria
de haber muerto, ¡camaradas!
¡defendiendo nuestros dioses,
defendiendo nuestra patria!

Buscar esa muerte honrosa
es buscar renombre y fama;
huir de esa justa lucha,
rehusar esa lucha santa,
es, a las indianas glorias,
poner otra nueva mancha;
morir luchando, es vivir;
es encarnar en el alma
de un pueblo agradecido
con amor sincero guarda
en nombre de los que caen,
en el altar de la patria,
y sucumbir sin luchar
por la libertad sagrada,
es más que debilidad,
una vergonzosa infamia.

Luchemos pues como buenos
contra las tropas de España
para que sepan que aún laten
en nuestras almas indianas
sentimientos de heroísmo
de aquella valiente raza
que ellos mismos encontraron
al llegar a estas comarcas.

Marchemos, pues, a la lucha;
marchemos, pues, sin tardanza;
y que el sol del nuevo día
si acaso muertos nos halla,
sea lámpara bendita,
que alumbra con dulce flama
ese túmulo glorioso,
esa sepultura santa,
de los que encuentren
la muerte por rescatar a la patria.

Enmudeció aquel guerrero;
y sus últimas palabras
retumbaron como un himno
entre las altas montañas
donde los genios benditos
de la libertad pulsaban,
los diapasones de oro
de sus dulcísimas arpas . . .

Poco después el tombé
sus roncos ecos lanzaba
y los escuadrones indios
armados de fuertes clavas,
en medio de las tinieblas
de nuevo emprendían la marcha.

El ejército insurrecto
cruzó la llanura basta;
y haciendo alto frente al muro
de la ciudad castellana,
se fue extendiendo, extendiendo,
en dos gigantescas alas.

El general español
que de las tropas indianas
observaba las maniobras,
cuando vio que a tiro estaban:
gritó a sus soldados: "¡Fuego!
¡Viva el Rey! y ¡Viva España!"
Sonaron los arcabuces
y sus mortíferos balas

abrieron sangriento surco
entre las filas indianas
que alzando un clamor inmenso,
clamor de dolor y rabia,
se arrojaron al asalto
de aquellas altas murallas
en las que, tras de sangrienta,
tenaz y ruda batalla,
el valeroso Popé
y el audaz cacique Jaca
hacían tremolar por fin
la bandera sacrosanta
emblema de justicia;
símbolo de venganza.

Canto IX

And in their churches and palaces
in their homes and garrisons
now filled with fire and burning flames.
Just as that Spaniard had said,
before your warriors, Jaca will lie the
          mass tombs
and the immense fire
over the great pain of defeat and disgrace
of those who only recently had made Tiguex,
and all of our race, a shameful slave.

Have the war drum break
the mortal calm so that on
arriving at the gates of that Castilian city,
those who defend it
will know that this proud Indian race
will retake by struggle that city
and this homeland,
which just as you have said,
Jaca, my valiant brother,
had wished to serve the crown of Spain.

Let us go forth,
the hour of liberty has sounded

for our enslaved nation
and so too, the hour of reprisal.
And if inconstant fate turns against us,
if Otermín defeats us,
if our Indian blood is not enough
to break the shackles that enslave us,
we shall always have the glory
of having died, comrades,
defending our gods,
defending our homeland.

This death is honorable,
it brings fame and honor.
To run from this sacred struggle
to reject this just war
is to place a new stain
upon the bravery of the Indian.
To die in struggle is to live,
it shall bring to life
the genuine love of the people
on the altar of those who have fallen.
For to die without struggling
for sacred freedom,
is more than weakness,
it is a shame and disgrace.

Let us fight like the best of them
against the Spanish troops,
so they will know that in our Indian soul
resides the heroism of the valiant race
which they themselves first found
when they first entered these regions.

Let us go forth to struggle,
let us go forth without delay
and if the light of the new day
finds us dead, let it be the holy lamp
that lights with its sweet aura
that glorious funeral mound,

that holy grave of those
who died to rescue the homeland.

That warrior was silent
and the last of his speech
echoed like a hymn
across those high mountains
where the holy architects of liberty
struck the golden chords of their harps . . .

Moments later the war drum
sounded its raspy echoes
and the squadrons of Indians
armed with strong spikes
and in the darkness
took up their march once more.

The rebel force crossed the vast plain,
stopping at the wall of the Spanish city,
then it opened wide,
opened like two enormous wingspans.

The Spanish general who
observed the maneuver of the Indian forces
waited until he saw
they were within firing range and shouted:
Long live the king and long live Spain!
The muskets roared and
their deadly slugs opened
a wide furrow in the Indian ranks
from which came the clamor of pain and rage,
and then leapt to the assault of those
        high walls,
where, after the bloody, vicious, and
        cruel battle,
Popé and the bold cacique Jaca
waved at last the holy flag,
the emblem of justice
        and symbol of vengeance.

Synopsis of Canto IX

As Canto IX begins, Popé describes the destruction and burning of Santa Fe as a scene reminiscent of Otermín's own resolve to have his troops be entombed in the ruins of the city rather than surrender it. Popé says that such destruction will occur just as in the words Otermín invoked before Jaca and his warriors. Popé orders the war drums to sound and the Indians to march to the walls of the city. Popé urges them to enter into battle, insisting that if fate turns against the Indian cause and if Otermín should be victorious, the death of the Indians shall still be valorous since they will have died defending their gods and their homeland. Popé reiterates the idea of finding an honorable death in a just struggle to rescue the homeland. The poet tells us that as Popé ends his speech, the chords of a hymn of freedom echo above in the nearby mountains. In the last part of the canto the Indian forces march to the sound of the war drum, and upon reaching the wall of the city they divide and open like two immense wings. Atop the walls the Spanish general watches the maneuver and orders his troops to fire upon the advancing warriors. A roar sounds as the surviving warriors scale the walls. The final view of the battle is of Jaca and Popé atop the walls, waving a banner that symbolizes justice and just reprisal.

Sombras franciscanas: Cross of the Martyrs, 2009.

Once A Man Knew His Name

E. A. Mares

(1987)

—dedicated to the memory of Popé, leader of the Pueblo Revolt, 1680, and to the memory of Alfonso Ortiz whose words inspired this poem and who requested a copy to read to his grandchildren.

I

My name is the promise of summer,
A cornucopia of food
Overflowing for the Pueblos.

My name is the harvest of gold,
The gathering of life-giving maize,

Fields of ripe squash, beans, and chile
Beneath the sun, wind, and stars.

As a child, I ran along the banks
Of the Río Grande. I nibbled
The sweet grass at the river's edge,
Blue grama, the little bluestem,
Chamomile, and the sunflowers.

I learned the Tewa stories. We come
From beneath Sandy Place Lake.
Our first mother is Blue Corn Woman,
The Summer Mother. Our first mother
Is White Corn Maiden, the Winter Mother.

All is sacred in our world:
Shimmering Mountain to the north.
Obsidian Covered Mountain to the west.
Turtle Mountain to the south.
Stone Man Mountain to the east.

Our hills are sacred.
Our shrines are sacred.
Our plazas are sacred.
Our dances are sacred.
From north to south,
east to west, these directions
and their colors are sacred

All is sacred for O'ke Owinge,
the pueblo the Spaniards called
San Juan.

The Spaniards said our spirits were devils,
Their faith the one true faith.
In the name of God
They destroyed our kivas.
In the name of God
They burned our katchinas.

In the name of God
They forbade our dances.
In the name of God
They flogged me and the caciques.
They took our Tewa names away
And filled our mouths
with the dust of our loss.

II

As a young man, I took in the colors of life. I
followed blue to the north, And my authority
returned to me.

I followed red to the south,
Yellow to the west,

White to the east,
And my authority returned to me.

I visited the sacred hills and mountains.
I knew the Summer People.
I knew the Winter People.
I knew my own name.
My authority returned to me.
At Taos Pueblo, inside the kiva,
I invoked P'ose Yemu,
He Who Scatters the Mist Before Him,
And my authority returned to me.

III

Our war leaders gathered,
And I spoke with authority.
I sent forth the runners
Like deer bearing the knotted cords
To the twenty-four pueblos,
To the six different languages,
To all the directions and their colors,
From Taos to the Hopi villages.

Los reconquistados: De Vargas Takes the Plaza, 2005.

We unraveled the last knot
In the searing light of day.
We struck everywhere at once.
We raked a fire across the sun.

We let those Spaniards go
Who had lived with us in peace.
We let them go. We drove the rest
South from Santa Fe,
Down the valleys of sweet rivers
To the mountains of Mexico.

The Spaniards tried, again and again,
to return to our land in the north.
I saw them marching to Santa Fe
and I called upon P'ose Yemu,
He Who Scatters the Mist Before Him.

The Río Grande rose, flooded,
Broke the ranks of the soldiers.
Confused, they scattered
Into the mist along the river.

We broke their arrogance
Like bits of dry straw.

We drove them away.
We let them go.

IV

Yet the Spaniards did return.
We fought them from our pueblos
Until tendrils of peace pushed up
Through the hateful crust of war.
Now we work the same fields,
Eat the same food.
We share our fiestas and our grief.
We've become compadres and comadres.
We work things out. We endure
like the earth and the stars
In their swirling galaxies.

My authority flows
Within and around the earth,
Within and around the mountains,
Like the waters flow
Through the pueblo lands.

I know my own name.
I know my own name.
I know my own name.

When Cultures Meet
Remembering San Gabriel del Yunge Oweenge

Orlando Romero

(1987)

The concept of San Gabriel means different things to different people. To this writer San Gabriel is a mystery with a capital M, for a daily diary or journal of the activities, indeed the very first encounter between the Native people and the first settlers, is not revealed to the extent that we would like. We do know from historical records that after a year here these settlers built a church and there was much celebration among both peoples. We know of Oñate's administration, his excursions outside of San Gabriel for riches and dreams that were never fulfilled, we know of various historical details except the daily and even mundane goings on of these people.

So what conjectures can we make? We can be assured that both people's way of life affected each other; another simple assumption is that material cultural exchanges must have been made. The settlers brought different seeds, for example, that to this day have affected our contemporary agriculture. And although the colonialists complained of the infertility of the land, we can be assured that seed did mix and that from the different varieties evolved, it could be that is the metaphor of San Gabriel . . . people are like seeds, the wind tosses them about, scatters them to the different corners of the world, and a new variety of fruit is produced, grafted, so to speak, upon the original hardy stock that is part of its origin. In contemporary terms it can be explained by population statistics on this very Pueblo of San Juan today, of 1600 people only 805 are counted as full blooded inhabitants.

Actually the key to understanding San Gabriel is not in statistics but in understanding the cultural legacy that has survived since 1598 to the present. The key word should be amalgamation for I doubt there exists an anthropologist or historian that can deny the fact that intermarriage did indeed occur here. And that in itself, no matter where it has occurred, has had an impact that has always had a strong influence. Just as Spanish influenced weaving or the Mexican Plateros influenced silversmithing or as the Matachines became a symbol of duality in shared ritual so too did this first encounter of these people result in a shared union. Poor Oñate, little did he realize that as he searched for riches in far-off lands the real riches lay not in the depths of the earth but in the people themselves. Maybe it was for the best that Oñate failed . . . the colonialist had to adapt not only to environment but to their new vecinos.

Imagine if you can, trade your shoes, and travel back in time, close your eyes for a second and pretend that you're either a Spanish colonial or a native; can you imagine what it must have been like to see each other for the first time? What other Pueblo in this region had aliens living in its midst for over ten years? Putting religious, material and cultural differences aside and knowing human nature, surely no one can deny that these two people were extremely curious about each other! It seems to me a curious note that the contemporary Chicano must seek his origin in the fabled kingdom of Aztlán when clearly here, in San Gabriel, these two people not only met but produced the new maize seed that was to be the legacy of the future! Can anyone in this prestigious gathering name me two other groups in this country that have shared as much as these two cultures, or for that matter, that have lived so closely in the same region?

Yes, there were disagreements, even abuse to the point that the Pueblo Rebellion is clearly justified. Yet after re-colonization and the reality that the Spanish were here to stay, Pueblo alliances were formed to defeat the much dreaded threat of marauding tribes that were a constant danger to both colonialist and Pueblo Native.

So, these two people lived as vecinos for nearly 400 years. And like all neighbors, disagreements were bound to occur, that seems to be a human trait. Yet they coexisted, and coexistence has always been the keystone to peace and understanding. These people got to know each other. It actually went beyond that. How many Hispanics in this area can say that they don't have some relative that is presently married to a Pueblo Native? Or how many Pueblo people in all of Northern New Mexico can say that they don't have Hispanic relatives?

Let me expand, strictly on a contemporary, day to day basis; my Grandfather said that as a young man living in Las Trampas, he wore teguas, that translates to moccasins. Later when I was ten years old, I used to help my Grandfather in his flour mill in Nambé. Many of the Pueblo people from Santo Domingo to Taos, used to bring my Grandfather their wheat to be ground in his mill. The Pueblo people in those days, about 1957, used to call us parientes. That word translates to relatives. There was not one Feast day in any Pueblo in this area where my Grandfather and I or our entire family was not welcomed. Many times my Grandfather had business in Española and being that he was headed in that direction, he would load up his truck with freshly ground flour, so that as he would put it, "my parientes wouldn't have to make an extra trip to the mill."

I remember . . . as if it was yesterday, when my Grandfather used to say, "I'm going to visit the Vigils or the Perezes, up at the Pueblo." He used to tell me that the Vigils and he had helped each other build their houses.

Maybe it is because I have the poet/writer's background that I remember things so vividly. It could be that I might be accused of romanticizing the bond that these two people shared, but I don't think so, after all I was there. And as such, I have personal knowledge that no anthropologist or historian has had privilege to experience, my memories are deep and true and as relatives there are few secrets that can be kept from each other, especially after 400 years!

In actuality it is our shared legacy, all you have to do is look at our architecture, our food, our deep respect for the land and the water and the entire sacredness of the earth. I don't consider that romantic. . . . ! Consider that a shared reality. Indeed, like parientes, relatives, it seems to me we have more in common than things we disagree in or upon. In fact, if there is a lesson to be learned from San Gabriel revisited, it is that this bond must be strengthened, nourished and continued. To do otherwise would be to deny our historical roots and the new maize seed that we cannot deny! It exists! And it also appears to me, that we must bring light to the past, so we learn from it, and with its light grow into the future, after all what are parientes for, if not to help each other? Maybe, just maybe, we will hear the word spoken once again, Pariente! Relative!

La Invasión Americana

Rafael Chacón

(c. 1874)

En Agosto de 1846 el General Armijo ordenó a mi padre Don Albino Chacón, (Juez de Primera Instancia y Alcalde Constitucional), llamar toda la milicia y los Pueblos de Indios para salir a encontrar las fuerzas americanas que ya venían avanzando á tomar posesión de Nuevo México. Como yo era cadete estaba sujeto a rendir servicio, y mi padre le dijo que si me excusaba, porque apenas tenía yo 13 años, era un niño sin experiencia. El

General le respondió: "No, señor, su hijo es cadete, y por lo tanto está sujeto a las ordenanzas; es militar, y por lo tanto también él tendrá que salir al frente." La disciplina de aquel tiempo se verá por el episodio histórico de Chapultepec, en donde los alumnos de la Escuela Militar, muchos de ellos de mi edad, murieron defendiendo la patria contra las tropas americanas en la toma de México. Me entregaron luego una pieza de artillería lijera con su equipaje y artilleros para que operase a mis órdenes. Marchamos al Cañoncito de los Apaches en donde había ya congregado como 10,000 entre milicia, Indios de Pueblo, compañías presidiales de Santa Fe, Taos y El Bado, y el escuadrón de Veracruz bajo el mando del Coronel Muñoz . . .

Un día hubo una desavenencia con la milicia, y en unos momentos hubo tal conmoción que ya estábamos para pelear unos con los otros. Despúes se apaciguó el motín y comenzamos a hacer trincheras y barricadas de rama de pinos y álamos: en este trabajo duramos tres días, cuando repentinamente ordenó el general Armijo que se retiraran los Pueblos de Indios y la milicia a sus casas, que él haría frente á los invasores con las tropas presidiales y con el escuadrón regular de Vera-cruz . . .

En Noviembre de 1846 llegó mi padre a la dicha casa [de su tía en Chimayó donde nos quedamos con la familia]. Allí vinieron dos veces los soldados de una compañía de dragones americanos para arrestarlo, pero logramos salvarlo en el Río Chiquito.

The American Invasion

Rafael Chacón

Translation by Enrique R. Lamadrid

In August of 1846 General Armijo ordered my father, don Albino Chacón, judge of first instance and constitutional magistrate, to call up the entire militia and Indian pueblos to go to encounter the American forces that were already advancing to take possession of New Mexico. Since I was a cadet, I was obliged to serve, and my father asked him if he would excuse me, because I was barely thirteen years old, a child without experience. The general responded, "No sir, your son is a cadet, and so is subject to military orders; he is a soldier, and so he too will have to go out to the front." The discipline of that time can be seen in the historical episode of Chapultepec [Castle] where students in the Military School, many of my age, died defending the country against the American troops in the taking of Mexico City. Later they delivered to me a light artillery piece with its equipment and artillerymen who would be at my command. We marched to Cañoncito de los Apaches where ten thousand had congregated, including the militia; Pueblo Indians; the presidial companies of Santa Fé, Taos, and El Bado; and the Vera-cruz Squadron under the command of Coronel Muñoz . . .

One day there was an argument among the militia, and at certain moments there was such commotion that we were almost ready to fight amongst ourselves. Later the disagreement was calmed, and we began to make trenches and barricades of pine and cottonwood boughs: we spent three days on this work when suddenly General Armijo ordered the Pueblo Indians and the militia to retreat to their homes, that he would confront the invaders with the presidial troops and the squadron of regulars from Veracruz . . .

In November of 1846 my father arrived at that house [of his aunt in Chimayó, where we stayed with the family]. Twice soldiers came there from an American company of dragoons to arrest him, but we managed to hide him out in Río Chiquito.

Comiendo elotes: Corn on the Plaza, 2005.

Doña Tules, Her Fame and Her Funeral

Fray Angélico Chávez

(1950)

Several years ago a university student working on a thesis wrote me for further data in connection with a quotation from Davis' *El Gringo* regarding the funeral expenses, or scandalously costly burial, of Gertrudis Barceló. I could not help the student because, at the time, I knew nothing about the subject except for a hazy recollection read somewhere, about her gambling salon in Santa Fe a century ago. But through the years, as I scanned many a document pursuing my own researches, the above query remained in the back of my mind, and I jotted down whatever I came across in connection with the name of Barceló. This surname is a rare one in New Mexico annals and so it struck my eye forcibly the few times I encountered it. It must be mentioned at the outset that these few Barceló facts that I gleaned do not coincide with what already has been written about this woman, dead almost a hundred years. Furthermore, there is no reason for me to discuss these points concerning her, save that the accepted indictment of her in the past has also been the indictment of a whole people.

Who Was Gertrudis Barceló?

The ultimate source for the woman's "Diamond Lil" reputation is Josiah Gregg, whose writings on New Mexico during the decade of the American occupation have been the bible of writers on the period ever since. Gregg introduces Tules[1] as a "roamer" of loose habits from Taos who came to Santa Fe where conditions were more favorable for her trade; he says that she here started her gambling salon and through it prospered so well that "now she is known as Señora Doña Gertrudes Barceló."[2]

Susan Shelby Magoffin, also writing for the eastern book trade of her day, describes Tules as "a stately dame of a certain age, the possessor of a portion of that shrew's sense and fascinating manner necessary to allure the wayward, inexperienced youth to the fall of final ruin. . . ."[3] The same writer saw Tules attending a ball and smoking cigarettes, like other women of these parts, an "old woman with false hair and teeth."[4]

Another writer used his imagination to describe her face, although he claims he saw her, as though marked by lines of unbridled passions, but he proceeds to quote Gregg. W. W. H. Davis also undoubtedly depended on Gregg when he wrote that "a few years ago, quite a celebrated female, known as Señora Gertrudes Barceló, led the van in gambling in Santa Fe. She was a Taosite by birth, but extended her adventures to the capital. . . . Here she struck the tide that leads to fortune . . . Her wealth leavened the social slump, and gained her admittance into the most fashionable and select circles . . ."[5]

Ralph Emerson Twitchell enlarged her questionable fame as "a woman of shady reputation" who was the one who revealed an anti-American plot in 1847,[6] and as a big-time operator of a luscious mirror-lined, thick-carpeted establishment of vice, who by her affluence worked her way into high social circles. Indeed, although she was the lawful wife of a certain José Sisneros y Lucero, she was the known mistress of General Manuel Armijo.[7] And so every writer on Santa Fe who re-lives those days of transition rehashes what was started by Mr. Gregg and Mes. Magoffin, and later amplified by other writers who followed them.

What I found is new but not sensational. The church registers of Tomé in Valencia County are the only ones in all New Mexico that contain any baptismal and marriage entries about the Barceló family. The name is altogether absent from the books of Taos. In 1823 there lived in the town of Valencia a widow by the name of Doña Dolores Herrero who on August 6 of that year married a Don Pedro Pino, bachelor. This woman was the widow of Don Juan Ignacio Barceló.[8] Since the family name appears in New Mexico quite sud-denly, we can suppose that the family itself came to Valencia at this period from some place like El Paso de Norte or any other part of Mexico—or from Spain via some other port in North America. The name itself is Catalán in northeastern Spain. Nor is there any proof that he himself came to New Mexico; if he did, he must have died sometime after his arrival in New Mexico, or else his widow migrated north alone with her children, all of marriageable age. Her family name, Herrero, is not a New Mexico name. Written many years later as "Herrera," at the time her grandchildren were baptized, it was undoubtedly confused with this very common local surname.

Doña Dolores Herrero Barceló had two daughters: María de la Luz Barceló who married Rafael Sánchez at Valencia, November 3, 1822, and Gertrudis Barceló who married Manuel Antonio Sisneros at Tomé, June 20, 1823.[9] Their mother married Pedro Pino two months after and went to live in Santa Fe some years later.[10]

The relationship between parents and daughters is established for sure by the baptisms for the following children: María Altagracia del Refugio Sanches (January 31, 1824), María Luisa Sánchez (March 5, 1826), Victoria Sánchez (March 5, 1830), and Teresa Sánchez (October 20, 1833), were the legitimate children of Rafael Sánchez (son of Manuel Sánchez and Gertrudis Chávez) and María Luz Barceló (daughter of Juan Ignacio Barceló and Dolores Herrera). Then: José Pedro Sisneros (October 19, 1823) and Miguel Antonio Sisneros (January 9, 1825) were the legitimate children of Don Manuel Sisneros (son of Hermenegildo Sisneros and Rita Lucero) and Doña Gertrudis Barceló (daughter of Don Juan Ignacio Barceló and Dolores Herrera).[11]

We may logically infer from the foregoing data, and the absence of previous Barceló names in New Mexico, that Gertrudis and her sister Luz were born elsewhere and came to the town of Valencia as young girls. They had a brother, Trinidad Barceló.[12] Gertrudis and her husband eventually came to live in Santa Fe where her mother now resided. It is well to mention at this point that members of her family, and her husband, were generally referred to as Don and Doña by the Padre of Tomé, a title which he bestowed only on families or individuals of the highest social standing in the community and district. That Tules started out as a low harlot in Taos and gained the title of Doña in Santa Fe by her sinful affluence is a figment of Gregg's imagination.

Doña Tules' Profession

The only word-picture that we have of Gertrudis Barceló's establishment in Santa Fe is the one provided through the pens of Josiah Gregg and Susan Magoffin, who were Puritans—at least in their moral outlook. To the so-called respectable American mind of those days (and to a large extent today), gambling, smoking, and drinking were vices in themselves. Gambling as a vice per se was and is a Puritan dogma stemming from another dogma— that to get something for nothing is sinful. Hence, the average American who smoked, especially cigarettes, or who drank wine or hard liquor or who played a game of cards, was made to feel that he was on the road to perdition. Liquor and cards and cigarettes were finally driven from outwardly respectable company to find harbor in frontier towns, among rowdy soldiers and sailors, or in places frequented by prostitutes. Therefore, we might not censure Gregg and Magoffin too much for being shocked at seeing even the women of Santa Fe sipping a bit of wine or enjoying a good, fat cigarette, or stopping at a monte-table to teach fortune at the turn of a card. We will not blame them too much, then, for concluding that Gertudis had started out as a poor

harlot and ended up as a prosperous madame. They were merely thanking God that they themselves were not like the rest of men.

As opposed to the Puritan, the Latin mind saw these things in a different light. To the Latin there was nothing in the law of nature, or in the Scriptures, that labeled tobacco, liquor, or gambling, as sins in themselves. Neither nature nor nature's god decreed that getting something for nothing was a sin: on the contrary, man got much of what he has from God and nature strictly for nothing. These activities were pleasant forms of recreation and relaxation, and of social wellbeing. True, the Latin realized that drinking leads to the vice of drunkenness, and gambling, to the vice of improvidence and the curse of family indigence, but precisely because they were forbidden neither by the divine or natural law, he did not feel that he had a right to prohibit them totally by his own law. In other words, total prohibition, whether of liquor or of gambling, is strictly Puritan.[13]

Little was needed to convince our first travelogue writers of the American era that a woman who ran a gambling house in Santa Fe was the personification of vice in its lowest forms. There is marked feminine antipathy when Susan Magoffin berates her for luring youth to final ruin, and likewise lack of logic when almost in the same breath she describes her as an old woman with false teeth and hair. All that we can say about the moral character of Gertrudis Barceló is what the impartial eye of sober historical research tells us. She made her living by running a house where open gambling, drinking, and smoking were enjoyed by all and sundry and no thought of being socially degraded. Many patrons enjoyed themselves immensely; other sinners gravely by excess, just as today some release their tensions with friends at a tavern and renew joyful friendships, while others throw their health and future away. Twitchell accused her, from posthumous gossip when she was over half a century dead, that she carried on sordid affairs with the leading politicos, but that kind of gossip has always circulated and still does today, about men and women in high government circles. Perhaps she did, but there is no contemporary proof.

Death and Burial of Doña Tules

Doña Gertudis Barceló, the wife of Manuel Sisneros, was buried from the Santa Fe Parroquia on January 17, 1852, having received the Sacrament of Penance, Extreme Unction, and Eucharist. The entry is signed by the pastor of Santa Fe, Don José de Jesús Luján.[14]

Now comes the statement by Davis, and repeated verbatim by Twitchell, that she was "buried with the highest honors of the church, at an expense of upward of sixteen hundred dollars for spiritual services in the internment ceremonies alone.... The bill was duly made out by the bishop of Santa Fe (Rt. Rev. J.F. Ortiz) with his name signed thereto and was presented to her executors and paid. Among them were the *derechos del Obispo* (fees of the bishop), one thousand dollars; *los posos* [sic], each fifty dollars, which means that each time the procession halted on its way to the burial, and the bier was placed upon the ground, the church made a charge of this amount, and the other charges were in proportion."[15]

The Bishop of Santa Fe at the time was John Baptiste Lamy, appointed as its first bishop in 1850, who had arrived in the summer of 1851. The priest who was pastor for the *parroquia* and who signed the burial entry was José de Jesús Luján. Where does Ortiz come in? Even if Davis is quoting an actual document, his ignorance of local customs is matched by his bigotry when in this matter he con-demns this exorbitant charging by the "Church" as an abuse resulting from two hundred and fifty years of unlimited sway in New Mexico, where it is an expensive thing to die and be buried.[16] This Ortiz mentioned by Davis as "bishop of Santa Fe" was Don Juan Felipe Ortiz, scion of the influential Ortiz family, who had served as Vicar of the Bishop of Durango up to the time of Lamy's coming. He still resided in Santa Fe, probably in the status of a retired clergyman. He was one of the three executors whom Gertrudis Barceló appointed in her will, drawn up on October 30, 1850, when she willed the Church thirty dollars for each ceremony to be requested. Ortiz, however, resigned as executor some months after her death in order to be legally free to collect and secure all her chattel rights and credits.[17] Perhaps, he himself did perform all those extra ceremonies as a retired clergyman and pocketed the fees without prejudice to the parish.

To understand this queer situation, we must remember that the now common passing of the collection plate on Sundays had been unheard of in New Mexico. The priest received his sustenance, after paying church expenses, from stipends given on the occasion of a baptism, marriage, or funeral. These stipends were small and fixed by the bishop's *arancel*, or list of minimum fees to be charged. Other means of support were the annual primicias (meaning "first-fruits" but used for "tithes"), which amounted to a pittance, paid by the head of each family in sheep or grain. However, few individuals ever paid anything because of the great poverty of the people; very many who could afford it, made it a point to avoid payment by asking for credit or *rebajos*, diminution of the fee. Authentic detail reports made as far back as 1777 are very enlightening in this matter; they state that the Spanish people of New Mexico did not support the church, taking delight in an immemorial custom of trying wholly, or in part, to avoid paying their just dues to the church.[18]

Certain abuses then crept in, which, at the same time, were not so much abuses as regrettable customs. A priest's policy from the nineteenth century on, when the missions were secularized, was to obtain from the rich as much as he could for the extra services which they demanded. The poor were charged the small fee listed in the arancel for the complete burial rite; often there was no fee for interment. But wealth and high position engender vanity, and so the rich vied with each other in the number of extra candles lit, of wailers hired, of stops made on the way to the graveyard, with special added ceremonies by the priest at each stop (*los pasos*, not posos as Davis has it), and so forth. One family tried to out-do another on the occasion of a funeral, as much as at a wedding, and the needy if not greedy priest made the most of this rivalry. Today, such rivalry has disappeared insofar as church rites are concerned because the lay mortician and funeral establishment have taken over these outward displays of vain show, and with a greater range of prices and varieties than any old Padre ever conceived.

Returning to Doña Tules, we can see that as a *rica* she had verbally requested all this pomp, or else her surviving relatives had insisted on one of these sumptuous funerals. Strangely enough, there is no *fábrica*, or burial fee, written next to her burial record. Hundreds of previous burials in this same register have fábricas that range from occasional ones of thirty-eight pesos to the more common ones of two or three pesos each, or else *de limosna*, free of charge. As for the total price adduced by Davis, we can see that it is not so exorbitant if we keep in mind that the church fees were still computed in terms of native pesos and not in American dollars. The *peso de la tierra* could not have been worth more than a dime; but supposing it was a quarter, her relatives got their four hundred dollars' worth in vain display.

And so, as "the wind leaves no shadow," let us leave none either on the character of a century-buried woman who brought to Santa Fe, a quiet frontier town of Mexico as well as of the United States, the noisy glamour of an open gambling house such as had not been seen before—something which as a girl she had seen perhaps in some far-away port like Havana, New Orleans, or Vera Cruz; and who at the same time was a respectable woman and faithful wife.

References

1. Spanish endearing diminutive form for Gertrudis; English, Gertrude.
2. *Commerce of the Prairies* (New York, 1844), Vol. I, pp. 239–240.
3. *Down the Santa Fe Trail* (New Haven, 1926 reprint), pp. 120–121.
4. Ibid., p. 145.
5. George Douglas Brewerton, *Overland with Kit Carson* (New York, 1930), p. 189.
6. *Leading Facts of New Mexico History* (Cedar Rapids, 1912), Vol. II, p. 233, note.
7. *Old Santa Fe* (Santa Fe, 1925), pp. 338–339.
8. AASF, M-56, Tomé; *San Felipe in Albuquerque, Informaciones Matrimoniales.*
9. M-56, Tomé.—The Padre uses Don and Doña before the names of the contracting parties.
10. B-72, Tomé, baptism of María Altagracia, expuesta en casa de Doña Dolores Barceló, vecinos de Santa Fe, December 22, 1832.
11. B-71 and B-72, Tomé.
12. Trinidad Barceló and his wife entered a complaint in 1837 with regard to some property in Pojoaque (Spanish Archives, I, no. 149). Gertrudis mentions him as her brother in her last will and testament.
13. This is no endorsement of gambling, but the statement of a historical situation. I have used the terms "Puritan" and "Latin" advisedly (instead

of "Protestant" and "Catholic"), for it is more a question here of customs and manners of social and racial groups than of religion and morals.— American English has borrowed the word "Puritan" from the sect of that name to mean anyone who is over-strict and rigid in manners and morals. Hence, a Catholic can be Puritan in this sense. As for Protestants, many of the early congregations in the United States built up their establishments through lotteries. Total prohibition of gambling, as did that of liquor, fattens the underworld and fosters organized crime. For a thorough treatment of these and other points, cf. *Pageant Magazine*, "Gambling: America's Ugly Child," by Murray Teigh Bloom, Vol. 5, No. 10, April, 1950, pp. 12–24.

14. Bur.-53, Santa Fe.—Twitchell's guess is that she died about 1851 (Old Santa Fe, p. 338). Ruth Lughlin Alexander in her novel, *The Wind Leaves No Shadow* (New York, 1948, p. 320), inadvertently gives the month as February instead of January; otherwise, although she depends on erroneous data from Gregg, Magoffin, Davis, etc., she writes a most sympathetic story about Tules.
15. *El Gringo*, p. 185; Old Santa Fe, p. 339.
16. *El Gringo*, p. 187.
17. Last Will and Testament of Gertrudis Barceló, Santa Fe Co., Rec. A, 1851–1864, pp. 4–7, 11.
18. N.M. Archives, Bibl. Nac. De Mex., 10, pt. 1.—This attitude persisted to our times, although it is fast improving in the more populated centers. While a modern priest barely makes a living in a country parish, an Anglo-American Protestant parish of a few families contributes enough to pay its minister with a family a standard professional living wage.

Tras la tormenta, la calma

Eusebio Chacón

(Imprenta de El Boletín Popular, *Santa Fe, 1892)*

Hay indiscreciones que resultan en consecuencias serias y enredadas, mas no por esto dejan de cometerse; sino que muy al contrario son fuente de muchas más y mayores, y el mundo, siempre necio, no se contenta con escarmentar en cabeza ajena sino que cada cual parece esmerarse por acopiar en su propia personalidad cuanta experiencia le puedan acerrear sus locuras é indiscreciones. En eso del amor son tantas las sin razones que se cometen que los libros andan llenos de ellas; y no porque en ellas haya originalidad ni novedad, sino que sucede con ellas como con las canciones viejas que entre más son, más bellas parecen. Del amor de Helena nació la perdición de Troya, del amor de la Caba se abrió la sepultura de la monarquía goda en España. Y aunque tan viejo es el amor, y aunque tan viejas las intrigas y resultados ya adversos ya propicios que consigo trae, sin embargo el mundo entero corre tras ellos y les sucede como al Conde del drama donde un loco conduce a un ciego para inauditos desastres. Tan arraigado está en la naturaleza humana el imperio del diocecillo alado que aun el sublime loco de la Mancha jamás habría sido immortal si no halla en un rincón de su mollera el recuerdo de una Aldonza rústica la cual muy en breve su imagen convirtió en princesa para gloria de las letras españolas. Esclavo de esa misma pasión dominadera, en mi tierra lo fue Luciano, joven de gallarda presencia y de gentil linaje y por saber aprovechar de la experiencia de otros se metió en un infierno de lances y percanses de los cuales sólo su buena suerte copulada de un poco de miedo le sacó. Y me duelo del mozo: mas no por eso dejan de entretenerme las bromas que los muchachos del día, y me divierte mucho oír serenarle algunas noches con aquellas rimas de Becquer:

> ¿Te embarcas?
> Ha tiempo que lo hice;
> Por cierto que aun tengo
> La ropa en la playa
> Tendida a secar

Pero en fin el diablo lo merece. Para diviertimiento de los enamorados voy pues a trazar la historia de ese amor de Luciano que tan apretado trajo al chico por indescrito.

Es pues el caso que en uno de los barrios de Santa Fe, mi amada patria, vivía una de esas morenas que endiablan a uno con sus miradas y al más pusilánime hacen atrevido y al más callado, hablador; llamábase Lola la chica y tan su enemigo era la fortuna que habíala dejado sin padres ni hermanos, y hacíale sus veces una su tía, matrona muy alegre y redonda, que de día comía muchas judías y cebollas y de noche roncaba como un sochantre por ambos respiratorios. La tía se llamaba Manuela, más por cariño le decía el vecindario, y era así conocida por el breve apodo de tía Mela.

La tía Mela era una alma de bien, no hay que dudarlo; y como no tenía hijos ni hijas amaba en extremo a su soberina, Lola, la cual como dijimos, era morena de las que hacen rabiar, y sólo tenía quince años. A esta edad, ¿cuál es la doncella que no arde a llamaradas en el divino fuego del amor? ¿Cuál la que no vive en un paraíso de ilusiones? ¿Cuál la que no ha dado flechazo con sus ardientes ojos y martiriza al niño alado teniéndole prisionero en sus redes? Lola no iba a ser una escepción a tan venerable costumbre, sino que al contratio su hermosura la destinaba a ser de las más ardientes amadoras de que la historia de Santa Fe tiene registro. Tan para amar había nacido que amaba a un joven obrero que se llamaba Pablo, y era del tan bien correspondida que no había enamorados más completos.

Pablo era el tipo del obrero de otros tiempos. No era el indolente, grosero, y sin ambición ni amor propio de hoy, que se contenta con vivir sin esperanzas ni dinero; que espera como el turco que un feliz acaso le traiga el pan a la boca y otro acaso le mueva las mandíbulas para comerle. No, Pablo no era tal obrero. Era pobre, mas su pobreza le incitaba a trabajar, a afanar para mejorar su suerte. Era sobrio, atento, cortés, modesto e industrioso: era ante todo cristiano, respetuoso con sus patrones, obediente y honorable. Amaba a Lola con ternura; la respetaba como respeta el hombre a la mujer que espera llevar al altar para hacerla su esposa. Me atrevo a decir que bajo sus toscas vestiduras había un ser verdaderamente noble. Tenía las manos callosas, el color del rostro algo quemada, pero era simpático y jovial. Las circunstancias del enamoramiento de estos hijos del pueblo tienen un colorido romántico y jamás me perdonaría yo a mí mismo si prosiguiera con la relación de esta historia sin consignar aquí tan importante suceso.

Pablo y Lola habían sido vecinos desde la niñez; juntos habían crecido, juntos habían recorrido en la infancia persiguiendo mariposas por los jardines, y en las noches de luna contemplando el cielo, por cuyo fondo acaso cruzaba alguna caprichosa niebla, ya figurando un lejano castillo, ya una batalla, ya un banquete de los dioses. La imaginación de estos dos niños se iba desarrollando simultáneamente y por una idoneidad de temperamento, amaban, deseaban, querían, admiraban una misma cosa; y en todo iban de acuerdo hasta en lo dulce y simpático de su carácter. Aquella semejanza en gustos y demás, luego que le niñez pasó y dio cabida a la juventud, se trocó en una pasión ardentísima.

Era una hermosa noche de primavera. Los jardines cargados de flores y las brisas cuajadas de aromas prestaban mil encantos a la situación. Sobre alguna flor se enamoraban las mariposas, y allá entre los copudos manzanos gemía alguna enamorada tórtola. La situación como queda dicho era de las más a propósito, y tal fue la que Lola y Pablo escogieron para decirse sus amores. Al frente de la puerta de la tía Mela crecía un viejo manzano que había presenciado en sus días muchas cosas y ahora iba a presenciar una escena amorosa que se representaba bajo sus cansados y macilentos brazos. Sentados en dos sillas, muy juntos, muy quietos contemplaban Lola y Pablo el disco de la luna, y escuchaban acaso algún lejano canto de algún enamorado. En el interior de la casa la tía Mela hacía rezar a un par de chicuelos adoptados y antes del final del rezo se había dormido a la par que los neófitos y muy de lejos bien podía escucharse, como ruido de molino, su áspero y nada musical ronquido. Entre tanto las horas volaban; Pablo y Lola sentían un amor profunda, inmenso, y sus manos se tocaban y sus miradas se encontraban con indecible ternura. Nadie pasaba por el camino, nadie los veía, y en medio de aquella calma de la noche sus labios se juntaron y se confundieron los latidos de sus corazones en un lánguido embeleso:

"Amor, oh dulce amor, en que se anidan de la ilusión las plácidas quimeras."

Estoy para exclamar con el cantor de Alberto, mi paisano y compañero; pero basta de digresiones, más vale que los héroes de esta historia hablen por sí solos y se den a concer en persona a los lectores.

—"¡Lola!" dijo temblando el mancebo.

—"¡Qué miedo, Pablo! ¡qué miedo!" tartamudeó la feliz morena; y sus labios volvieron a juntarse en otro beso que duró . . . ¿Cuánto duró poetas? Dicen por ahí que un beso no se mide por el tiempo sino por el amor que lo engendra; y el amor es inmenso en dos almas tiernas cuando se aman a los quince años y por primera vez.

—"Sabes que te amo con toda mi alma, Lola mía."

—"Qué dicha Pablo; siento que las lágrimas me brotan de placer."

—"Mi corazón te adora."

—"Y el mío te idolatra."

—"¿Será tu amor siempre constante? ¿O te avergonzarás algún día de haber amado al humilde obrero de rostro tostado?"

—"Nunca, Pablo de mi corazón; no trocaré tu amor por nada de la tierra."

Pero, ¿es posible trasladar al papel aquella escena de amor? ¡Insensato de mí, que tal cometido he atentado! Decid lectores, ¿quién se atreve a retratar al sol? ¿quién al huracán? ¿quién a aquellos objetos que embotan el arte y la constancia del hombre? Insensato de mí, que quiero decir cuanto ellos se dijeron. Bien que sus ojos y besos y sus almas con su mudo pero tierno lenguaje se hablaron más que sus lenguas; ¡y ese lenguaje del alma y de los ojos nos se puede retratar! ! En resolución diré que tanto se enamoraron Pablo y Lola que las horas se pasaban sin que ellos lo notaran, y el sol del otro día habríalos sorprendido diciéndose amores, si una casualidad no trae por allí a otra vecina muchacha también. Y algo inclinada a lo romántico. Llamábase Pascuala, y era tan decidida como aquella otra Pascuala del cuento.

Si será mentira
Si será verdad
Sólo nuestros nietos
Lo averiguarán.

Pero el caso es que había una muchachona de rancho que se iba a casar. Preguntóle el cura que si cómo se llamaba y ella en brío dijo:

—Pascuala, ¿ *pus* cómo?

—¿De dónde es vd.?

—Del rancho, ¿ *pus de ónde*?

—¿Y quiere vd. casarse?

—¡Sí! Se entiende que este *sí* es un superlativo forte.

No menos intrépida era esta Pascuala que ahora venía a interrumpir los dulces coloquios de Pablo y de Lola. Días hacía que andaba perdida de amor por el simpático obrero, bien que él no lo sabía. Era la hora en que la alondra empieza a ensayar su canto matutino cuando Pascuala se salió de su cama y asomó a la ventana. La claridad de la noche era tal que sólo siendo ciega no hubiera visto lo que pasaba debajo del manzano a la puerta de la tía Mela. Conoció también a los actores de aquel episodio, y loca de celos se precipitó a la calle exportulando de una manera terrible ante los dos amantes. Sorprendida Lola huyó a su casa y Pablo se quedó a combatir el encono de la ofendida Pascuala.

"Sí," decía esta,—"infiel, ingrato, que así te entregas al amor de esa repulgada coqueta y no haces caso de mis desvelos. Mira, corazón de palo, alma de tirano, como no te dueles de mí, y así, insultas mi corazón, engreído."

—"Pero Pascuala," interponía el turbado manchebo: y apenas formulaba la frase cuando ya Pascuala se le adelantaba con otro flujo de palabrería.

—"Ingrato, cómo me alegraré que esa melindrosa, ojos de zorrillo, te pegue un parche: mira, si me amaras a mí, que te había de ser más fiel que una tortolita;—y al decir esto la Pascuala lloraba, gemía, y acabó por echarse al cuello de Pablo. ¡Cristo y que bochorno pasó el muchacho! Quería hablar pero se le hacía un nudo en la garganta. Y tan violenta fue aquella escena que hubo de despertar a más de una vieja chismosa, que no bien se llegó el día y ya la relación corregida y libremente aumentada de aquel episodio de la medianoche, andaba vagando por los cuatro rumbos en alas de la furia.

Tal es la historia verdadera del principio de estos amores. La celosa Pascuala se quedó en Babia, y el amor de Pablo y de Lola, con excepción de aquella interrupción, corrió manso y tranquilo sin encontrar más contratiempos ni turbaciones por algún tiempo.

Pero es hora ya de buscar a Luciano que todo este tiempo ha sido relegado al olvido. Al sexto mes de estar Pablo y Lola enamorados, ya la fama de la belleza de esta se había esparcido como un fuego en las selvas, y como era natural, muy en breve llegó a oídos de los estudiantes de San Miguel, a cuyo número pertencía Luciano. No era Luciano un joven aplicado, ciertamente no era un modelo. Era el tiempo de recordación para los exámenes finales, y en lugar de atender a sus deberes gastaba su tiempo en leer El Don Juan de Byron, El Estudiante de Salamanca y otras composiciones por el estilo, de cuyas páginas iba cobrando una muy fuerte afición a las deshonestidades que en ellas se esparcen. De tal manera se despertó su fantasía que sólo anhelaba la ocasión para probarse un temerario Don Juan, o un Félix de Montemar. Todas aquellas cosas que leía le parecían a él haber pasado tal cual se pintaban y nada creía más propio de la vida estudiantil que todas aquellas blasfemias indecorosas, inmoralidades y faltas de honor. Principió por enamorarse y por escribir versos a la graciosa morena, por el estilo de los siguientes:

De los ojos de la luna
Traje dos finos diamantes
Para poner en los tuyos
Morenita de ojos grandes.

Y en otra ocasión fingiendo haber obtenido una cita de la bella Lola, explayó todo su intelecto en la siguiente composición digna de archivarse para los siglos de los siglos, amén; y es como sigue:

Y ese tu mirar divino,
Oh queridísima amiga,
Diciéndome que te siga
Está por aquel camino.
No interrumpa tu camino
Ni el viejo con su garrote,
Que aquí ya se viene al trote
Este pobre peregrino.

Es de advertir que aún no se ha podido averiguar a qué viejo en particular se refería aquí el inspirado compositor. Pero dejemos esas averiguaciones a un lado y adelante con el cuento. Luciano se deshacía por verse libre del Colegio para consagrarse con libertad a enamorar a Lola y después . . . después aquello era harina de otro costal. Faltaba un mes completo para la distribución de los premios. Excitado hasta lo último por aquello de:

Yo a las cabañas bajé
Y a los palacios subí
Y donde quiera que fui
La virtud atropellé.

El indiscreto muchacho se escurrió una noche por uno de los balcones de su alma mater, y palpitándole el corazón como fuelle de herrería, se encaminó hacia la case de la tía Mela. Precisamente acababa de salir la luna y para la bienandanza del rondador estudiante, el amante de Lola se acababa de perder de vista doblando una esquina. Por lo que a ella concierne aún permanecía de pie e inmovil bajo del viejo manzano, y no se apreció de la llegada de Luciano hasta que éste no la sacó de su contemplación diciéndole:

"Buenas noches, ¡hermosa Lola!"

Lola se sobresaltó, y dando tres pasos atrás y volviendo bruscamente la cabeza, dijo: "Buenas noches."

Un momento después ya se había encerrado, y el pulido alumno de San Miguel se quedó solo. ¡Solo! con un caos de esperanzas desvanecidas, y con un abismo de amor en su corazón. ¡Solo! y aquella mujer que tanto le robaba la calma lo dejaba con el silencio de la noche.

—¡Qué chasco! Luciano estaba aturdido. El que soñaba con recoger material aquella noche para escribir un romance por lo menos se quedó en

tinieblas. Sin embargo, rehaciendo sus desbaratados pensamientos se arrimó al tronco del manzano y meditó:

—"Desengaño," se dijo, ¡qué severa lección me has enseñado! Pero en lo sucesivo sabré aprovecharla bien y esa esquiva morena que hoy huye de mí en un día no muy lejano suspirará por verme llegar a este copudo manzano. "¿Por qué se asustaría conmigo? ¿Será que tiene un amante ya? ¿Quién será él que dobló la esquina? Yo vi un bulto allí y después oí la voz de uno que cantaba en esa dirección. No hay duda que ella tiene un amante. Es preciso caminar con cautela en este negocio. Mañana tornaré a este sitio a esta misma hora. Volveré a probar mi fortuna y entonces . . . traeré mi vihuela. Dicen que canto bien: me haré de un puñal para más seguridad. Bueno."

Y al decir esto se rascaba el chico la cabeza y se hacía todo ojos para ver si distinguía a la puerta de la tía Mela, algún objeto que se pareciese a Lola. Nada veía. Rodeando luego la casa distinguió luz por una de sus ventanas; se acercó a ella y estudiando su interior vio un candil encendido, un catre de tijera con una cama, una mesa con vasos y flores, y a la cabecera del catre un antiguo crucifijo ante el cual oraba de rodillas una joven: era Lola. Contemplóla Luciano por un momento.

—"Reza, murmuró, y en seguida se alejó de la ventana.

Tomó el camino que conducía al colegio y media hora después dormía muy tranquilamente en su cama. El chico se hacía todo ojos para ver si distinguía a la puerta de la tía Mela algún objeto que se pareciese a Lola. Nada veía.

A la noche siguiente volvió a repetir su excursión bien armado de puñal y de vihuela, resuelto a no dejarse chasquear otra vez. En esta ocasión no se atrevió a hablarle a Lola por no sobresaltarla; sino que dejándola que se retirase a su cuarto fue a colocarse cerca de su ventana, y aguardó a que rezase y que se fuese a la cama; lo cual no bien había hecho la doncella cuando un canto suave acompañado de vihuela llegó a su oído:

> Despierta, vida mía,
> Despierta de ese sueño,
> Ven a escuchar mi canto,
> Ven a escuchar mi acento.
>
> Si el mundo es dulce Carmen,
> Donde el amor florece,
> De sus rosas más lindas
> Un don vengo a ofrecerte.
>
> No temas, que es de noche,
> No temas, que todo duerme,
> La noche es blando seno
> Donde el amor se mece.
>
> Si los ojos azules,
> Son del color del cielo,
> Son de amor los tuyos
> Pues, los tienes tan negros.
>
> Despierta, vida mía,
> Despierta de ese sueño,
> Ven a escuchar mi canto,
> Ven a escuchar mi acento.

Tal fue la canción del estudiante. Tan lánguida, tan suave, tan dulcemente tierna resonó en medio de la calma y de la noche que todo parecía un sueño. Azorada la pobre joven se revolvía en su cama, y quería y no quería asomarse a la ventana para poder escuchar mejor. Sabía quien era su trobador, y aquella voz simpática bien merecía ser escuchada. Venció al fin la curiosidad de la mujer. Levántose Lola, alzó un tanto el bastidor, mas no bien lo había hecho cuando una mano se introdujo por la ventana y depositó en la de Lola un billete, y una voz de afuera dijo al mismo tiempo:

—"Lea vd."

Lola creyó desmayarse de miedo y dejó caer el bastidor con fuerza, y el billete se le escapó de las manos. En el exterior se oyó una queja y un ¡malhaya! muy enfático. El bastidor acababa de coger y de machacar muy de lo lindo un precioso dedo. Después se oyeron unos pasos y después nada más.

A la mañana siguiente lo primero que vio Lola al levantarse fue el billete de la noche pasada y recogiéndolo con cautela lo desdobló y vio que decía:

Bella Lola:

Amo a vd. como nunca se ha amado. Por vd. soy capaz de morirme y de matar. Correspóndame vd. Sé que vd. es pobre y yo rico. ¿Pero, qué importa? Ámeme, vd. Es vd. demasiado Hermosa para vivir en la obscuridad. Responda.

EL DE ANOCHE.

—"¡El de anoche! Murmuró Lola y rompió el billete en mil pedazos.–"El de anoche," se volvía a repetir, y luego temblaba. Se acordaba de Pablo; y se acordaba de su amor.

Excusado es decir que Luciano no bien llegó la siguiente noche cuando volvió a tomar su puesto cerca de la ventana, y a entonar la misma canción, y a introducir el mismo billete, o majar dicho, otro dictado en los mismos términos; y de nuevo tornó a machacarse un dedo y a decir, ¡malhaya! De nuevo tornó Lola a asustarse y a correr medrosa a su cama para volver a encontrar la esquela de *El de Anoche* a la mañana siguiente. La serenata de Luciano se parecía a la de aquel que no sabía más que un verso y toda la noche lo cantaba a la puerta de su amada. Era pues el verso como sigue:

> A tu puerte planté un pino,
> Y a tu ventana un peral,
> Para que que comieras peras
> La noche de navidad.

Tantos pinos y perales plantó allí el trovador que cierta noche el Viejo amohinado tuvo que asomarse por el balcón y decirles:

—"Hijo, ya tienes un bosque plantado a mis puertas y ventanas. Mañana no podrán pasar los carros por mi patio de seguro. Vete ya y deja dormir."

Si la cándida de la tía Mela no durmiese tan profundamente, bien pudiera despachar a Luciano a plantar jardines de amor muy lejos de Santa Fe. Pero la buena señora nada oía. Era la hora en que dormía y nada le podia arrancar de su profundo sueño. ¡Y oh, desventura que no lo hiciera! Oh, destino cruel, que por vías mil y complicadas encarrilas la suerte de los mortales y a veces haces complices de tus maquinaciones a la inocencia y la simplicidad. Oh tía Mela, si en vez de roncar y de sonar tal vez en nabos y cebollas y en los nuevos potages de mañana hubieras velado y vigilado con un ojo lo que pasaba a unos pasos de ti a la ventana de la hermosa parienta, habrías por lo menos contrarestado el éxito de una aventura que después te había de salir tan amarga y fatal.

Por allá en mis mocedades no sé en que libro latino leí el proverbio de que *guta cavat lápiden non ví sed saepe cadendo.* Con esto en la mente y con aquello de otro de que *audaces fortuna juvat;* el flamante Luciano continuaba asediando a la bella morena; y pudo tanto su constancia que al fin hubo de rendirse aquella tieran beldad. La humanidad ama la adulación: La mujer la necesita como parte de su existencia, y Luciano bien comprendía esto cuando entonaba su canción a la ventana de Lola. Del canto se pasó a las palabras, de las palabras a la amistad, de la amistad . . . cuál otro Lucifer en forma de serpiente que descubriendo bellas mentiras y efímeras delicias ante los ojos de la primera mujer la sumergió en un mar de desventuras, así Luciano con dorada hipocresía derribaba la felici-

dad de Lola. Lola temblaba, y sin embargo comenzaba a amar el peligro y escrito está que quién ama el peligro en el perece. Semejante a la mariposa que se deja facinar por la luz de los faroles, y en un momento dado se arroja al fuego, así Lola se iba acercando a la funesta llama del amor de Luciano y se dejaba facinar. Aquel joven corazón iba padeciendo un cambio radical que debía producirle lágrimas infinitas, y sin embargo se dejaba facinar. Del canto Luciano pasó a las palabras; pero palabras que la iban haciendo perder el juicio y abandonarse a las más extrañas aberraciones de la mente; palabras que al oído de la crédula joven parecían la quinta esencia de la miel y a cuyo lado eran groseras las del humilde Pablo; palabras que en fin como las de Luzbel escondido entre las ramas del árbol de la ciencia en el paraíso terrenal. No había que dudarlo: Luciano ganaba terreno, y con tenacidad cerraba el cerco y la presa iba a ser suya. Habíale confiado Lola el secreto de sus amores con Pablo, y Luciano luchaba por destruirlos. Hablábala de la condición humilde de su amante ponderábala su belleza en seguida, y como conclusión lógica deducía que ella estaba destinada a moverse en una esfera de admiradores y de lujo que pertenecían a los obreros. En resolución tan pertinez anduvo el astuto Luciano que arrancó de los labios de Lola una solemne promesa de abandonar a Pablo y de ser suya cuando él quisiese con condición que en saliendo del Colegio se casase con ella.

—"Acepto," exclamó y le tendío la mano.

—"Selle vd. el contrato," repuso la doncella y le presentó los labios.

Un beso estalló en las tinieblas que parecía romper las fibras de la alma. Era el sello de la traición y de la infidelidad.

Lector amado, quisiera presentarte a Lola revestida del magnífico ropaje de las heroínas, bella y virtuosa, adornada de mil prendas y acrisoladas en la victoria alcanzada contra el furor de las pasiones. Quisiera que siempre se presentase a ti tan dulce, tan simpática como la vio nacer mi fantasía, y la vio crecer al lado de Pablo, amándole con ternura, y haciéndole feliz. Pero desde este momenta sólo podré presentarle un ramo deshojado, una flor marchita, una ilusión que fue, un sueño que pasó. Sin embargo, ámala tú como yo la amo, por su debilidad funesta; compadécela tú como yo la compadezco por su desgracia; y en vez de despreciarla sabe que no fue ella quién labró su desventura sino aquel malvado Luciano que tenía dolor en su alma cuando la prometía casarse con ella; y de todo a todo la engañaba sólo para satisfacer un diabólico capricho. ¡Aquel beso! ¡Aquel maldito beso! ¡Cuántas de las que empezaron así se arrastran hoy en el cieno de la inmoralidad más vergonzosa! Y sin embargo son más criminales los Lucianos que las Lolas.

Mas para no cortar el hilo de esta narración diré que después de aquel beso todas las noches entraba por la ventana de Lola un joven armado de puñal, y después de un largo rato volvía a salir murmurando un horrible chiste y con una sonrisa diabólica en los labios.

Caminaba el asunto a las mil maravillas; y adonde iban a parar aquellas aventuras difícil sería de conjeturar si una casualidad no detiene de súbito su marcha y da giro diferente al que llevaban. Pablo no tenía pelo de tonto, y ya empezaba a tener barruntos de la infidelidad de su morena. Había sorprendido en ella un cambio inexplicable y se quebraba la cabeza por hallar un modo de desentrañar aquel misterio de su cambio, si era que tal existía. Lola por su parte tiempo hacía también que estudiaba algún plan para deshacerse de Pablo sin que su reputación padeciese menoscabo, y no acertaba encontrar uno que le cuadrase. En su apuro ocurrió al locuaz Luciano, pero aquel estaba tan árido de planes como su corazón lo

estaba de buenas intenciones. Andando así las cosas, Pablo el obrero, cierto de que debía de haber gato encerrado en algún lugarcito, y resuelto a encontrarlo costara lo que costare, se dirigió a la casa de la tía Mela una noche que era la víspera de la distribución de los grados de San Miguel. A lo largo de la casa corría una tapia que no se que gobernador mandó edificar para que los indígenas no le barrenaran el casco a flechazos, y detrás de esta tapia se detuvo nuestro obrero haciéndose fuerte para lo que pudiese sobrevenir. De aquel punto se distinguían claramente los objectos en torno de la ventana de Lola y aun se veía gran parte del interior, pues la luz estaba encendida, y era muy corta la distancia. Se veía el catre, parte del crucifijo y la mitad de un vaso lleno de flores; y en el fondo blanqueado del aposento se destacaba la sombra de la graciosa Lola, que sin duda resultaba de estar este interpuesto entre el candil y la pared. Embelesado en la contemplación de aquel cuadro estaba Pablo y no sentía correr las horas. Dio al fín las once el reloj de la catedral, y de pronto el ruido de unos pasos vino a turbar el silencio que en torno reinaba y Pablo se hizo todo ojos para ver y todo oídos para escuchar. El corazón le latía con violencia. Observó, detuvo el aliento, apretó los dientes y crispó las manos: alguien acababa de llegar sigilosamente y como agitado a la ventana. Oyó en seguida los acordes de una guitarra, y bien pronto resonó a media voz un apacible canto. Se abrió la ventana; el rumor de un beso vino a helar el corazón del pobre obrero, y antes de que este se persuadiese de que era realidad y no ilusión lo que veía ya el recién llegado se introducía en la habitación como un ladrón en la noche.

La mente de Pablo se nubló de coraje y echando mano a su pistola la amartilló, metió puntería, y con pulso sereno un momento después habría puesto una bala atravésde su rival y de su infiel amada. Pero al momento de dar fuego para cometer un doble asesinato, otra idea más feliz le vino a la mente, y obrando de acuerdo bajó el arma, la volvió a su lugar, y echando a andar con pasos rápidos y descompuestos se dirigió a la puerta de la casa. Entró sin llamar y halló a la tía Mela roncando como se ronca cuando el cuerpo está fatigado y la conciencia tranquila. Acercándose a ella y moviéndola bruscamente para que despertase le decía al oído:

—"Tía Mela, tía Mela, despierte. ¡Qué sueño! Tía Mela!"

La buena señora se revolvía de uno a otro lado, sin duda soñando que algún espíritu malo se la llevaba y al cabo de un rato abrió los ojos colorados como brazas y frontándose acabó de roncar y preguntó azorada:

—"¿Qué hay? . . . qué. . . . qué. . . . Pablo! Ah, eres tú! ¡Qué susto!"

—"Yo soy, tía Mela. No tenga vd. miedo," replicó Pablo, "Pero levántese y venga conmigo."

La pobre matrona abría los ojos, y no acertaba en que pensar: mas obedeciendo, y vistiéndose a la carrera, volvió a preguntar.

—"Y bien muchacho, ¡Qué susto! ¿Qué quieres?"

—"Quiero que me autorice a defenderla. Vd. no se puede defender. Yo soy amigo, la defenderé."

—"¿Pero, qué hay muchacho? Acaba. No me tengas suspensa, tartamudeaba falta de aliento la tía Mela."

—"Hay ladrones en su casa, tía Mela."

—"¡Jesús! No me digas muchacho. ¡Socorro, vidas mías! Socorro, Socorro, que soy una mujer desamparada!" y la tía Mela se retrocía las manos con deseperación lastimera.

Pablo no dijo más. Arrastreándola casi la llevó al cuarto de Lola; y todo esto pasá con tanta celeridad que aunque Lola y Luciano oyeron los gritos no tuvieron tiempo de prevenirse, sino que cuando aún estaban suspensos por saber lo que pasaba, ya la puerta se había abierto de par en par con un fuerte empujón que Pablo le dio y como el relámpago en un momento, éste, y la medrosa tía se arrojaron dentro. Fue tan repentina su llegada que Luciano ni aun pensó en tirarse debajo del catre. El candil estaba encendido, el cuarto sembrado de zapatos, camisas, calzones y calcetines, y sobre el catre yacían en uno la morena infiel y el estudiante veleidoso. Tornó la tía a dar de gritos y a hacer aspavientos; tornó a pedir socorro, y esta vez no tanto de miedo como de dolor. Se figuraba que un ogro tenía en sus rapantes garras a Lolita; que la tierna joven estaba desmayada, y que el ogro cometía con ella cosas contra su voluntad. ¡Oh, lo que puede el amor! Y Pablo estaba lívido. En su rostro se veía la determinación y en su diestra relumbraba la terrible compañera. Luciano tenía el color de la cera y pestañeaba, y Lola se cubría la cara. En aquel momenta los dos criminales hubieran querido que la tierra se abriese y se los tragase.

—"Ved," dijo al fin Pablo a la tía Mela, y la boca se le ponía azul de rabia y sus ojos despedían relámpagos.

—"¡Socorro, Socorro!" tornaba a gritar la pobre señora, y presa de un inaudito dolor corría por la habitación como fuera de sí.

—"He ahí al ladrón," volvió a decir Pablo. "Tía Mela, tía Mela, le roban a vd. la virtud de su sobrina, mas no es lo peor. Es que ella se deja robar, se deja prostituir."

Al oír estas palabras Luciano se creyó perdido. Temiendo por su pellejo saltó de la cama para huir, y Pablo que creyó que le iba a arrebatar la pistola, dio fuego y le hirió una pantorilla. Lola se echó al otro lado de la cama; la tía Mela cayó tan larga desmayada gritando que la habían muerto. Luciano se arrojó por la ventana en paños menores como estaba; y como quien va a poner un pico en Flandes. Pablo se arrojó en pos de él. Al ruido acudió la gente del vencindario y encontraron aquella casa en el mayor trastorno y a la pobre mujer acabándose. Trajéronla al Padre como ella lo había suplicado, y muy en breve ya la estaban velando yerta y descolorida. Aquel susto fue mortal.

Media hora después corría con las ganas del miedo un encamisado por las calles, y le seguía muy de cerca uno que parecía endemoniado y que corría también. Para el uno era cuestión de vida; para el otro de honor y de venganza. Habían corrido dos horas; la noticia de que la tía Mela y su sobrina habían sido asesinadas cundió como peste. ¡Tanto se aumentan las cosas pasando de boca en boca! El pueblo se amotinaba, ladraban los perros, repicaban las campanas, se montaba la artillería del fuerte y las tropas estaban sobre las armas, y el encamisado y su perseguidor corrían. Por fin al doblar una maldita esquina no vio el primero a uno que venía en dirección opuesta y dándose de frente con él le hizo caer a un buen trecho y él mismo quedó mal parado viendo estrellitas en medio de la calle. Aquel encontró su perdición: un momento después le asió con mano de hierro su tenaz perseguidor. Si Pablo no hubiese estado tan ciego de coraje habría reído harto al ver la facha de su rival un día antes tan ufano; y ahora tan ridículo, verdad era que parecía una copia fidelísima del Caballero de la Mancha en sus penitencias de la Sierra Morena, con la única diferencia que aquel era un magnífico loco y este un insigne cobarde. Sin aguardar a hacer apologías al otro aporreado, nuestro Pablo se echó a Luciano por delante, y estimulándole con algunos puntapiés y con muchos apodos, que venían al estudiante como de molde, le hizo emprender la marcha de nuevo, y se lo llevó a la casa de la tía Mela. Llegaron allí cabalmente cuando la infeliz acababa de boquear por última vez y de entregar su alma cándida a su Creador. Sin andarse con

ceremonias y sin curarse de la solemnidad de la ocasión el encamisado y su persiguidor se abrieron paso por entre los circunstances, y arrastrando el segundo al primero hasta donde estable tendida la que fue en vida la tía Mela, dijo con voz que puso espanto a todos.

—"Mira, cobarde, la hechura de tus manos. ¡Contempla esa muerta un momento antes llena de vida; gózate en tu obra, villano, y si aún tienes corazón para sentir, horrorízate, que ha sido víctima inocente de tus maldades! ¡Oh, tía Mela, continuaba enterneciéndose ante el cadáver; ante los ojos del mundo parecerá una calamidad, tu repentina muerte, pero dichosa tú que no has podido sobrevivir a la deshonra! ¡Infeliz, que no morí también contigo, para no ver deshonrada a la mujer idolatrada! ¡Y porque ella lo quiso! ¡Deshonrada! Y yo engañado por ella en el momento que yo más la amaba. ¡Mujer inconstante, mujer pérfida!"

Pablo hubiera perseguido con un largo discurso digno sin duda de insertarse en el *Tesoro de la Elocuencia Española* de Campani, pero el dolor vino en su ayuda y sejó de un tajo el tierno botón antes que fuera rosa. Por lo que a Luciano concierne se asemajaba a un idiota; su desencajado rostro y su mirada estólida le daban el aspecto de uno que acaba de volver de una soberana borrachera. Admirábanse los circunstantes de verle en tal catadura; pasmábanse de oír los deslices de Lola; tapábanse un ojo las viejas para no ver; asombrándose los chicos de mirar tantas extrañejas; discutían unos el problema de un sumario linchamiento y otros, más piadosos, opinaban por el vapuleo; y el señor cura que aún no se atrevía a asomar a la puerta ni siquiera el sobrante de su excelente nariz por temor a la ronda se hacía cruces y conjuraba al infeliz a que si era demonio o difunto hiciese el favor de ausentarse *sin die* del medio de aquella buena comunidad. Al ver la solicitud de su

Reverencia, Pablo volvía a hacer temblar a la asamblea con su voz, diciendo:

—"¡No hará tal, Señor Cura! Digo que no hará tal, ya Vd. ha llenado sus obligaciones para con los muertos, llénelas ahora con los vivos."

—"Pues, ¿qué hay hijo mío?" Interrogó su Reverencia.

—"Hay que esa mujer que allí veis tendida se dejó morir de dolor por no ver a sus sobrina deshonrada por este vil cobarde," señalaba a Luciano.

—"Lola era mía; prosiguió, y este despreciable la ha deshonrado. Tengo para mí que con falsas promesas la arrastró a su ruina y yo vengo aquí a cuidar que esas promesas se cumplan. Sí, debe haberla prometido mucho, pues Lola era pura y buena, y por el solo deleite del pecado no se dejaría desflorar. Lola era mía, y mi alma la adoraba como adora a sus fetiches el indígena. En ella ponía yo mi complacencia; mas ahora ya todo ha concluido entre nosotros. Sin embargo, aún la amo lo bastante para salvarla de mayores caídas. Padre, allí está Lola; el engañador está aquí. Por la ley natural se pertenecen, y yo desde ahora para siempre renuncio a todo reclamo que mi corazón tenga al corazón de Lola. Si usted no quiere ver a esa joven insensata correr mañana a la prostitución para ocultar su locura primera, cáselos, cáselos. Yo lo quiero, yo lo mando. Yo respondo en mi consciencia y ante Dios por lo que venga después."

Era tan terrible el ademán de Pablo que sin poderlo remediar todos volvieron a estremecerse y a admirarse y pasmarse. Lola estaba anonadada; Pablo sombrío y amenzador, mientras que Luciano, ayudado de algunas almas compasivas, variándose como un azogado, se calzaba las botas trocadas y se ponía los calzones al revés, pues alguien le trajo sus haberes que tan vergonzosamente había abandonado al enemigo en el aposento de Lola, y el cura le había ordenado que se vistiese, porque no era decoroso que se estuviese en camisa en presencia de tanta señora.

Por lo que a su Reverencia concierne, dando muchas vueltas a su rosario e invocando a toda la corte celestial para que le acorriesen en tal aprieto, y dándose piadosos golpes en la barriga, con aire grave se dirigió a Luciano, y dijo:

—"A ver, muchacho, ¿qué respondes a los cargos que se te hacen? ¿Son todos verdaderos?"

—"Todos, padre mío," respondió Luciano, con tono suplicante.

—"¿Y amas a Lola y la tomas por esposa?"

—"Si padre."

—"Y tú, niña; Ven, ven acá, continuó dirigiéndose a Lola. "¿Amas tú a Luciano y lo tomas por esposo y compañero?"

Un sí casi imperceptible salió de los labios de la joven, y bajo la cara encendida como un tomate. Un sordo rumor se esparció por la asamblea. Y Pablo estaba blanco como el jaspe.

—"Hacéis propósito ambos de reparar las faltas pasadas y de dar buen ejemplo? ¿Y os arrepentís de todo corazón de lo que habéis cometido?" tornó su Reverencia a preguntarles y ambos a una voz tornaron a replicar en la afirmativa.

Se dieron las manos, el sacerdote alzó los ojos al cielo, levantó la diestra en alto, hizo la cruz sobre los dos jóvenes, y pronunció la bendición. Pablo derramaba una lágrima furtiva y Lola que lo viera echándose a sus plantas con sus ojos arrasados de llanto, exclamó:

—"¡Perdóname, Pablo!"

Pablo tomando por última vez aquella hermosa cabeza entre sus manos, respondió:

—"El perdón de Dios te acompañe como te acompaña el mío," y en seguida desapareció.

Hoy, al pasar yo todas las tardes junto a la puerta de la difunta tía, en vano busco aquel rostro alegre de la cándida señora, y me dan ganas de llorar. En su lugar, herederos absolutos de su casa, habitan Luciano y Lola, pidiéndose mutuamente perdón por las faltas pasadas. Tienen ya un chiquillo muy lindo a quien llaman Pablo, y en las noches de luna cuando mi alma está triste voy al árbol de su puerta de donde puedo escuchar de vez en cuando una playera o vespertina de que Luciano tiene un variado o inagotable repertorio.

The Calm after the Storm

Eusebio Chacón

Translation by A. Gabriel Meléndez

There are indiscretions that lead to serious and tangled consequences, but this does forestall their happening. On the contrary, they are the source of greater and more serious indiscretions, and the world, foolish as it is, is not satisfied in merely learning a lesson from another's misstep; rather it seems that each person seeks to shine by copying each and every example that another's folly and indiscretion can provide him. In matters of love, so many foolhardy things are done that books are filled with them. Not because there is something new or original here; rather they are like the old songs: the more there are of them, the merrier. Over Helen's love, Troy was lost and for lady Cava the grave of the Goths in Spain was dug. And, while love is ancient and love's intrigues are just as old, and the results love brings so adverse and, yet, so fitting, still the whole world chases after it, finding itself, like the count in the play, in the situation of a crazed man leading a blind man to unheard-of disaster. The supreme will of the miniature-winged god is so rooted in human nature that even the sublime fool of La Mancha would never have become immortal had he not had in some recess of his mind a rueful Aldonza, who, by his fancy, he was able to change to a princess, albeit for the glory of Spanish letters. In my land, Luciano, a gallant, young man of honorable lineage, was a slave to that same domineering passion. And because he did not know how to make the most of the experience of others he found himself in a fix of incidents and mishaps from which only his good luck and some sniveling saved him. I feel for the lad, yet I am amused by the ribbing the boys give him, and it pleases me to hear them serenade him with Bécquer's verses:

> Do you sail?
> I did so some time ago,
> In fact, I still have
> my clothes strewn on the beach to dry.

In any case, the devil can have him. To amuse myself with the matter of lovers, I will go over the story of Luciano's love affair, one in which indiscretion got him in such a tight jam. The case is that in one of Santa Fe's barrios—my beloved homeland—lived one of those dark women who can bedevil you with their looks; the kind that makes the weak of heart, bold, and can turn taciturn men into orators. The girl's name was Lola, and luck was such a stranger to her that she had been left without brothers, sisters, or parents. She was in the care of a matronly, plump, and happy aunt who ate peas and onions by day and snored like a choir director at night through both nostrils. The aunt was named Manuela but was affectionately known by the nickname Tía Mela.

No one should doubt that Tía Mela was a good soul, and since she had no sons or daughters of her own, she loved her niece, Lola, in the extreme. Lola, a dark-skinned beauty who made the men rage, was only fifteen. At this age where is the young woman who does not smolder with the divine fire of love? Which the girl who does not live in a world of fantasy? Which the girl who has not let loose the arrow of her burning eyes to torture the winged child and trap him in the net of her gaze. Lola would not be the exception to such an ancient custom; on the contrary, her beauty destined her to be the fieriest lover in the history of Santa Fe. So inclined to affection was she—she loved a young laborer named Pablo and was so loved by him in return—that one could say there had never been two more complete lovers.

Pablo was a worker of the kind that belongs to another time. He was not apathetic or coarse, he did not lack ambition, and he did not lack self-esteem as is the case today. He was not the type content to live without hope or money or wait like a Turk until some stroke of luck brings forth his daily bread, lays it in his mouth, and even moves his jaws to eat. No, Pablo was not this kind of worker. He was poor, but his poverty pushed him to work and struggle to improve his lot. He was sober, attentive, courteous, modest, and industrious. He was above all a Christian, respectful of his bosses, obedient, and honorable. He loved Lola tenderly. He respected her as the woman he hoped to take to the altar to make his wife. I dare say that under his rough exterior was a truly noble person. His hands were calloused, the skin of his face was somewhat burned, but he was jovial and good-natured. The love story of these two young commoners had a romantic tinge to it, and I could never forgive myself if I would go on with my narration of this story without writing down here such an important beginning.

Pablo and Lola had been neighbors since childhood. They had grown up together. As infants they had chased butterflies in the same gardens, and, on moonlit nights, they had imagined in the fog of some cloud a faraway castle, a battle scene, or a banquet of the gods moving across the backdrop of the heavens. The imagination of these two

children developed together and matched their disposition. They loved, desired, wanted, and admired the same things. They were in agreement in all things, even to sharing a sweet and pleasant character. Their childhood likes and dislikes gave way in adolescence to a burning passion.

The gardens, filled with flowers and breezes saturated with fragrance, provided illusion to their circumstances. Butterflies nestled among the flowers, and in the copious apple trees a dove swooned. The time and place, as I have said, were ideal, and Lola and Pablo picked just such a moment to confess their love to one another. In front of Tía Mela's house grew an old apple tree, a tree that had seen so many things and now would see this love unfold under its bending and haggard branches. Seated side by side, Lola and Pablo contemplated the round form of the moon and perhaps heard the love song in the distance. Inside the house, Tía Mela had put a couple of adopted children to pray and even before the prayers had ended, the neophytes had fallen asleep. From a distance the harsh, cavernous sound of her snoring could be heard. The hours seemed to fly. Pablo and Lola felt profound and immense affection. Their hands touched, and they exchanged unspoken tenderness by their gaze. No one passed by the road, no one saw them, and in the middle of that calm night, their lips met, and the beating of their hearts melded together as a single, long delight:

"Love, oh sweet love, where placid fantasies nest in sweet illusion."

I am driven to exclaim with the singer Alberto, my friend and countryman, but enough digression. It is best that the protagonists of this story speak for themselves and introduce themselves to the readers.

"Lola," said the young man, trembling.

"I'm frightened, Pablo, so frightened," blurted the woman as their lips met in another kiss that lasted . . . Poets, tell me, how long did it last? They say that a kiss is not measured by time but by the love from which it is born, and love is immense in two people who at age fifteen love each other for a first time.

"Lola, you know I love you with all my soul."

"What good fortune, Pablo. I feel I will cry the tears of joy."

"My heart adores you."

"And mine praises you."

"Will your love be constant forever? Or will you feel shame one day to have loved a humble, brown-faced worker?"

"Never, Pablo, I would not trade my love for anything on this earth."

But is it possible to transfer that scene of love to the page? How foolish of me to try and take up such a task. Tell me, dear readers, who would try to paint the sun, the hurricane, or those things that art holds as the essence of humanity? How foolish of me to want to repeat all they said. Their eyes, their kisses, their souls said more in their silent and tender language than what was spoken by their tongues. And that language, the language of the soul and of the eyes, cannot be painted! In short, I shall only say that Pablo and Lola were so in love that they did not notice the hours they spent together. The sun of a new day would have found them speaking lovingly to each other had not happenstance brought forth another neighbor girl moved by love. Her name was Pascuala, and she was as strong willed as the legendary Pascuala.

If it be a lie,

If it be true,

only our grandchildren will

ever really know.

In the story of Pascuala, a country girl is about to marry. The priest asks her name, and she responds in a spirited way:

"Pascuala, what do you think?"

"Where are you from?"

"Well, from the ranch, where else would I be from?"

"And you want to get married?"

"Yes!" (It must be understood that this came as a strong exclamation.)

This Pascuala, who now comes to interrupt Pablo and Lola's sweet conversation, was no less bold. For days she had been smitten with love for the likable worker. At the hour the lark begins to sing its morning song, Pascuala got out of bed and looked out the window. The brightness of the night was so clear that only if Pascuala had been blind could she have missed the scene that played itself out under the apple tree at Tía Mela's door. Recognizing the protagonists of the scene and filled with jealousy, she hurried to the street and stood in front of the two lovers. Surprised by this, Lola ran to her house, and Pablo stayed to fend off the ire of an offended Pascuala.

"Yes," she said, "faithless traitor. You give yourself to the love of that disgusting flirt, and you do not heed my yearning. Look, you heartless tyrant, how is it you do not have compassion for me but instead injured my captive heart?"

"But, Pascuala," the stunned young man interrupted, only beginning to speak when Pascuala launched a new flurry of words.

"Ingrate, how I would delight if that sweet cake, with the eyes of a fox, would give you a hot patch. Look, if you were to love me, I would be more faithful than a little dove," and saying this, Pascuala, cried, moaned, and threw her hands around Pablo's neck.

Christ, what a predicament. Pablo wanted to speak, but a knot had lodged in his throat. So startling was the scene that it caused more than one old busybody to wake up, and although the day was still young, the tale that had begun at midnight had been changed and liberally amplified and was bantered to the four corners on wings of zeal. Such is the true beginning of this love story. Jealous Pascuala was left in a quandary. Pablo and Lola's love affair went on, save that one brief interruption, and for some time flowed calmly and meekly without further setbacks or confusion.

But it comes time to seek out Luciano, who has remained forgotten to us all this time. Six months after falling in love, talk of Lola's beauty had spread like fire in the forest and, as might be expected, came to the attention of the students of St. Michael's College, one of them being Luciano. Luciano was not a dedicated young man, and he was certainly no role model. It was closed week before final examinations, and instead of tending to his studies, Luciano spent his time reading Byron's *Don Juan, The Student at Salamanca,* and other such works, becoming obsessed with the dishonest behavior that runs throughout them. In this way a fantasy was born in him that caused him to dream of the occasion he might prove himself a don Juan or a Felix of Montemar. He believed that all the things he read had actually happened as they were described and came to believe that the life of the student was just about blasphemy, shamefulness, immorality, and breeches of honor. He was smitten and took to the idea of writing verses to the dark-skinned woman in the following manner:

> From the eyes of the moon
> I have picked two fine diamonds
> The thought in mind to place them
> In your great eyes, dark woman.

Another time he pretended he had made a date with beautiful Lola, and he opened the gate to his intellect in this next composition, one that merits being filed away for all eternity. It goes like this:

> And there is your divine sight,
> Oh beloved
> Calling me to follow you,
> Down by the road.

> Let nothing block your path,
> Not even that old man
> With his big stick
> For, though a poor pilgrim,
> I am making my way to you.

One should note that it is still unknown which old man with a big stick inspired our poet. But let us leave those inspirations off to one side and move on with the story. Luciano could not wait to be free of college, to be able to freely pursue and seduce Lola, and then to . . . well, what comes later is another matter. There was still a month to go before graduation and the awards ceremony. Luciano continued to be enthused with thoughts like these:

> Down to the cabins I went
> And up to the palaces I climbed
> And wherever I went,
> I crushed all virtue.

One night the indiscreet boy scurried down the balcony of his alma mater and with his heart beating as fast as a blacksmith's bellows, walked toward Tía Mela's house. The moon was coming up and to the student's good fortune; Lola's lover turned the corner and was lost from sight. As for her, she had not moved from under the old apple tree and did not notice Luciano until he broke her thoughts by saying:

"Good evening, lovely Lola!"

Lola started, took a few steps back, and turning her head abruptly said, "Good evening." A moment later she was inside the house, and the persnickety college student was left standing by himself. Alone, with his hopes crushed and with a pit in his heart. Alone, and that woman who stole his peace had left him in the silence of the night. What disappointment! Luciano was stunned. Luciano, who had hoped to gather enough material that night to fill at least one novel, was left in the dark. Nonetheless, piecing together his fractured plan he went up to the apple tree and thought: Illusion! What a bitter lesson you have given me! But in the future I will make the most of it, and that evasive dark woman who flees from me today in a not too distant day will swoon at seeing me arrive at this bushy apple tree. Why was she startled? Could it be she already has a lover? Who was it that turned the corner? I saw a shadow and later the voice of someone singing from that direction. There can be no doubt she has a lover. It will be necessary to proceed cautiously in this business. I shall return here tomorrow. I will try my luck again, and then we'll see. I'll bring my guitar. People say I sing well, and, hah, I shall find a dagger to bring along as well.

Having said this young man scratched his head and looked wide-eyed again to see whether he could perceive someone resembling Lola at Tía Mela's door. He saw nothing, but going around the house he saw a light in a window. He moved closer and saw a candle burning, a folding cot and a bed, a table with flowers and vases, and at the head of the cot an ancient crucifix before which a young woman knelt and prayed. It was Lola. Luciano gazed upon her for a moment.

"Pray," he whispered and quickly moved away from the window. He took the road to the college and a half hour later slept peacefully in his bed.

The next evening he went out again. He was armed with a dagger and his guitar, having decided not to be disappointed again. This time he did not chance to startle Lola by speaking to her. He let her remove herself to her room and went up to her window. He waited for her to finish her prayers and go to bed. The young woman had only just done this as a gentle song and the sound of a guitar reached her ears:

> Arise, my love,
> Wake from your slumber,
> Come and hear my song,
> Oh come and hear its timber.

> If the world is but a sweet garden
> Where love flourishes
> I come to offer you
> One of its lovely roses.

> Be not afraid, that it's dark
> Fear not that everything sleeps
> For night is the soft breast
> Where love gently sways.

> If blue eyes are
> The color of the sky,
> Your dark eyes
> Are the color of love's passion.

> Arise, my love,
> Wake from your slumber,
> Come and hear my song,
> Oh, come and hear its timber.

The student's song was so smooth, so gentle, so sweet and tender in the calm of the night that everything was transformed like in a dream. Astonished, dear Lola went back to bed. She both wanted and did not want to peek out the window to better hear the song. Her curiosity finally won out. She got up and raised the window, and as she did a hand came through the opening and placed a folded paper in her hand.

It goes without saying that the next night had barely fallen when Luciano returned to his post near the window and began to sing the same song and place the same note, better said, another note with the same wording, and again, he smashed his finger and said, "Damn it!" Lola was again frightened and ran to her bed, only to awaken the next morning and find the note from "The Night Visitor." Carefully unfolding it, she saw it read:

Lovely Lola:

I love you as I have never loved anyone before. I am capable of killing and dying for you. Please talk to me. I know that you are poor and I am wealthy. But what does it matter? Please love me back. You are too lovely to live out your days in obscurity. Please reply.

Last Night's Visitor

"Last Night's Visitor!" Lola murmured, and she tore the note to bits. "Last Night's Visitor," she repeated and began to tremble. She remembered Pablo and her love for him.

It goes without saying that the next evening had barely arrived when Luciano took up a position near the window and began to sing the same song and then went on to place the same note, or better said a second note written in similar form, and then again he stubbed his finger and cried out, "Damn!" Lola once again became frightened and ran to her bed and again, the next day, found a note from "Last Night's Visitor." Luciano's serenade resembled that of someone who only knows one verse that he sang the whole night at the door of his lover. It was the verse that follows:

I planted a pine tree at your door
And a pear tree by your window,
So that one day
You will be able to eat pears on
Christmas Eve.

This troubadour planted so many pines and pear trees that one particular evening a grumpy old man had to look out from his balcony and shout:

"My son, you have already planted a forest at my door and windows. So many that tomorrow the wagons will not be able to enter my courtyard. Go away and let me sleep."

If naive Tía Mela had not slept so soundly, she might have been the one to send Luciano to plant love gardens far from Santa Fe. But the good woman heard nothing, and nothing could pull her away from her deep sleep. And, oh, what misfortune that she did not do so! Oh, cruel fate, in a thousand ways and by the complicated tangle of human fortune you, at times, make innocence and simplicity accomplices to your machinations! Oh, dear Tía Mela, if instead of dreaming of onions and turnips for the next day's stew, you had kept vigil, scrutinizing with one eye what was happening just a few steps away at the window of your beautiful relative, you would have been able to reverse the outcome of an affair that later would become so bitter and tragic for you!

In my youth I remember reading in some Latin text, the proverb: *guta cavat lapidum non vi sed saepe caendo*. With this proverb in mind and another, *audaces fortuna juvat*, an ardent Luciano continued to pester the lovely woman. His resolve was such that in the end the tender beauty surrendered. Humanity loves adulation. Woman needs it for her existence, and Luciano understood this well as he sang his song at Lola's window. From song he went on to words, from words to friendship, from friendship to . . .—well, like another Lucifer in the guise of a snake placing beautiful lies and ephemeral delights before the first woman and then pushing her into a sea of misadventures, so too Luciano did, with shimmering hypocrisy, strike down Lola's happiness. Lola trembled, and yet she began to love the danger—and it is written that he who loves danger will perish by it. Like the butterfly who is seduced by the light of the lanterns and at a given moment flies into the fire, Lola was drawn closer to the disastrous flame of Luciano's love and was seduced. Her young heart was going through a drastic change that would produce a sea of tears, and yet she let itself be seduced. From song, Luciano had moved on to words that caused Lola to lose judgment and give in to curious thinking. These words at the ear of the credulous young woman seemed like pure honey. By comparison, humble Pablo's words seemed coarse and vulgar. Luciano's were like Luzebul's words of knowledge, spoken as he lay hidden in the tree of the earthy paradise. There was no doubting it, Luciano was gaining ground, and as he tenaciously closed the circle, the prey would be his. Lola had broken the secret of her love for Pablo, and Luciano worked to destroy it. Luciano would speak to Lola of her lover's humble origins and then ponder her beauty a minute later. He would, logically, deduce that she was destined to move among a circle of admirers and in luxury, apart from the life of workers.

Luciano continued with such persistent resolve that he got Lola to make a solemn vow to abandon Pablo and as he desired, to be his, with the proviso that upon his leaving college she would marry him.

"I accept," he exclaimed and extended her hand.

"Seal the contract," the maiden said and gave him her lips.

A kiss strong enough to tear the fibers of the soul flashed in the dark. It was the seal of treason and infidelity.

Dear reader, I would like to present Lola made-up in the magnificent dress of a grand heroine, virtuous and adorned by a thousand jewels, pure in her victory over the fury of passion. I would like her to take shape before you sweet and kind, just as she was born in my imagination and as she grew at Pablo's side, loving him tenderly and bringing him happiness. But now I can only present a leafless branch, a faded flower, a vanquished idea, a dream at its close. Nonetheless, I ask you to love her as I love her, to have compassion for her as I have compassion for her, with her tragic flaw and in her fall from grace. Rather than disdain her, know that she did not fashion her misfortune, but that it was Luciano who had planned it in his soul when he promised to marry her, deceiving her throughout just to satisfy a devilish whim. That kiss, that damned kiss! How many have started just like this and today drag themselves through the muck of the most shameful immorality. Still, every Luciano is more criminal than every Lola.

So as to not interrupt my story, let me say that every night after that kiss a young man armed with a knife entered Lola's room through a window, and after a long time he would reemerge and with a devilish smile on his face, murmuring a horrid joke.

Things went on in this way. What these episodes might have led to would have remained a matter of conjecture had it not been for happenstance that all at once arrested their progress and set them spinning in a different direction. Pablo was not the least bit slow and was having deep suspicions about his dark woman. He was surprised by the unexplainable change in her. He beat his head trying to unlock the secret of this change. For her part, Lola had been thinking of a plan to drop Pablo without damaging her reputation, but she had not found a plan to her liking. In her quandary she approached silver-tongued Luciano, but he was as barren of plans as his heart was barren of good intentions. With things going on this way, Pablo the worker, sure that something was up, determined to find out at any cost what it was and made his way to Tía Mela's house the night of the presentation of awards at St. Michael's. An adobe wall that some governor had ordered built so that the Indians would not drill arrows into his head ran the length of the house. Our worker stood behind this wall, prepared for whatever might come. From that place he could make out everything around Lola's window. Even the interior of her room a short distance away could be seen as it was lit from the inside. There was the cot, part of the crucifix, and a vase half-filled with flowers; at the back of the whitewashed bedroom, Lola's graceful shadow cast by the candle could be seen on the wall. Pablo was transfixed by the scene and did not sense the hours flying by. The clock on the cathedral eventually tolled eleven, and not much later some movement broke the silence. Pablo became all ears and all eyes. His heart beat furiously. He looked, held his breath, grit his teeth, and clasped his hands. Someone arrived at the window quietly and quickly. He next heard the strumming of a guitar and the diminutive voice of a pleasant song. The window opened, and the smack of a kiss froze the wretched worker's heart. Before he could believe what he was seeing, the man entered like a thief through the window.

Pablo's mind filled with rage. He pulled out a pistol, cocked it, and took aim; a moment later he would have placed a bullet in his rival and another in his unfaithful love. But at the very instant of committing the double murder, a happier thought came to him, and he lowered the gun to his side and walked briskly up to the door of the house. He did not knock but went in and found Tía Mela snoring the way a person snores when the body is tired and the conscience is clear. Going to her and shaking her awake he said in her ear:

"Tía Mela, Tía Mela, wake up. What a dream, Tía Mela!"

The good woman tossed from side to side dreaming, no doubt, that an evil spirit was taking her away. After a time she opened her eyes, which were as red as embers, and rubbing them, she stopped snoring and asked:

"What's up, what, what . . . Pablo! Oh it's you! What a scare!"

"It's me, Tía Mela. Don't be scared," replied Pablo.

The pitiful matron kept opening her eyes and did not know what to make of this. She nonetheless did as Pablo asked, got dressed quickly, and again asked:

"All right, young man, What a fright you have given me. What do you want?"

"I want you to give me permission to defend her. You cannot defend yourself. I am your friend, and I shall defend you."

"But what's this about, boy? Go on. Don't keep me in suspense," stuttered Tía Mela as she lost her breath.

"There are thieves in the house, Tía Mela."

"Christ! Please say it isn't true, boy. Help! Oh my gracious! Help, help me, I am a defenseless woman!" And, Tía Mela twisted her hands in wrenching desperation.

Pablo did not say more. Dragging her by the hand he took her to Lola's room. All this happened so quickly that while Lola and Luciano heard the shouts they had no time to react. As they tried to understand what was happening, Pablo threw the door open. In a flash he and the squeamish aunt were inside the room. Their entrance was so sudden that Luciano had not even thought to hide under the cot. The candle was burning; the crucifix was hung on the wall; the withered flowers were on the table; the room was planted with shoes, shirts, underpants, and socks; and, on the cot, the unfaithful dark woman and the uppity student lay as one. The aunt again began to shout and make wild gestures in the air. She shouted for help, this time not as much in fear as in pain. She believed a rapacious ogre had her Lolita in his talons. She imagined the sweet girl had fainted and that the ogre was having his way with her. Oh, what love can do! Pablo was livid. His face was filled with determination; in his right hand the dreaded companion could be seen. Luciano turned the color of wax, and he blinked his eyes continually. At that moment the two wrongdoers might have asked the earth to open up and swallow them.

"Look," Pablo said, at last, to Tía Mela as his mouth became blue with rage and his eyes shot daggers.

"Help, help me," the old woman again shouted. As if gripped by pain she ran uncontrollably through the room.

"There's the thief," Pablo repeated. "Tía Mela, Tía Mela. He steals your niece's virtue, but this is not the worst of it. It is she who permits this, she who prostitutes herself."

Hearing this Luciano thought himself lost. Fearing for his life, he jumped from the bed, and Pablo, thinking Luciano would try to pull the gun from him, fired, hitting Luciano in the calf of his leg. Lola threw herself to one side of the bed. Tía Mela fainted and dropped to the floor, believing she was dying. Luciano jumped out the window in his shorts, and Pablo, like someone on his way to work, followed him. The ruckus brought out the neighbors, who found the house in an uproar and the poor old woman fading fast. They took her to the priest as she had begged them to do, and soon they were watching over her discolored, stiff body. The scare had been fatal.

A half hour later a man in his skivvies driven by fear ran through the streets followed by a man possessed. For one of them, this was a matter of saving his skin, for the other, a matter of saving his honor and getting his revenge. Two hours had passed, and the rumor that Tía Mela and her niece had both been murdered spread like the plague. The story spread from mouth to mouth. People gathered, dogs barked, bells rang, the troops at the garrison saddled up, and a naked man and his pursuer ran through the streets. Then, turning a corner, the lead man in the chase failed to see another man coming from the opposite direction and bumped headlong into him. He fell back a few feet, where he was left to see stars in the middle of the street. The run-in brought him down, and a moment later his pursuer grabbed him with an iron fist. Pablo might have laughed had he not been totally consumed by rage seeing his rival—so arrogant only the day before—looking so ridiculous now. The truth of it was that he looked just like the Knight of La Mancha in his penitence in the Sierra Morena. The difference was that the other was a complete madman and this one a complete coward.

Without waiting for an apology from the battered one, Pablo fell upon Luciano and, moving him with some well-placed kicks and calling him by several names that fit the student perfectly, made him keep walking and took him back to Tía Mela's house. They arrived back just as an unfortunate Tía Mela took in her last full breath and gave her soul up to her Creator. Without ceremony and without taking notice of the seriousness of the occasion, Pablo dragged the man in his underwear to the spot were Tía Mela lay. He said with a voice that frightened everyone:

"Look, coward, the work of your hands. Think about this dead woman who was filled with life just a moment ago. Enjoy your work, villain, and if you still have the heart to feel something, you must feel its horror. She has been an innocent victim of your evil deeds."

"Oh, Tía Mela," he continued tenderly before the body. "For everyone your unexpected death must seem a calamity, but fate has made it so that you will not have to survive dishonor. Woe is me, at your feet an abyss of shame opens before me. Woe is me, that I did not die with you so as to not see my beloved woman dishonored. And all because she wanted this! Dishonored! And, I, deceived by her at the moment I most loved her. Fickle woman, faithless woman!"

Pablo would have continued with a long speech worthy of being included in *The Treasure of Spanish Eloquence* by Campani, but pain came forth and cut away the stem of this bud before it could grow. As for Luciano, he looked ridiculous, his contorted face and stupid gaze gave him the appearance of someone who is supremely drunk. Those present were surprised to see him in such a fix. They were astounded to hear of Lola's indiscretions; the old women covered one eye to avoid the sight while the children were wide-eyed seeing so many strange happenings. Some of those present talked of a swift hanging, and others, the kinder ones, spoke of a beating. The resident priest, who still had not dared to stick his great nose out the door, crossed himself and damned the fallen Luciano, wishing that he were a demon or a dead man so as to exhort him to leave *sine die* from the midst of that good community.

Hearing the priest's plea, Pablo again made the crowd tremble with his voice and said, "You'll do no such thing, Father! I say you will not allow as much. You've done your duty for the dead, now, do your duty to the living."

"What do you have in mind, son?" The priest asked.

"You have that woman lying there who let herself die before she would see her niece dishonored by that vile coward," he said and pointed to Luciano.

"Lola was mine," he went on, "and this despicable fellow has dishonored her. I can't help but think he dragged her to ruin with false promises, and I am here to see that those promises are kept. Yes, he must have promised her a great deal, since Lola was pure and good and would not have given in to the pleasure of this sin and let herself be besmirched. Lola was mine, and I adored her like the Indians adore their fetishes. I placed my joy in her, but now everything is done between us."

"Nonetheless, I still love her enough to want to save her from greater pitfalls. Father, there is Lola, the deceiver is here. By natural law they belong to each other, and I, from today forward, give up any claim my heart has on Lola's heart. If you do not wish to see that unthinking young lady enter a life of prostitution to hide her first wild act, marry them, marry them. This is what I want, this is what I order. I will be responsible in my conscience and before God for what comes later."

Pablo's attitude was so forceful that none was able to challenge it. They shuttered. They were surprised and shocked. Lola was shocked. Pablo was somber and wounded. Luciano, helped by some considerate folk, was shaking like a victim of mercury poisoning. He put his boots and underclothes on backwards, which someone had brought from where he had shamelessly abandoned them in Lola's bedroom. The priest had ordered him to dress, seeing that it was not proper for him to be in only his underwear among so many respectable women.

As for the reverend, he kept turning and turning his rosary, invoking the heavenly court to assist him with this predicament. He gave himself some pious blows to the stomach, and with a grave air he turned to Luciano and said:

"Let's see son, how do you respond to the charges brought against you? Are they all true?"

"Every one of them, dear Father," Luciano answered in supplication.

"And do you love Lola and take her for your wife?"

"Yes, Father."

"And you, child, come here," he continued as he directed himself to Lola. "Do you love Luciano and take him as your husband and friend?"

A barely audible "yes" came from the young woman's lips as she lowered her face, now red as a tomato. A hush went through the crowd. Pablo was as white as ash.

"Do you both intend to mend past faults and provide a good example? And do you repent with all your heart from what you have done?" the reverend father asked again, and both at once replied in the affirmative. They gave their hands to each other, the priest raised his eyes to heaven, and he raised his right hand and made the sign of the cross over the two young people and gave his blessing. Pablo shed a furtive tear, and Lola, seeing this, dropped to his feet. As her eyes filled with tears, she exclaimed, "Forgive me Pablo!"

Pablo took that beautiful face in his hands for the last time and answered, "May God's mercy, and mine as well, go with you." And with this, he left. Now, every evening when I go by the door of the deceased aunt I feel like crying. Lola and Luciano, heirs to all her estate, live in her house. They live asking each other for forgiveness for past faults. They have a lovely child they call Pepe. On moonlight nights when my soul is melancholy, I go to the tree by the door from where I can sometimes hear a vesper song from Luciano, who knows an infinite and inexhaustible variety of them. ☼

COLOR PLATES

Murallas de lumbre

PHOTO ESSAY ON THE MURALS OF SANTA FE

Miguel A. Gandert

▲ [Previous page] *Lady of Justice* (1972). Sam Leyba, Pancho Hunter, Gilberto Guzmán, and Gerónimo Garduño with Artes Guadalupanos de Aztlán, a group started in 1971 by brothers Sam, Albert, and Carlos Leyba, Gerónimo Garduño, and Gilberto Guzmán. Acrylic mural on south and west walls of small building, upper Canyon Road. Sponsored by Román Salazar, CCRG Mayoral Candidate (Citizen's Coalition for Responsible Government). 8 x 30 feet.

▼ *Cara de Tres Culturas* (1972). Albert Leyba, Carlos Leyba, and Gerónimo Garduño with Artes Guadalupanos de Aztlán. Site of COPAS Community Service Provider (Corporación Organizada para Acciones Servidoras). Sponsored by New Mexico State Office of Economic Opportunity. 4 x 20 feet.

Multi-Cultural Progression (1981). Zara Kriegstein, Felipe C. de Baca, and team. Acrylic mural on Empire Builders Supply building, Cerrillos Road. Sponsor: Henry Culver. 15 x 80 feet.

Acequia Madre (1992). Frederico M. Vigil.
Fresco at Acequia Madre Elementary
School. Sponsors: Santa Fe Arts
Commission, Michael and Marianne
O'Shaughnessy. 26 x 10 feet.

Tratado de Guadalupe Hidalgo (1997). Frederico M. Vigil.
Interior fresco in Old Santa Fe County Court House.
Sponsors: Santa Fe County, McCune Foundation.
16 x 38 feet.

[Above and right] *Las Tres Caras del Mestizo* (1986). Carlos Cervantes with Artes Guadalupanos de Aztlán. Acrylic mural on Alto Street and Alameda facing the Santa Fe River. Funded by New Mexico Arts Division, Art in Public Places Program, and National Endowment for the Arts. 8 x 35 feet.

History of New Mexico (1982). Zara Kriegstein, Cassandra Gordon Harris, Gilberto Guzmán, with Rosemary Sterns, Frederico M. Vigil, David Bradley, and the Multicultural Mural Group. Acrylic mural on Halpin Building, Guadalupe Street. Sponsored by New Mexico State Archives and Records Center. 18 x 110 feet.

PART IV

Nuestra Cornucopia

PLACE, WATER, FOOD

Oración al Río Grande/
Prayer to the Rio Grande

A. Gabriel Meléndez

(2009)

Río Grande
bravo del norte
weave
your harsh
and wild course south
spill your past
over the dark volcanic riverbed of my soul,
mark us, the living, with your power
for all the generations to come,
you, river of earth
song that begins at the foot of pine trees and
descends from the four sacred mountains
of our Indian-brothers-cousins, abuelas,
    compadres, vecinas, uncles,
tatarabuelos, genízaros,
river that seeks the heart of the valley,
shed your torrent of earth,
stone, sun, moon,
footsteps,
strands of hair, bones,
lips, animal hooves,
horse's manes, water striders,
uñas de gato,
trout fins, caliche, cottonwood branches,
treebark,
talco,
ristras,
relámpagos, aserrín,
capulín, manzanas, albercoque,
estrella de la mañana,
quelites, calabazas, yerba buena, juansinmiedos,
santoniños, pedrodeurdimales, bartolos, lloronas,
    chufunetes,

Un puño de tierra: Catron's Last Land Grant, 2008.

altamisa-de-la-sierra, descansos, matachines,
    vía crucis,
arco-de-monarcas, comanches, malinches, llantos,
    lágrimas, sudor de manito,
sangre de manito, malvas, mana estefanitas, saliva,
    piedra turquesa,
piedra lumbre, varas de san josé, santoseñor-
    deesquípulas,
shimmering light, waves of life, particles of
    resurrection:
Río Grande, sáname con tus aguas,
heal me with your waters,
cobíjame con el suave bálsamo de tu cauce,

cover me with the soft balm of riverearth

santíguame,

bless me,

purifícame,

cleanse me,

carry me into the sea

when it is time

to leave

this life

for another.

El Río de Tesuque

Anónimo

(La Aurora, Santa Fe, New Mexico, August 1884)

Algunas horas de infinito solaz y de
plácida calma disfrutamos el jueves, en
la tarde en ese pintoresco lugar, cuya
naturaleza, en parte cultivada, en parte
silvestre necesitaría el pincel más
diestro para describirla dignamente.
El arroyo que dulcemente allí serpentea,
en medio de fértiles y seductores
plantíos, convida al viajero, agobiado
de fatiga a pasar las colorosas horas de la
tarde debajo de los umbrosos árboles
que majestuosamente se desarollan en
su lecho para cautivar la vísta del
meditabundo poeta. ¡Cúan más poéticos
fueran los alrededores de eso sonriente
paisaje si la mano del hombre edificara
hermosos "Chalets" para el deleite y
comodidades de las familias que desearen
veranear en ese casi desconocido edén!
Allí los enfermos hallarían la deseada
salud; las almas entristecidas, la señalada
alegría; los bardos, la inspirición más fecunda;
los amantes a las melodías

escucharían de continuo los armoniosos
    conciertos
que las aves contadoras no cesan de brindar
a los rústicos campesinos,
hoy dueños y señores de tanta
belleza y riqueza tanta.

Down by the Tesuque River

Anonymous

Synopsis by A. Gabriel Meléndez

We enjoyed a few hours of peace, calm, and relaxation on Thursday evening at this picturesque place whose natural setting, in part under cultivation and in part untamed, requires a most exacting brush to paint it in an apt way. The river that sweetly winds its way between the fertile and seductive fields invites the weary traveler to spend the burning hours of the afternoon under the shady trees that majestically grow on its banks—a sight that inspires the meditative poet. Oh, how much more poetic these surrounding would be if men built beautiful "Chalets" for the enjoyment and comfort of those families who would want to summer in this unknown Eden! There the sick would find the health they seek, those with beleaguered spirits would find joy, the poets would find inspiration in abundance, lovers would find the melodies and the harmonious concerts of the birds that continuously sing and give to the rustic farmer who is today the owner and lord of so much beauty and richness.

Sum-Sum-Summertime

Marie Romero Cash

(2007)

During the rainy season, the acequias brimmed with water. My dad's great-uncle, Tío Fortino, was in charge of the nearby acequia that ran along the edge of his property and that of the Apodacas, and also parallel to our street. The mother ditch, or acequia madre, originated a long distance away near the upper end of Canyon Road and traveled down Hickox Street, eventually arriving at our street and continuing down to the State Penitentiary, where it ultimately served the gardens. From this main ditch, a small stream ran from Galisteo Street down through Houghton Street. At certain points the water was diverted to different neighbors as their turn came up. This irrigation system served our neighborhood gardens and also provided a bit of recreation for bored teenagers on hot summer afternoons. The sidewalk that ran along West Houghton from Galisteo Street was built over a culvert tunnel, and when you walked along this sidewalk your footsteps made a hollow sound. The boys would crawl more than one hundred feet through the tunnel from beginning to end when there was no water, emerging triumphantly at one end of the small concrete bridge on Galisteo Street.

The water in the acequia was crystal clear and had a layer of fine sparkling sand at the bottom. Horny toads flitted past the edges, taking cover under rocks and vegetation. Tío Fortino had a nice orchard on his property with apricot, apple, and peach trees, and among other things, grew great stalks of sweet corn in his garden. Dad and our neighbors used the water to irrigate our family vegetable gardens, which were grown in the large lot down the street that also served as our baseball field, although the water from the acequia couldn't travel to our gardens on its own. My brother Emilio assisted in diverting the acequia to serve this purpose by removing several bricks from the main diversion nearby, thus redirecting the flow to the crops planted in the open

field (which is now part of my backyard on Lomita Street). When the watering was completed, the bricks were replaced and covered with a layer of dirt, averting any suspicion of tampering. We also used this water for household purposes, cooking and bathing, before indoor plumbing. A community well at the north side of the street next to Tío Fortino's house also served the neighborhood. It was an old stone well, and we used a bucket tied with a rope to haul water.

During the rainy season in mid-July, the arroyos filled with water and overflowed to create large ponds on the hill directly east of our house on Rosina Street. At this location, Jimmy, Cousin Junior, and the rest of the neighborhood boys spent days hauling rocks and logs to dam the culvert into one big pond, which served as a swimming hole. Cousin Junior recalled, "We spent most of the day gathering rocks and sticks and stacking them in a row on the edge of the culvert. One of us would tramp mud and leaves down to hold the rocks in place, while the others gathered different sized rocks. By the time the water started to pool, it was early afternoon and time for a swim. You wouldn't believe how much water we managed to divert, it was pretty deep. Anyway, I decided to dive in, and as I hit the cool water with a running jump, the momentum carried me to the bottom of the pond. There was a broken Coke bottle lodged between the rocks, and I dove right into it. I came out of the water fast, holding my bleeding hand. My cousin Emilio dragged me over to his bike and rode me home, where my mother applied a bandage. I didn't get to swim for a few days, but once it healed I was back there again. We started being more careful about gathering glass and sharp rocks before we built our dam."

The boys also tied long ropes to the branches of two large elm trees near the edge. Pretending to be Tarzan, they rode the rope across the short distance and catapulted themselves into the center of the pond. Cloudbursts provided an added bonus when such abundant rain fell that we were able to wade in the pond every afternoon. The monsoon season usually started in mid-July and continued into August, but the pond primarily relied on the acequia water to keep it full.

The pleasures were often short-lived, however, since the damming was so effective that it kept water from reaching the State Penitentiary, located where Cordova Road and Cerrillos Road now intersect, about six blocks southwest of our neighborhood. As soon as the problem became evident early in the day, prisoners from the penitentiary, accompanied by a guard, were ordered to walk the entire length of the acequia system, starting on Acequia Madre Street (where the mother ditch began). After walking down several city streets, they eventually discovered the dammed area. In order to free up all the boards and rocks, one of the prisoners dove into the deep end of pond. The others broke up the top of the dam with shovels, releasing a gush of water, and they watched as it slowly gathered momentum and flowed in the direction of the penitentiary. It wasn't too long before the rain resumed and the boys began gathering and stacking river rocks to rebuild their dam, and swimming was on the next afternoon's schedule again. If it was late Friday or Saturday, the guards wouldn't bother to break up the dam over the weekend, but they arrived like clockwork on Monday morning, prisoners in tow. The boys were so fascinated with the demeanor, mannerisms, and tattoos of the prisoners that they would deliberately dam the culvert just so they could spend a few moments talking to them.

Los duraznos de mi casa en el arroyo de Chinguayé (Octavilla)

Inspiración de Primavera

Robert Lara Vialpando
(1979)

Ya salieron las hormigas,
ya la tierra calentó
son indicios que la vida
veraniega comenzó.
Por eso hay que principiar
nuestros pechos a llenar
de aire puro que da aliento,
que nos trae felicidad.

Deja la obra "vida mía"
sal del trabajo penoso,
trinos de amor sonoroso
te canta un jilguero aquí.
Y alegre con su trinar
te está cantando por mí
te dice que te sé amar
con ardiente frenesí.

De la flor la dulce miel
chupetea la colemena
se ha parado a sustentar,
para así poder volar
en su volido emigrante,
como la nuez elegante
que se halla en el piñonal.

Perdiéronse las urracas
en las cimas de los montes,
y salieron los zinsontes
como un brillante clarín,

chirriando las chuparrosas
en las flores del jardín,
y en las ondas del paisaje
se olía a1 puro jazmín.

Sal al campo de tu casa
refleja el nuevo sembrado,
que en el surco del arado
se ha plantado nueva mata,
mira a1 gañan en los ranchos
con esperanza sembrar,
ve a los duraznos florear
en los campos de tu casa.

Peaches at My Home in Arroyo of Chinguayé (Octosyllabic Verses)
Inspired by Springtime
Robert Lara Vialpando
Synopsis by A. Gabriel Meléndez

This local bard describes the coming of spring as the ants come out with the warming earth. He urges us all to fill our lungs with the pure air of the season for it brings great joy. Speaking to the love of his life, he urges her to leave her hard work and listen to the goldfinch that is singing a pleasing love song. The goldfinch's trill sings out the poet's burning love for his friend and lover.

The poet describes how the swarm of bees sucks the sweet nectar of the flowers. The act sustains the bees and allows them to fly. Their flight in the distant sky looking like pine cones blowing in the piñon trees.

The poet speaks of magpies that are lost from sight on the crest of the hilltops but says the mock-ingbirds have emerged and sound like brilliant trumpets, the hummingbirds are humming among the flowers of the garden and the smell of pure jasmine moves across the countryside in waves.

The poet urges his love to go out to the fields that surround their home. There he assures her she will see how the furrows of the plow are sprouting new plants. He asks her to understand how the young man working his fields anchors his hope to the new planting, noting how the peach trees in bloom in the surrounding fields give the first sign of this future hope.

Nuestra Cornucopia
Alfredo Celedón Luján
(2008)

Some things never change, like *pelando el chile*—yes, we still peel chili, make that chile. Simón—"the more things change, the more they remain the same." Santa Fe has changed, but *norteños* have not. Grocery shopping, for example, gives one clue to how The City Different has become The City Divided. Grocery stores are a by-product of the socioeconomic and population shifts that have transfigured Santa Fe.

In some stores chichi is in, but chile is out because there's a new "Santa Fean" in town, one who has little or no experience with the ways of northern New Mexico. New Santa Fean and norteño choices for grocery stores are as disparate as the contrast between old school downtown and modern day downtown.

Norteños and *norteñas* long for the plaza, back when Santa Fe High, Harvey Jr. High, St. Michael's, and Loretto Academy were around the corner, *cuando la plaza era de la gente*, and the businesses were local and practical: Woolworth's, Goodman's, Dunlap's,

JC Penney, Livingston Furniture, El Paseo, the Lensic, *las cantinitas*, Safeway, Maytag, and Sears.

The megaboutique into which la plaza has morphed is more appealing to new Santa Feans, of course, because it's the only plaza they've known: the town square surrounded by coffeehouses, galleries, restaurants, and shops where guests and tourists sip their lattes or double espressos and buy glitzy, expensive mementos. The dichotomy between the old plaza and the new town square is reflected in the grocery store chasm as well.

In some stores local is *qué loco*, while in other stores it's passé. As the demands for organic foods and health supplements soar, stores like Whole Foods, The Market Place, and Wild Oats have become meccas for shoppers who feel comfortable in them—make that those who can afford to shop in them. Those stores appeal to BMW, Mercedes Benz, Land Rover, Hummer, hiker, bicycle rider, hippie, transplant, environmentally correct, yippie, yuppie, sensibility, and sustainability types.

The other stores remain the domain of the natives and immigrants: Smith's, Albertson's, Sam's, Lowe's . . . food emporiums with Fords, Chevys, Hondas, Toyotas, and pickup trucks parked in their lots . . . stores that attract white- and blue-collar, no nonsense, thrifty, no-political-agenda, everyday shoppers . . . those who don't necessarily shop for food in designer threads. Santa Fean and norteño life-styles and shopping preferences are self-discriminating. "Dime con quien andas shopping, y te diré quien eres."

It's a quandary. What to do: shop uptown, downtown, or the south side of town? Are you looking for *menudo* or tripe; tortillas or white bread; posole or hominy; chile verde or green chili peppers? Do you need a supply of food for when three generations of *familia* come to *cenar*, or do you need ginseng, whole grains, echinacea, and

a massage while you shop? Are you looking for a painkiller o *un remedio*? Are you homeopathic? Do you want real cookies or vegan decadence? Are you looking for a package of powdered chile at the Rancho de Santa Fe display, where you can buy guacamole mix, *azafrán*, white corn posole, or *chipotle* salsa while listening to top 40s rock 'n' roll that "soothes the soul . . . the days of old?" Or are you shopping for minerals, amino acids, and antioxidants while you listen to piped-in audio learning and world music for the inner life? Do you need whey, guey, soy protein, or are you *soy quien soy*?

In the good ol' days we shopped for food once a month. We rode on the back of a flatbed or pickup truck or in the back seat of a '55 Ford Fairlane to go for *los groceries* at el Pigele Wigele *en la esquina de* St. Francis *y* Cordova (where Wild Oats now is) or el Safeway downtown *cerca del* Sears. Most of the cashiers and stockers *eran conocidos; hablaban español; eran primos, compadres, comadres, vecinos*. Shopping for food was the business of getting something substantial to eat. The food was organic without the label. Everybody knew everybody. The *extranjeros* were few and far between. Spanish, English, and Spanglish were spoken in these stores, *donde nos entendíamos unos a los otros*. The dialogue was authentic northern New Mexican.

"Y tus hijos?"

"Todos bien."

"¿Todos vivos?"

"Algunos vivos, algunos tontos, pero todos comen."

Pura risa.

Today, grocery shopping is a trip. With the exception of Lowe's, English is the dominant shopping language with occasional Spanglish sprinkled in. Some shoppers yearn for tofu, sprouts, the *New*

York Times, the Wall Street Journal, the Reporter, red chili hummus, tortilla chips, and pita bread. Others crave avocados, jalapeños, the Santa Fe New Mexican, La Herencia del Norte, pork fat for chicharrones, tostadas, and the makings for salsa, ese. Where one shops is related to what one reads . . . strange, but true.

Whether one snacks on potato chips, pure-beef bologna sandwiches, and sardinas con cebolla . . . or whether he/she delights in celery, carrot sticks, and the deli will determine one's favorite grocery store. Do you like carne, or are you a vegetarian? Can you eat the by-products of farm animals, or must you eat something that never had a face? Are you in the mood for reading from a classic novel at the in-the-grocery-store café, or do you just wanna buy your food y a volar sin alas? The answers to these questions have polarized shoppers in their quest for food in Santa Fe.

Of course, there are cross-eaters. Some norteños and norteñas have become vegetarians. Imagine the surprise when my own daughter claimed she was vegetarian. "But, hija," I told her "you make your own carne seca, and you eat bacon sometimes."

"That's different," she said.

Why argue with a seventeen-year-old's logic? "Ok, hijita, you're a vegetarian."

Other locos have switched to healthy low-fat diets and healthier life-styles (even if their grandparents lived more than ninety years eating papitas, carnitas del ranchito y huevos frescos every day). Some hummus eaters, though, have taken to the local cuisine. They love to say "red," "green," "Christmas, please," or "Veggie tamales."

"Veggie tamales?" I wonder, recognizing the oxymoron that would offend any upstanding pig.

For sure the northern New Mexican palate has evolved much like the mezcla of the people and the language. We now often crave the exotic: tofu, raw fish, stir fry, watercress, curry, tandoori lamb, wonton soup, egg rolls, calamari, Gino's Pizza, and even Maine lobster in landlocked Santa Fe, ése. We eat Greek, Italian, Thai, and Vietnamese. Yes, norteños also park their SUVs and Beamers in the lot, Simón. They also read the Times, the Post, and classical literature. We follow the market. We enjoy generational, intellectual, and tactile stimulation. "Somos quienes somos."

So every autumn, during harvest season, you will not find us norteños or norteñas shopping for herbal supplements at Whole Foods or Wild Oats. In a pinch, however, we might stop if there's green chile roasting in their parking lots. For the most part, we will be looking for real deals on chile verde along Cerrillos Road. We will buy out the freezer bags at our favorite store for packing el chile. We will be pelando y empacando. Our hands will get red hot enchiladas, so we will have to be very careful when we blow our nose or rub our eyes, and extremely careful when we take a leak. Jokes about el chile will meander with the lingering bouquet of chile rescoldado.

For example, we were pelando chile under the portal one day. We had a couple of sacks steaming in a cooler to loosen the chile skin. Newspapers were spread on top of the table for wrapping the peels, stems, and seeds. There were pans of water for rinsing, cookie sheets on which we would stack the peeled chile, a cutting board and knives for chopping, and one quart freezer bags for packing. Another cooler was full of cokes, water, and frías. We had chicarrones frying in the grill; mom had made some fresh tortillas. The garlic was diced. I had put my SOL cap on to remind myself that some of this chile would be going to primo Larry, my tías, and other relatives in Califa. We sat around the wooden table, peeling chile, pulling the stems, cleaning out the seeds, mitotiando, and telling stories and jokes . . . yeah, in the old day people went around the pueblitos in carros de bestias or carts selling their goods—leña, fresh vegetables, tools . . . odds and ends, whatever. One day a farmer was selling bushels of chile straight from his jardín. And it was healthy, macizo . . . long, firm chile . . . largo, you know? Behind him a man was selling old and rusty shovels—square shovels, spades, round shovels, snow shovels . . . shovels de todas clases, but they were old—palas viejas. Bueno—there they went, early in the morning, calling out their goods. The farmer yelled, "¡*Chile largo!*"

Behind him the merchant yelled, "¡*Palas viejas!*"

"¡*Chile largo!*"

"¡*Palas viejas!*"

There they went.

"¡*Chile largo!*"

"¡*Palas viejas!*"

Es que all the women from the village came out of their houses with smiles on their faces . . . looking for that healthy chile.

Another time two spinsters arrived for a dance at the El Rancho Bar. They parked and got out of their car. It was a brisk autumn night. The band was on a break. In the dance hall most of the women had lined up at the restroom, while the men went outside to pee. That's the way it was back then. Juanito was tirando el choro (relieving himself) between two cars, unnoticed, as the two women walked by. It was cold. One of the women pulled her shawl over her shoulders, turned to the other, and said, "Pretty chilly."

"Thank you, ma'm," Juanito said, "thank you."

Peeling chile, while telling stories and jokes, is ingrained in our northern New Mexican consciousness and heritage. For us, returning to the fall chile peeling ritual each year is like salmon running to their spawning grounds or squirrels storing nuts for the winter. It's in our DNA. In our cultural cornucopia some of our elders still hang *ristras* to dry, and then they *despepitar* el chile. For them, ristras are not just decor. And in the fall norteños and norteñas shop for *calabacitas*, not squash; a "punkin," not a pumpkin; *cebollitas*, not onions; frijoles, not pinto beans; chile, not chili peppers. During the harvest season, our portales and the aisles of our favorite stores will echo our *antepasados* with *palabras, dichos y chistes* rich with wisdom, playful rhythms, and crafty puns . . . *herencias* not found at Whole Foods, The Market Place, Wild Oats, or any place where chichi is in and chile is out. ☼

PART V

Los Barrios

HOME SPACES

Barrio de Analco

Francisco X. Alarcón

(1995)

Los adobes
del barrio más antiguo
de esta nación
hablan náhuatl

Analco
Analco
"al otro lado
del río"

El Palacio Real
Se estableció
En la ladera norte
del Río de Santa Fe

aquí en la ladera
sur del río
es donde la Raza
vivía
los tlaxcaltecas
los aliados indios
los sirvientes
los mestizos

el lomo
el músculo
las verdaderas manos
del imperio

en los gruesos muros
de San Miguel
la iglesia más antigua
de esta nueva tierra

Los Chileros: A New Mexican Cornucopia,
Santa Cruz, 1993.

todavía puedo oír
sus oraciones
mitad náhuatl
mitad español

¿acaso sabían
que al venir al norte
estaban regresando
a Chicomóztoc

la tierra mítica
de las siete cuevas
la patria original
del pueblo nahua?

éstos son los campos
que tanto cultivaron
las viejas acequias
que limpiaban cada año

éstos son los pisos
que seguido barrían
las vigas que dispusieron
en los techos de las casas

éstas son las ollas
que moldearon en barro
su comida que todavía se sirve
en la mayoría de las mesas

la cuidad en realidad
de sus sueños
mestizos.

The Neighborhood of Analco

Francisco X. Alarcón

The adobes
of the oldest barrio
in this nation
speak Nahuatl

Analco
Analco
"on the other side
of the river"

El Palacio Real
was established
on the north side
of the Río de Santa Fe

but here on the south
side of the river
is where la Raza
lived

the Tlaxcalans
the Indian allies
the servants
the mixed bloods

the backbone
the muscle
the real hands
of the empire

on the thick walls
of San Miguel
the oldest church
in this new land

I can still hear
your prayers
half in Náhuatl
half in Spanish

were you aware
that coming north
you were coming
back to Chicomoztoc

the mythical land
of the seven caves
the original homeland
of the Nahua people?

These are the fields
You went on tending
the old acequias
you cleaned out in spring

these are the floors
you kept on sweeping
the vigas you placed
on dwelling roofs

these are the pots
you molded out of clay
your food is still served
on most tables

the whole city
is an outgrowth
of your mestizo
dreams

De la capital

Correspondiente Especial *El Independiente*
Bonafé

(El Independiente, *Las Vegas, New Mexico, 1892)*

Santa Fe, Oct. 1—Cualquier observador mediana-
mente curioso no puede menos que notar el cambio que ha ocurrido en Santa Fe y en algunas otras
plazas del Territorio, de algunos años a esta parte,
cambio que claramente indica que poco a poco nos
vamos "americanizando." Muchos son los indicios
que ponen esto de manifiesto y hacen conocer que
las costumbres y usos anteriores van lentamente
desapareciendo y cediendo a prácticas nuevas a
imitación de las que están en boga en los estados.
Casi todos los jóvenes de veinte años abajo hablan
el idioma inglés con más o menos perfección y se
han olvidado o no hacen aprecio de los juegos y
diversiones que eran la regla en años anteriores, y
hasta algunos de los más avisados o más pretencio-
sos imitan el tono y manera de los recien venidos
monstrándose más turcos que Mahoma en esto de
hablar el inglés a todas horas del día y de la noche;
teniendo casi por mengua hablar su propio idioma.
En los juegos de diversión nadie se acuerda ya de
la pelota con chuecos, de la barra, ni del juego de
la iglesias; el vocabularío del baseball llena la boca
de toda la juventud, desde los más grandes hasta
los más pequeños y muestran igual entusiasmo por
este juego insípido que sus colegas de los estados.
Ya no hay peleas de gallos, ni se juega a la teja ni
a los demás juegos juveniles que eran el deleite de
los neo-mexicanos en tiempos pasados, y las car-
reras a caballo y a pie son pasatiempos que han
caído enteramente en desuso. La gente ya no se
divierte y parece haber perdido su alegría y con-
tento anteriores, siendo muy raros y contados los
bailes de gusto que se daban tan a menudo antes, y
los bailes de mesilla de los cuales hubo tiempos en
que se daban tres o cuatro noches se han descon-
tinuado enteramente y no hay quien siga esa clase
de especulación. Las únicas danzas que se notan
en esta época presente son los bailes que algunas
veces en el año dan los bomberos o alguna otra
sociedad con el objeto de reunir fondos, y para
eso, a esa clase de bailes no asiste la generalidad
de la gente. Todo esto prueba que nos hallamos en
una época de transición y en camino para adoptar
las costumbres de la nación en que pertenecemos.
Es muy probable que en el término de cincuenta
años o antes se habrá generalizado el uso del idioma inglés y habremos adaptado las prácticas de
los ciudadanos de la gran república. Esto no quiere decir que nuestro pueblo abandonará el uso de
su idioma nativo, sino que todos, por convencia
propia, aprenderán la lengua que se habla general-
mente en el país a que pertenecen.

La comisión de la penitenciaria ha estado en estos días teniendo su sesión regular con el fin de recibir las propuestas semestrales para el aprovisionamiento de dicha institución y al mismo tiempo para despachar otros negocios de rutina que regularmente se presentan en cada reunión del cuerpo, tales como la confirmación de guardias, de los cuales siempre hay un surtido nuevo cada vez que expiran los seis meses de pórroga. En la actualidad varios comerciantes de Santa Fe y de otras partes del Territorio han metido propuestas para proveer los diverosos artículos y provisiones necesarias, pero todavía se ignora quienes habrán sacado los contratos.

La expedición que salió hace dos o tres semanas en busca de Pedro García acusado de doble asesinato cometido en el condado de Bernalillo, de lo cual dimos cuenta en una carta anterior, ha regresado sin haber conseguido atrapar al pájaro volante; pero el lunes pasado volvieron a salir otros oficiales con la misma embajada y se dice que esta vez si tienen buenos prospectos de prender al fugitivo, porque han descubierto que García acostumbra dormir con mucha frequencia en cierta casa situada a algunas millas de San Pedro y allí se espera cojerlo como en una trampa al día menos pensado.

Se ha recibido de Taos la lamentable noticia de la muerte de Doña Refugito Martínez de Sánchez digna esposa del Hon. Pedro Sánchez cuidadano prominente de aquel lugar y uno de los hombres de mayor reputación en el Territorio. Los muchos amigos del señor Sánchez en esta ciudad simpatizan con él en su duelo y le acompanan en el pesar que debe haberle ocasionado la pérdida de su fiel compañera.

También nuestro amigo Don Carlos Conklin ha recibido la triste noticia de la muerte de su hija política, esposa de su hijo mayor Don Francisco Conklin, la cual ocurrió ayer en la ciudad de Kansas, donde hacía tiempo vivía en compañía de su esposa. Deja dos niñas de tierna edad las cuales echarán menos los cariñosos cuidados de su madre, pero tendrán el consuelo de albergarse bajo la sombra de su padre y de sus abuelos que con su ternura les harán olvidar su orfandad.

La cosecha de fruta ha sido muy abundante en esta ciudad, especialmente en lo que toca a manzanas y peras, habiéndose recogido de las primeras por lo menos cien mil libras y de las segundas probablemente la mitad de esa cantidad. Las cosechas de grano han sido regulares aunque no tan abundantes como se esperaba por razón de que la excesiva abundancia de las lluvias perjuidicó algún tanto los sembrados. Sin embargo, ha sido general la abundancia y la cosecha recogida suplirá a muchas familias a manera de que pueden provisionarse sin trabajo para todo el año que viene.

El señor arzobispo de Santa Fe, acompañado de su secretario se halla actualmente en la ciudad de México asistiendo a las festividades de la coronación de Nuestra Señora de Guadalupe, a la cual se cree que asistieron millares de personas de todas partes del mundo. Regresará su señoría antes del día 15 en cuya fecha se espera arribarán a esta capital el cardenal y los prelados que vienen a asistir a la imposición del patio y á efectuar la consagración del señor arzobispo de Santa Fe.

Han regresado del norte los oficiales de la corte del primer distrito judicial, después de haber tenido una semana de cortes en el condado de San Juan, donde se juzgaron algunos causas criminales. En Río Arriba y Taos no se pudo tener cortes por falta de fondos para los gastos.

Ultimamente el difunto banco nacional de Albuquerque, de que es recibidor el señor Schofield, y cuya quiebra dejó engolillada la suma de sesenta mil pesos pertenecientes al Territorio, ha pagado un tercer dividendo de diez por ciento a los acreedores del banco completando con esto un treinta por ciento del déficit, y por su puesto, la tesorería Territorial recibió la parte que le correspondía.

From the Capital

Special correspondent to *El Independiente*
Bonafé
Translation by A. Gabriel Meléndez

Santa Fe, Oct. 1—Any halfway interested observer cannot but note the changes that have occurred in Santa Fe and in some other towns of the Territory in recent years up to now. These changes clearly indicate that little by little we are becoming Americanized. There are many indicators that show this and make known that the customs and earlier practices are slowly disappearing and giving way to new practices in imitation of those that are in fashion in the "States." Almost all the young people, twenty years old or younger, speak English with greater or lesser perfection, and they have forgotten or do not appreciate the games and diversions that were the rule in previous times, and so, even—the most pretentious—imitate the tone and manners of the recent arrivals and show themselves to be more Catholic than the pope in this matter of palavering English at all hours of the day and night and have ceased to speak their own language.

In games and sports no one even remembers the game of *pelota y chuecos*, or that of the bar or the game of churches. Baseball terms fill the mouths of the smallest to oldest of our youth. All are on par in their enthusiasm for this game with their counterparts in the "States."

There no longer are cockfights, nor does anyone play *teja* or the other games for young people that were the joy of the Neomexicanos in the past.

Horse races and foot races have fallen out of use completely. The people don't seem to enjoy themselves and seem to have lost the happiness and contentment of other times. The joyous dances that were common are now rare and few in number, and the salon dances, which at one time were held three or four nights of the week, have been discontinued, and there is no one who invests in that kind of activity. The only dances to be noted and given once or twice a year are the Fireman's Ball or a dance sponsored by some other organization for the purpose of raising money, and that, the general public does not attend this kind of function. All this supports the idea that we are in a period of transition and on the road to adopting the customs of the nation to which we belong. It is possible that within fifty years or less, the use of English will be generalized, and we will have adopted the practices of the citizens of this great Republic. This does not mean that our people will abandon the use of its native language, but all, for convenience will learn the language that is generally spoken in the country they are a part of.

The Penitentiary Commission has been in session these days. Its regular session is for the purpose of accounting for the weekly budgets for the support of that institution and to dispatch other routine business presented at the regular meetings of the commission, business like the appointment of guards, of which there are many, at the end of the six-month probationary period. At present several businessmen in Santa Fe and other parts of the Territory have submitted proposals to provide various goods and necessary supplies, but it is still not known who has gotten the contracts.

The party that left two or three weeks ago in search of Pedro García, accused of a double murder committed in Bernalillo County that we reported on in previous correspondence, has returned without having caught the bird in flight. Last Monday,

Sueños impuestos:
Speed, Saguaros,
Sleeping Mexicans, 1974.

though, other officials went out with the same charge, and it is reported that on this occasion there are good indications that the fugitive will be arrested, since it has been learned that García has the habit of sleeping at a certain house a few miles from San Pedro. The hope is that he will be snared in a trap there any day now.

From Taos has come the regrettable news of the death of doña Refugito Martínez de Sánchez, the worthy wife of the honorable Pedro Sánchez, a prominent citizen of that place and one of the most well known men of the Territory. The many friends of Mrs. Sánchez in this city sympathize with him in his sorrow and the grief occasioned by the lost of his faithful companion.

Also, our friend, don Carlos Conklin, has received the sad news of the death of his daughter-in-law, the wife of his eldest son, don Francisco Conklin, which happened yesterday in Kansas City where he lived with his wife for some time. She leaves two small children who will miss the loving affection of their mother, but they will be consoled by the protection of their father and their grandparents who with their tenderness will make them forget their orphanhood.

The harvest of fruit has been very abundant, especially that of apples and pears, with at least a hundred thousand pounds of the first and half that amount of the second gathered. The harvest of grains has been average, though not as abundant as expected because of the excessive rains that damaged some of the fields. The amounts have been abundant, however, and the harvest taken up will supply many families so that they can stock up without difficulty for all of the coming year.

His excellency, the archbishop of Santa Fe, in the company of his secretary, is presently in Mexico City attending the festivities around the coronation of Our Lady of Guadalupe. It is believed that thousands of people from all over the world attended. His excellency will return before the fifteenth, when the cardinal and other prelates will arrive in this capital to preside over the dedication of the courtyard and ordain the archbishop of Santa Fe.

Officials of the court of the First Judicial District have returned from the north after having had a week of court in San Juan County, where several criminal cases were heard. Court could not be held in Taos and Rio Arriba because of the lack of funds to pay the cost.

Lastly, the defunct National Bank of Albuquerque, whose receiver is Mr. Schofield and whose bankruptcy left it seventy thousand dollars in debt to the Territory, has now paid a third installment of 10 percent to the bank's creditors, thus paying off 30 percent of the deficit. To be sure, the treasury of the Territory received the portion it was entitled to.

Los Caminos del Barrio

J. Chris Abeyta

(1999)

Los caminos del barrio todavía son de tierra
Tienen viejitas andando en procesión . . . rezando
y los jóvenes corriendo

Hay casas hechas de adobe
y casas que hacen de cartón
de allí yo saco mi corazón

Los caminos del barrio te llevan
dentro de casas y almas
Entre los árboles y las yerbas
Entre la muerte y la vida

Olores te llenan de memorias
de leña en la madrugada
y de comida en la tardecita

Hay música con guitarras y acordeón
tocando la bamba y cuatro milpas
el mosquito y las mañanitas

Los caminos del barrio todavía
son de tierra caminos de tu alma
tierra de tu corazón

The Roads of the Neighborhood

J. Chris Abeyta

Translation by Rosalie C. Otero

The roads of the neighborhood are still unpaved
Where old women walk in procession . . .
        praying
And children run

Adobe homes
And cardboard houses
From where I fill my heart

The roads of the neighborhood
Take you inside homes and souls
Betweem orchards and weeds
Between life and death

Aromas fill your memories
Of wood burning at dawn
And cooking in the evenings

There is guitar and accordion music
Playing "La Bamba" and "Cuatro Milpas"
"El Mosquito" and "Las Mañanitas"

The roads of the neighborhood are still unpaved
Roads of your soul
Roads of your heart

Espaldas del pinto: Dreams of Freedom, 1985.

Corrido de la Prisión de Santa Fe

Alberto "Al Hurricane," Amador "Tiny Morrie,"
and Gabriel "Baby Gaby" Sánchez
(1980)

Amigos, quiero contarles
una tragedia muy triste,
esta tragedia ha pasado
en la prisión de Santa Fe.
Han muerto arriba de treinta
y unos ni saben por qué.

El año ochenta corría
cuando empezó la cuestión.

El día dos de febrero
hicieron revolución.
Unos cuantos prisioneros
allá en aquella prisión.

Como costumbre esa noche
a los presos vigilaban.
Al capitán y sus guardias
en una gran descuidada,
los tomaron prisioneros
sin darles tiempo de nada.

Con los guardias secuestrados
por delante los llevaban,
sabiendo de su importancia.

Al cuarto centro llegaban,
la cerradura rompieron
y la prisión controlaban.

Algunas celdas salieron
y a la enfermería se fueron,
unos encontraban drogas
otros no más se pasaron,
muchos otros confundidos
no sabían qué había pasado.

Negociaban unos presos
con el gobierno estatal,
decían de la injusticias
que pasan en el penal.
El gobierno se alistaba
con la Guardia Nacional.

Muchos encendieron fuego
para llamar la atención,
la capilla donde rezan
llegó alcanzar salvación,
lo demás quedó rompido
por todita esa prisión.

Uno de los presos dice
-Yo los quiero aconsejar,
que si a balazos llegan
los guardias voy a matar,
y al capitán sin cabeza
yo se los voy a entregar.

El encierro protector
era la número cuatro,
Allí se encontraban muchos
que los tenían señalados.
Con un escuadra de muerte
la vida les han quitado.

Allí en la número cuatro
muchos perdieron la vida,
unos muy atormentados
les dieron muerte sufrida
Ya por esos corredores
corría la sangre fría.

En la cara de un cadáver
se puede ver el terror
al verlo da escalofrío
ha muerto sin compasión.
Una varilla en los sesos
causó su condenación.

Detrás de aquella muralla
una crueldad sucedía
Se oyen gritos por clemencia
y alaridos de agonía.
Eran los llantos de angustia
de presos que perecían.

Sus celdas y dormitorios
los prisioneros quemaron,
el gimnasio ardía fuerte
el humo desenfrenado
Cubre el cielo como nube
todito fue destrozado.

A los guardias secuestrados
les dieron liberación,
unos salen malheridos
por entre la destrucción.
Uno se salvó la vida
escondido en la prisión.

Por fuera de la prisión
se encuentran padres queridos.
Muchos leían las listas
en busca de conocidos.

Pidiéndole a Dios del cielo
la salvación de sus hijos.

Pobres de aquellas familias
que por sus seres lloraban.
Nadie podía avisarles
lo que en la prisión pasaba.
Quiénes estaban ya muertos
ni cuáles vivos quedaban.

Algunos presos se entregan
para escapar la maldad,
los otros no resistieron
a la Guardia Nacional.
Muchos no tenían culpa de
la horrible atrocidad.

Bomberos y reporteros
entran con la policía.
Después de ver tantos cuerpos
un comandante decía,
-Estas torturas y muertes
es el vivir pesadilla.

Apareció el arzobispo
saliendo de ese presidio,
consolaba a las familias
y le rezaba al Eterno,
que nunca en la vida pase
esto que aquí ha sucedido.

En fin se acaba el tumulto
trienta y seis horas de infierno,
para los brutalizados
el alboroto fue eterno.
Y las familias envueltas
todavía siguen sufriendo.

Ballad of the Santa Fe Prison Riot

Alberto "Al Hurricane," Amador "Tiny Morrie,"
and Gabriel "Baby Gaby" Sánchez
Translation by Enrique R. Lamadrid

Friends, I want to tell you
a tragedy quite sad.
This tragedy has happened at
the Prison of Santa Fe.
Over thirty have died,
and many do not know why.

The year 1980 had started
when this whole thing began.
The second day of February
they waged a revolution,
a bunch of prisoners
there in that prison.

As was the custom that night
they watched the prisoners.
The captain and his guards,
in a great oversight,
were taken prisoner
without a moment's notice.

With the guards held hostage
they went with them in front,
realizing their importance.
They reached the central guardroom,
they broke the lock
and were in control of the prison.

Some left their cells
and went to the infirmary.
Some found drugs

others just went along,
many others were confused
not realizing what had happened.

Some prisoners negotiated
with the state government,
telling of the injustices
that occur in the prison.
The government got ready
with the National Guard.

Many lit fires
to attract attention.
The chapel where they pray
was spared destruction,
the rest was destroyed
throughout that prison.

One of the prisoners says
-I wish to give you advice,
if you come in with gunfire
I will kill the guards,
and the beheaded captain,
I will deliver to you.

In the protective cell block
it was number four,
there many were found
who were marked for revenge.
With a death squad
their lives have been taken.

There in number four
many lost their lives,
some mercilessly tortured
were given death with suffering.
And through those halls
cold blood ran.

In the face of a dead man
terror can be seen.
To see it gives one the chills,
he has died without compassion.
A piece of rebar in his brain
caused his condemnation.

Behind that wall
a great cruelty happened.
Pleas for mercy are heard
and cries of agony.
They were the tears of anguish
of prisoners who were perishing.

Their cells and dormitories
the prisoners burned.
The gymnasium burned hot,
the smoke without control
covers the sky like a cloud,
everything was destroyed.

The guards held hostage
they were given liberty,
some emerged badly wounded
from all the destruction.
One saved his life
hidden in the prison.

Outside of the prison
are the beloved parents.
Many read the lists
in search of names they knew,
asking God in heaven
for the salvation of their sons.

Those poor families
who wept for their loved ones.
Nobody could advise them
of what happened in the prison,

which were already dead
and which remained alive.

Some prisoners surrendered
in order to avoid the evil.
The others did not resist
the National Guard.
Many were without blame
for this horrible atrocity.

Firemen and reporters
enter with the police.
After seeing so many corpses
a commander declared,
-These tortures and deaths
are a living nightmare.

The archbishop appeared
exiting the presidio.
He consoled the families
and prayed to the Eternal,
that what has occurred here
never in this life should happen again.

In the end, the tumult ended,
thirty-six hours of hell,
for those brutalized
the riot was eternal.
And the families involved
still continue suffering.

Memories of el Camino del Cañón

Lydia Armenta Rivera
(1999)

As I walk along the Santa River bank, up the canyon toward the Sangre de Cristo Mountains, I can remember a different rhythm, a slower heartbeat of days and a time that is cast to the winds, and I cannot help but follow the river, the acequias, physically as well in memories.

Originally El Camino del Cañón, Canyon Road was used by the Indians as a means of survival. The ideal location of the canyon land, next to the natural element of necessity, water, was an ideal place to plant their crops; also this beautiful path along the river was used as a trail that led to Pecos. The Indians of different tribes communicated and traded with one another first by sending a runner, and later, by horseback through this terrain. This trail was eventually called, THE WINDSOR TRAIL. At one point in time, *la gente* were asked if they would give up LA ACEQUIA DE LOS ARMENTAS, as it was called at that time. This acequia was an irrigation canal that ran direct in the path from the mountains beyond the reservoir; the road would be carved from the earth. The people gave their permission to do away with the acequia, for the sake of progress?

Memories of adobe structures that were homes with families, *uno de los vecindarios del pueblo*, where who that lived in this barrio felt privileged to know that they lived close to nature with the gift of blessed water and within walking distance to those precious mountains with their mysterious paths that intrigued and beckoned. Almost every home had a simple physical beauty, which I would dream of exploring, hoping I would be invited to see and experience the mystery of each house. My young childhood mind feared as well as marveled at the wonder of the awesomeness and strength of Picacho Peak, Atalaya, and Sun Mountain, the Sangre De Cristo Mountains, which cradled the environment as well as taught us the role of survival. These majestic peaks that were and are so strongly visible beyond the canyon made me wonder who was God; was He a rock or a mountain?; but then God was everything and everywhere! This was the wonder of my quest. Did others wonder about Him? Who and why were we living here; where did we really come from; where did we really go? Well, I knew others talked about this, at least at St. Francis School, and so did my family, who gathered at my grandma and step-grandpa's every morning to greet the new day, as the elders drank coffee and we sipped on grandma's hot, liquorless toddy. In the evening, I looked forward to visiting my grandma's house again, and I especially remember how I loved the aroma and light the kerosene lamp provided; I looked forward to listening to dichos and cuentos, but was terrified to hear *cuentos de las brujas, del Coco, y de los fantasmas.*

The children of our extended family were nurtured and asked to share our childhood ideas and experiences. The vecinos knew each other intimately. There was a beautiful exchange of respect and good manners; and the usual salutation to be heard was "Buenos días le de Dios" or "Buenas noches le de Dios," but if a person was at a distance, or if one was not too familiar with the other, a simple nod of the head was acceptable. This was the general gesture, greeting, salutation for El Pueblo de Santa Fe.

I can recall the four seasons of the year in my environment and from time to time became aware of the beauty with which my life was filled. I imagine other Santafesinos probably felt the same way. Autumn was for me the beginning of the year. The aroma of roasted green chile and fried potatoes garnished with onions, and sometimes with stick chorizo, freshly made stove-top tortillas, and in the evenings roasted piñon permeated our mountain canyon *vecindario*, our entire environment. Most children from Canyon Road walked to school and back home, unafraid, and felt protected by the knowledge of the familiarity of la gente who lived in those adobe houses. What a wonderful sensation it was to run our shoe-covered feet through those tree leaves. I can recall those red chile strands that almost every family had hung in the sun; those vivid colors that handsome Elesio Vigil and Tommy Macionne, "El Diferente," had the capacity to capture with their pallet and paintbrush; the horsenut trees that produced and produced those round horsenuts that fell and dropped to the ground on the clean swept dirt over the white picket fence at the elegant compound of El Zaguán. My brothers would pick the nuts and carry them home in a large *saco de papel* (paper sack) to the delight of my mother, who would throw them in our kitchen wood stove as we eagerly awaited the loud sound the nut made when it popped open. What a delight of excitement and caring those simple experiences produced!

Green, gold, orange, and brown leaves began to be sprinkled with snow. Little blue jays shrugging the frost, not really knowing which way to go, *urracas* (magpies) constantly chattering, lingering foliage, stubborn life, refusing to see winter's approaching conditions. Storms that blew, came, and then left the earth with an immaculate blanket of snow that covered our barrio's imperfections. I can remember the heavily packed snow that my two brothers and other schoolboys used to slide on by holding onto a vehicle, which transported them for a distance; muddy dirt roads that looked like chocolate slush, which *los caros y las trocas* had splashed on the whitewashed and adobe-colored houses; snowballs that boy, Lupe, threw in my eyes, as I wailed, "I'm going to tell my Mama on you."

There was Perciliano's Grocery and Gas Station and directly across the street was the cleaners. Sara and Sylvia Chávez lived in an ideal two-story house;

los Raels; los Moyas; los Roybals' family store and bar, which later belonged to Sylverio Martínez and still later became Claude's Barand Lounge; Gormely's; and Mrs. Rael's tamale factory, which she operated from her home; the Canyon Road Bar, with all its shadowy mystery; the Salazar store; Abarato store; los Vigiles; Tonita Contreas and her family; Marianita and Juan Romero and their family; don Pedro Vigil and family; my friend Stella Hernández and her mother; los Ortiz family, los Carrillos, who shared their well water with my aunt Verna and my grandmother, Andreita Armenta Romero; when the acequia water was murky or frozen, the water was carried *en cajete* to wash their clothes before my great-grandmother, Albina Lucero, had the convenience of running water installed; our home de los Armentas on the corner of Acequia Madre and Canyon Road; that majestic, two-story adobe house of the Bemizers and the Guerras; *los hombres del barrio*, carpenters and mason builders who could not find much work in winter, who stood against that majestic two-story Bernizer and Guerra adobe house wall in midwinter, warming their bodies *en la resolana* as their bodies were protected from the wind and cold and instead received the sun that splashed its rays on them and that unique house sheltering them as they gathered world and local news. Adolfo Romero and his family; our wonderful church, the el pueblo's home base; those weekly trips to Saturday confession; and Grandma warning us to attend mass on Sunday, lest "Ya ande ese cornudo jalándoles las covijas."

Msgr. Patrick Smith, to whom we, as a barrio and pueblo, owe so much for instilling us with pride for our culture, those wonderful Mexican movies (also American movies) that he showed at the Patrick Smith Center, which taught los jóvenes to preserve our Spanish language and heritage; los Garcías; Tom Domínguez's Canyon Road Grocery and Liquor Store and his family; los Armijos, los Gabaldones, los Martínez family, los Rodríguez, los Alarids, and all those numerous families, too many to mention; and of course, Upper Canyon Road, which was, and is, for me, a woodland of enchantment; Cerro Gordo, Atalaya, Picacho, and the entire east side of nuestro pueblo were included as friends and neighbors or as a parish.

Spiritual and material preparations for Christmas began on Advent Sunday, when the priests would announce the Christmas season; after that everything seemed to accelerate. On December 12, people celebrated El Día de Nuestra Señora de Guadalupe. My father, Rubel Armenta, was exceptionally busy at this time, as were the men who worked for him, hauling, splitting, chopping, and delivering wood for fuel as well as for the luminarias, as were don Ríos and his workers. Stacks of interlocked ocote were stacked in front of many of las casas de la gente. Los vecinos ignited *la leña* and gathered around the *lumbre de las luminarias* while they exchanged greetings; some people sang *cánticos*, while during this seasonal time, *los chamacos* had been saving money they had earned in order to buy Grandma, Grampa, Mamá, Papá, brothers and sisters, a best friend, and perhaps that favorite teacher, a little gift, which expressed affection. It was not unusual to see many of la gente walking to and from La Plaza, carrying *parquetes*, while some of the people took the Santa Fe bus transit, and still others rode by in the family vehicle, which usually was a practical troca.

Crismes would come and go. *El mes de enero* always seemed a lengthened, frozen, storm-filled time. Howling winds that blew snow, forcing us to stay inside our casas. *Febrero loco* was a great time for me since that was my birthday month and Valentine's Day, but Lent, a time of spiritual renewal, would also start during this month.

Banderita de papel: American Bi-Centennial Kid, 1976.

March would either drop a prolonged white sheet of snow that produced some loneliness in most people, I believe, but what was even more unwelcomed by me was that gushing wind. April brought hope and showers, and May ushered in with a carpet of green, some flowers, and tree blossoms. June weddings, church bells ringing, beauty surrounding us for the entire summer; my brothers and all the boys from the east side swam at La Crotcha, as they would dam up the water near the bridge by the Sosoya house. We thanked God, prayed for our needs and rain. As July and August arrived, so did the chile venders in their trucks filled with that year's freshest crop! Mamá as did the other women, would rush out to inspect and purchase some of the best *melones*, calabacitas, maize, chile verde, cebollas, you name it, the venders had it! We prayed and thanked God for all our blessings as Mama told us to do and with the next breath went out to play.

"EL CAMINO DEL CAÑÓN" is no more as it was, only a few traditional families live here. The houses remain, but most of la gente sold their properties, and "y casi la mayoría de la gente mayor se ha muerto." Their ghosts and memories linger. These memories and many more sustain me as well as yours do, I imagine. It is wonderful to remember and know what our ancestors stood for; what their struggles were; the combination of over the *tapia* gossip; the new, the old news, joy, tragedies, the good and bad of life; and though many of la gente del barrio y de todo Santa Fe have died, their seeds, their memory, will live in us. The only thing we can leave behind is a memory. I hope we can accept the positive as well as the negative, for once it is done, it is gone unless recorded, and once recorded it, cannot be erased, at least not that easily.

Shine Boys: A Story About Santa Fe

Vincent Younis

(1995)

From the very start of the day things in Santa Fe always had a very certain flavor to them. It was just the way all the elements would come together and make Santa what it was at the time, The City Different. And that it was in a lot of ways, from the river park to the local gente to all the turistas that came from what seemed everywhere on the earth, just to see the sights that this beautiful town hidden in the Sangre de Cristos had to offer.

When Pablito and I would walk from our barrio to the downtown area we would pass some of those sights. They were some of the most beautiful sights in the whole country, though we probably saw them in a different light than the turistas did. First there was the church, the Santuario of Nuestra Señora de Guadalupe, with its massive walls and school behind them. Our Lady of Guadalupe. "Our" Lady? After that we would come to the river park with its giant cottonwood trees that seemed to reach the sky from both sides of the río. During the primavera the trees would shed this stuff that looked like snow and all the turistas would walk along the river looking like a bunch of locos in a spring snow storm.

Next, we would come to the Loretto Chapel where the Miraculous Staircase was built and where

the turistas would flock like the cottonsnow. The legend was that the church sisters needed a staircase to get up to the choir loft and couldn't find anyone to do it for the money they had to offer. One day a man came to them and told them that he had heard about the project and he was interested in doing it. They told him about the pay and he said it was fine. The day after he finished building it, none of the sisters could find him to pay him. When they checked out the staircase, they found it didn't have any nails in it. Since it was so miraculous and he had done it for free, gente said that Saint Joseph had appeared to do it and then disappeared after it was done. That was way back when the church had been making money ever since on that staircase. A miracle still, after all those years.

When Pablito and I would walk around town it was as if we were someplace not on this earth. Santa was different and also a very special place to a couple of kids looking to make some money shining shoes. We'd been shining shoes for about a year and knew all of the hot spots in town.

We also knew the not so hot spots. These were all things some chavalos had taught us. They were now grown up and doing paper routes, so they didn't need the shine money anymore. The way to make shine money in the summer was with the gringos who came to Santa to spend money on a good time. Our plan was to try and make sure one of our special shines was part of their spending attack. Pablito was my best camarada in the whole world and even for as young as we were we had seen a lot of Q-vo times together. Pablito was a tall chavalo with fair skin and a frail frame that made him look like the son of a great basketball player. But that wasn't the case by any means. His jefito and jefita were the typical Chicano five foot five. The always joke was about him being the mailman's son. That theory never meant much as the mailman was a black man from somewhere down south and had been the mailman for Pablito's familia for the last twenty years.

Gente say that the mailman, Mr. Dodson, had moved here because of heavy racial tensions in the South. Mr. Dodson said it was more mellow here in Santa. There were racial tensions here, but it was between the Chicanos and the gringos. They were so busy hating each other they had no time to be hard on the blacks. But, being that there were so many Chicanos, only the gringos seemed like the odd man out. Pablito and I had seen a few gringo turistas get their asses kicked by some pachuco around town just for being a gringo. With the pachucos, the thing to do was stay away, even for the chavalos doing shoes and selling papers downtown. My gramita used to tell Pablito that they were marijuanos and that stuff had made them all loco in the head. I knew one of the younger brothers of a pachuco and they seemed like they had this thing with mala suerte— for some reason or another at least one member of the familia was in some sort of trouble. Always. Sometimes more than one—it seemed like that was the only way some of them could spend time with their fathers. For the women at home, visiting the pinta was a very regular thing.

Pablito and I would start our daily trek by going to the local bars. There were three main bars in downtown Santa: The El Cid, the Plaza Bar and the infamous Mariposa. All three had the personality of three train wrecks happening at the same time, but that seemed normal to us. After all, we had shoes to shine and places to go, and we had to start somewhere. Why not jump-start the day with a train wreck?

The Mariposa was probably the craziest of the three and we always went there first. By the time we would get there the hard core would be there already, trying to get a free drink to take care of their cruda. Also in the mornings the gente who worked in the offices downtown would be getting their heads straight for the day ahead. For some, a shine was part of that ritual. And sometimes we would catch a shine off someone who had an important meeting and needed to look extra sharp.

Some of the borrachos would be trying to get credit until the first of the month when their cheque would come. It was always something different, but somehow always the same. The trouble was that the gente working behind the bar had heard it all before and weren't in the mood to hear it again. That didn't keep the borrachos from trying. I guess maybe they forgot how many variations on the same line they had created in their desperation. And they forgot important details. One of my favorites was the one where the sister was sending a cheque at the end of the week—the same sister who had died in some dramatic fashion just last month.

There were a lot of different kinds of gente that truly hung out in the bars. Actually, for two young shine boys, it was better than TV. After all, TV lacked the 3-D flavor of the Santa bars' regulars.

Caline and Calina were two drunks who were so in love with each other they would have probably died for each other. If not for that, someone would have already shot them just for the way they stank. There was a truly special smell that went with them. It was almost a Technicolor smell: unwashed clothes, BO that could kill at twenty paces, trash-can rummage, alcohol-rot, stale puke and urine. People were always chasing them from bars because of the smell. It was really bad, but I guess they didn't like the pictures in their minds about where the odors came from. I remember one time Pablito and I overheard Caline telling Calina how he had gotten thrown in jail for public drunkenness and while he was in the drunk tank some big old gringo started to kick his ass because he stank so bad. When the jailers figured out what was going on they let Caline out of jail. Seems like they didn't want to see him get killed while they were working. Nothing personal, you understand, just too much paperwork. Caline and Calina's lives, besides drinking, revolved around their old stories which they told each other again and again. Then they would get a big laugh out of it and take another drink from the bottle of wine they had just bought. To say the least they were a helluva pair to draw to.

The local available single lady who hung out at the bars was a lady by the name of Queenie. Now this was a lady, the real thing, and she obviously believed it. She was so fat she couldn't sit in just one bar stool, and she would wear all these loud clothes. I mean L-O-U-D. Yellow and purple and green and red things around the neck and long, long earrings that hung down almost to her shoulders. But probably the funniest thing about her was that she always had one stocking clumped down around her ankle. Drunk or not she always looked that way. My jefita told us never to make fun of her out loud because she was crazy and she didn't know better. She told us that Queenie had lost her mind when she was going through the change of life, so we never teased her to her face. We would just laugh to ourselves and make bad jokes when she wasn't around.

Another interesting "regular" with a difference was Rita Dompes. She was the first woman I had ever seen knock a man out with her fist. She was mean to gente that she didn't like or to turistas who would bug her at that bar. Even though she was attractive in her own way she hated it when people would compliment her on how she looked. She had an apartment above the Mariposa and knew the owners real good. So whenever they needed someone to help out they would call on her. On days when she worked and the bosses weren't around, she would give drinks to her camaradas. If we happened to go into the bar when she was kind of drunk she would always give me and Pablito some kind of candy or chips. She liked most of the shine boys, except for the ones who would sniff glue in the back. I remember one time she had gotten really drunk while working. Pablito and I were making the rounds and she asked us to give her a shine. That wasn't the joke, the joke was that she was wearing tennis shoes, the old canvas kind that couldn't be shined. The whole bar was in tears from laughter. We didn't see anything funny about it, but then again we weren't drunk either.

Next to the Mariposa was the only pool hall in Santa and next to that was the bus depot. That combination made for some helluva times in the downtown area. It seemed like all the people that were coming through or into Santa on the bus would get off and see the pool hall and say to themselves, yea I'll go over there and shoot a few games while I wait for the next bus, or my ride or whatever. What they didn't know was that the locals didn't want strangers where they were gambling and would let them know it as soon as they walked in the door. There was always some kind of shit going down at the pool hall. Both of us would try to make it to the bus depot every time a bus would come in to see if we could find a customer who might want to look his best on his trip west. It was real rare for anyone to be traveling east, for some reason, but we never figured out why. And, even if there wasn't a shine in it for us, we would just go to check out the pretty girls who always seemed to be on the bus. One thing that Santa was never lacking was pretty chavalas.

One time during the summer we had talked this rich looking Tejano into letting us do his expensive boots for him while he waited for the next bus. He had this beautiful girl with him so we took him outside to some benches so his señorita friend could sit next to him. We sat his girlfriend so we could both check out her legs as we did the shine. After we finished and got paid we left and laughed about how we had gotten over on him and his girlfriend; we thought we were pretty hot stuff.

The turistas in town used to ask the locals some really stupid questions, but the weirdest was probably if American money was good down here. That question used to make a lot of gente mad and so they tended to start fights with turistas. Once this turista asked Pablito and me about the foreign money thing and we told him to give us a five dollar bill and we would go and exchange it for him. He fell for it and we stayed out of town the rest of the day.

The gentleman who owned the bus depot was a large man by the name of Lou D'Amico. We had heard stories about how he had come to Santa from New York, but it didn't matter because everyone in town knew him and respected him. That and because the story was that he was somehow tied to the Mob in New York and if anyone messed with him or his business they would have to answer. Mr. D had three nice-looking daughters and the pachucos at the pool hall were always going to the bus depot to check them out and try and get their phone number. They knew they had to be careful, because of Mr. D's connections, but somehow that made the game even more fun.

We weren't old enough to get in on the phone number game, but we'd stop by to check the place out on a pretty regular basis. Once in a while Mr. D would ask us to touch up his shoes for him. At first we were kind of scared because his shoes were so expensive and we didn't want to mess them up with cheap shine. But he didn't seem to care and when we did his shoes he would always tip us good and then go over to one of his pinball machines and open it and rack up some free games for us

to play. Pablito and I were both pinball fanatics so free games were heaven sent. Pablito was dog nuts at the game but to be truthful I could kick his ass on any given day. We had this thing between us about who was the best on the pinball machine; it was good honest competition and fun, and it didn't mess up our friendship.

Not only the gente in town but also the turistas would go to Woolworth's at lunch to get some of their world famous Frito pies and cherry cokes. This seemed to be the lunch of the day for most people at least twice a week in Santa. After they would get their food they would go across the street to the plaza and sit and eat while the locals would cruise in their caruchas checking out all the mamacitas in town. Lunch time in Santa was made for the locals; if you weren't from there you'd never understand. To be able to eat in town was one reason we worked shining shoes, and it was worth it.

Juan G., Green Eyes, and Yankee were some of the main vatos who hung out at the pool hall. It seemed like they would play endless games of pool. We would go there in the morning and see them start to play, and at night before we went home they would still be playing the same game, with the same gente, and probably the same money. It didn't matter if they won or lost, they were friends and they all kept themselves clean, which meant keeping their shoes shined, which meant paying us to do it. The vatos at the pool hall had probably all been shine boys once in their lives so they always treated us all right. On Saturdays they would take a break from the games and hang out on the corner by the bus depot so they could check out the girls in town buying stuff at the shops.

One time Yankee was standing outside the pool hall on a Saturday, kind of drunk. He was talking to all the turistas. This one Tejano stopped to ask him something and before you know it. Yankee had struck up a full-fledged conversation with the gentleman. The Tejano had on this nice expensive cowboy hat with a turquoise and silver hat band. Yankee couldn't give him enough compliments on it. Finally Yankee asked if he could just put it on for a minute. The Tejano was kind of reluctant at first but then said all right. Yankee was a Tejano-hater at heart, and as soon as the man gave him the hat, he threw it down on the ground and started to stomp the shit out of it. So naturally the Tejano started to kick Yankee's ass and before anyone knew it there was a mini riot in front of the pool hall. The cops carted Yankee and the Tejano off to jail. Yankee got out of jail the next day because the Tejano was going back home the next day and didn't want to press charges.

Living around so many different kinds of people used to make me wonder where my place was gonna be when I got older. It was especially tough to try to figure it out, since most of what I saw was bits and pieces of people, never a whole picture. The rest of their lives, beyond the shines or the drinks or the pranks, I could only guess at. And I didn't really know enough about life in general to make guesses that were close to reality.

In Santa during the summer months almost every afternoon it rains. Not a bad rain, but a cool summer rain that cleans the streets and makes everything smell fresh again. The bricks around the plaza would be red and bright again and the flowers in the park would shine with all the colors that I didn't have in my shine box. The paper boys would get on their bikes and chase each other around the plaza, splashing each other with some kind of extra energy that only came with the rain. Most of the paper boys were ex-shine boys—the money they got from the shines went into the wheels they needed to do the paper routes. Most shine boys would become paper boys when they got old enough. After all, it took time to save up the money for the bike so they could move up in the world. Paper boys made better money than shine boys, but then again it was more work.

Pablito and I would go over to the paper and watch the men load the trucks up with papers, then give the chavalos their papers for their routes and to sell in town. We both planned on selling papers in town when we got old enough. We both figured, since we knew just about everyone, it would be a breeze to sell out every day. After the trucks were loaded, if there were any papers left, we would try to make some kind of deal so we could bring a paper home to our familias.

One day we were at the paper kind of late and one of the bosses was standing outside. He looked at us and called us over to where he was standing. Naturally we went because we thought he wanted a shine. He told us that he had a whole bunch of fliers that weren't put in the papers so he needed someone to deliver them. He told us he would lend us a wagon he had inside and when we were done we could just bring it back and leave it with one of the dock workers. He also told us he would give us ten bucks each. It seemed too good to be true. Having heard all the con-jobs at the Mariposa, we shook our heads no, thinking this couldn't be for real. Then the guy pulled out a roll of bills, peeled off two tens and handed one to Pablito and one to me. We were in some kind of shock. Nice, but still shock.

The paper guy went inside for a minute and when he returned he had the wagon. He told us to go ahead and load up the fliers and gave us a small map of where they had to be delivered. The fliers were small and thin so there were really more than what it looked like. We both put our shine boxes on top, figuring we would drop them off at the pool hall before we started delivering the fliers.

After we had delivered for about a hour we stopped and sat down to rest. Pablito was telling me how hard we had just worked and how there was still a big ass pile of fliers to be delivered. I knew he wasn't into doing this anymore. To tell the truth, neither was I. Without making a real decision about it, we pulled the wagon down to the river and dumped the rest of the fliers right there in the sand. Then we walked back to town, pulling the empty wagon. By the time we got to the paper, the guy we had talked to wasn't there anymore so we left the wagon and split back to the pool hall to get our shine boxes before we went home. Who knows, after all, we might pick up an extra shine or two on the way?

We didn't go back to the paper for a long time after that, thinking that maybe they had found the undelivered fliers and would call the cops on us or something worse, like sending us to the DHome. We had heard that if you ended up the Dete,' the cops would call your parents. The parents would have to go over there to the Dete' and sign some papers to get you out. And then you had to see a probation officer. Pablito and I had never been there but we had both heard some real messed up stories about how they treated kids, and both of us hoped like hell we would never end up there. ☼

PART VI

Los Cambios

A Legacy of Change

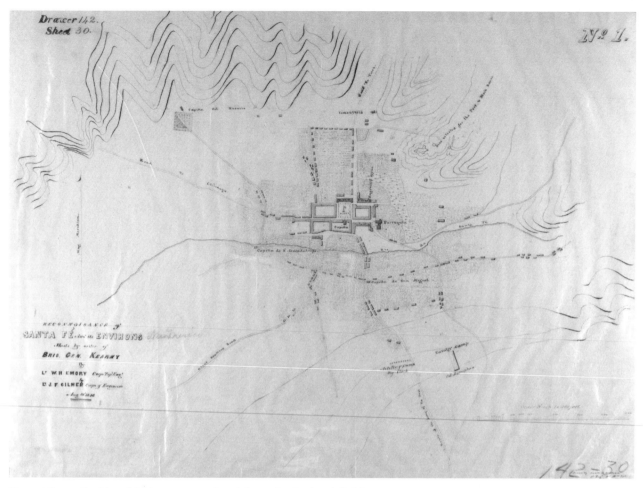

Plan of Santa Fe, New Mexico, surveyed and drawn by 1st Lt. J. F. Gilmer,
U.S. Corps of Engineers. National Archives, Cartographic Branch, RG 77,
Fortifications File, Drawer 142, Sheets 30 and 30A.

Nuevo México
en el año 1950
Lo que observo en el estado de Pujacante un alma del otro mundo que vino a visitar sus antiguas querencias

Enrique H. Salazar

(From El Independiente, *Las Vegas, New Mexico, May 14, 1908)*

Un Neo-Mexicano que murió en Nuevo Mexico a principios del siglo veinte, a los cincuenta años de haber muerto, sintió deseos de visitar el país que lo vió nacer y morir, y donde disfrutó la parte que le correspondía de goces y penas, y pidió y obtuvó licencia para hacer jornada al mundo de los vivos, cual lo han hecho muchos otros, según cuentan los escritores de obras de imaginación—los novelistas y otras autoridades respetables. Su nombre e historia de antes no son necesarios ni vienen al caso. Basta decir que en vida fue hombre de bastante instrucción y experiencia y conoció muy bien el estado que guradaba su país natal desde el año 1837 hasta 1900, que fue el período de la duración de su existencia.

Entró al territorio por la frontera del norte con intento de visitar los puntos principales de Nuevo México de su tiempo y con viva curiosidad de saber lo que había pasado durante los cincuenta años de su ausencia, pues no tenía la más mínima noticia porque en la morada de las almas no se publican periódicos, y las ánimas errantes que de vez en cuando obtenían licencia para volver al lugar donde vivieron nunca se ocupaban en dar cuenta de lo que pasaba en el mundo de los vivos.

El habitante del otro barrio recurrió con interés las localidades del norte y encontró muchas poblaciones nuevas y vastas áreas de terreno bajo cultivo, observando al mismo tiempo que toda aquella gente era de otro aspecto y de raza diferente a la que antes habitaba aquellos lugares. Unicamente en sitios apartados y poco productivos halló aldeas y poblaciones habitadas por los antiguos pobladores del país que poco a poco habían sido arrollados allí por la ola de inmigración de los nuevos colonos. Por regla general, el país no parecía más rico ni más próspero que en su tiempo, pero había mucha más gente, entre cuya mayoría se notaban señales de miseria y pobreza más o menos manifiestas. Echábanse de menos los inmensos rebaños de ganado vacuno y lanar que antes se veían en las campiñas y unicamente se observaban de vez en cuando pequeñas partidas de ganado en terrenos de particulares. Recorrió de esta manera los antes llamados condados de Taos y dondequiera se observaban los mismos cambios en el carácter de la populación [población]. El Valle de Taos estaba llena de una populación dense y se veían varias plazas que tenían el aspecto de ciudades más o menos grandes. Los indios de los pueblos habían abandonado enteramente las costumbres de sus antepasados. Según le informaron después, el Valle de Taos tenía más de 200.000 habitantes todos ellos pertenecientes a diferentes nacionalidades.

El visitante no había preguntado ni se había informado de nada hasta que llegó a Santa Fe que era el punto donde vivió, y allí le esperaban varias sorpresas. Sorprendió no hallar ni traza de la antigua capital y que todo estaba trasformado y sus moradores era gente nueva que había venido de otras partes. Supo que los descendientes de los antiguos pobladores se habían dispersado refugiándose en aldeas y poblaciones remotas del condado y una pequeña proporción residía en caserías distantes algunas millas de la ciudad donde todavía conservaban algo de sus antiguas costumbres, aunque enteramente desviados de la vida común de la demás gente. Dijéronle también que ya Santa Fe no era la capital de Nuevo México y que el nombre de Nuevo México no era ya más de un recuerdo, y el país que antes abrazaba se había convertido en un estado de la Unión, que se llamaba Pujacante. Que le habían puesto ese nombre porque varios senadores influyentes del oriente detestando el nombre de Nuevo Mexico y admirando sumamente todo lo que se relacionaba a las tribus indígenas se habían enamorado del nombre de Pujacante, el cual, según ellos, tenía una significación misteriosa y terrible en los ritos y ceremonias de los indios.

Por tal razón opinaron que el nombre sería muy original y característico, y a la par, muy propia para el nuevo estado, y como ellos eran los árbitros del negocio plantaron el nombre al nuevo estado de manera que ya los Neo-mexicanos de antes no tenían otro nombre que el de Pujacantes. Cuando dijeron al visitante que ya Santa Fe no era la capital, al punto se le ocurrió que sería Albuquerque, y le contestaron que no, que dicha ciudad estaba muy menoscabada por razón de que ya dos veces la había invadido el Río Grande y había hecho canal por la plaza; que esto había ahuyentado a la mayoría de la gente la cual había fundado una plaza nueva cerca de Belén. Supo además cuando quitaron la capital a Santa Fe la trasladaron a Albuquerque, pero después de los estragos hechos por el río la misma fue mudada a Americanópolis, que era la plaza nueva fundada por los de Albuquerque.

Toda la parte central del Río Grande estaba tan atestada de gente, que se calculaba que desde Albuquerque hasta la frontera había nada menos que medio millón de habitantes. También le informaron que el condado de San Miguel estaba dividido en cuatro o cinco condados y que las plazas de Las Vegas y las poblaciones circunvecinas se habían convertido en una gran ciudad que contaba más de 100.000 habitantes.

Respecto a las demás condiciones prevalecientes en el estado de Pujacante le dijeron que estaba dividido en más de 60 condados y que su populación según el último censo excedía de dos millones y medio de habitantes. Como el visitante fue en su tiempo muy aficionado a política, preguntó como estaban ahora los partidos y le respondieron que no había partidos Republicano ni Demócrata; que ambos se habían demolido y desbaratado y se habían organizado dos partidos nuevos cuyos principios se destinguían por sus respectivas actitudes hacia al capital y el trabajo. Que el partido que defendía al capital se llamaba el Imperialista y el otro el Laborante; y que el primero estaba en poder y tenía mayoría en el Congreso; que ahora había ejército permanente conteniendo dos millones de soldados; que la marina de guerra americana era la más poderosa del mundo, y que los Estados Unidos tenían también una escuadra aérea compuesta de máquinas voladoras que constituían una arma potente en la guerra; que en los cincuenta años pasados la nación había tenido varias guerras con naciones poderosas y había salido vencedora; que el Canadá formaba ya parte de los Estados Unidos y que tres estados de la República Mexicana habían sido anexados hacía poco tiempo a la Unión.

El visitante no quedó nada a gusto al saber los cambios que habían ocurrido en lo que era antes Nuevo México, y renunciando a visitar lo demás del país se volvió triste y pesaroso a la tierra de las sombras, tomando la resolución de no volver a procurar informarse acerca de lo que pasara en el mundo de los vivos, porque estaba seguro de ver ultrajados sus sentimientos y recuerdos con lo que estaba sucediendo.

New Mexico in 1950

What a Visitor from Another World Observed in the State of Pujacante When He Returned to Visit His Old Hunting Grounds

Enrique H. Salazar

Translation by A. Gabriel Meléndez

Fifty years after his death a Hispano New Mexican who died in New Mexico at the beginning of the twentieth century felt a desire to visit the land of his birth and death, the land where he had had his share of suffering and joy, and he asked for, and was given permission, to journey to the land of the living, something that many other dead folk have done as writers of imaginary works, novelists and other respectable authorities relate. His name and history from his time in life need not be mentioned, nor are they important here. Suffice to say that in life he was a man of much learning and experience who knew well the condition of his homeland from the year of his birth in 1837 to 1900, which was the extent of his existence.

He entered the territory by crossing the northern border with the intent of visiting what had been the major localities of New Mexico in his day and with true interest in knowing what had happened in the fifty years of his absence, because he hadn't had the least bit of news. In the region of souls, newspapers are not published, and those errant souls that did obtain permission to visit the places where they had lived never took up the matter of telling what was happening in the land of the living.

This inhabitant of the "other neighborhood" traveled with much interest through the places of the north, and he found many new towns and vast tracks of land under cultivation. He also noted that all these new people had distinct features and were of a different race from those who had lived in these same places before. Only in remote and uncultivated places did he find villages and towns inhabited by the old settlers of the land. These, little by little, had been tossed there by the wave of immigration of the new colonists. In general, his homeland did not seem to be richer or more prosperous than in his own time, but there were many more people, and in the main, indications of misery and poverty could be seen in greater or lesser degree.

Absent were the large herds of cattle and flocks of sheep that were once seen in the countryside, and only once in a while did one find small herds of animals on private lands. In this way he traversed the counties once called Taos, and everywhere he observed the same changes in the character of the population. The Taos Valley was filled by dense population, and several towns having the appearance of medium-size cities could be observed. The Pueblo Indians had entirely abandoned the traditions of their forebearers. According to the information he was later given, Taos Valley had a population of two hundred thousand inhabitants, and all were of different nationalities.

The visitor did not ask, nor was he told, more until he got to Santa Fe, the city where he had lived. There several surprises awaited him. He was astonished at not finding even a trace of what had been the ancient capital. Everything was so changed, and the residents were new people who had come from elsewhere. He learned that the descendants of the original settlers had been dispersed and taken refuge in the remote villages and towns of the county and that another group of them lived in some dwellings a few miles from the city, where they still managed to keep some of their ancient costumes, but they kept to themselves and were completely apart from the general life of the rest of the people. He was also told that Santa Fe was no longer the capital of New Mexico, the name New Mexico was nothing more than a memory, and the homeland he had once embraced was now a state of the Union called Pujacante. He learned that it had been given that name because several influential senators from the East hated the name New Mexico, and, since they admired everything concerning the Indian tribes, they had fallen in love with the name Pujacante, which according to them had a mysterious and ominous meaning related to the rituals and ceremonies of the Indians.

Because of this they were of the opinion that the name was highly original and very characteristic and on a par with the new state. As they were the arbiters of this matter, they imposed the name on the new state so that the New Mexicans of old had no other name than that of Pujacantes.

When they told the visitor that Santa Fe was no longer the capital, he immediately imagined that it would now be Albuquerque, but they responded no, saying that that city was very diminished because it had been flooded by the Rio Grande on two occasions. A canal had been dug through the plaza, and this had caused most of the residents to flee the city. He was told they had founded a new town near Belén. He also learned that when Santa Fe was removed as the capital that the capital had been moved to Albuquerque, but that in the wake of the damage caused by the river it was moved to Americanoplis, which was the new town established by the people of Albuquerque. The whole of the middle Rio Grande Valley was so crowded by people that it was estimated that from Albuquerque to the border there were no fewer than half a million inhabitants. He was also told that San Miguel County was divided into four or five counties and Las Vegas and other nearby townships had all become one large city having more than a hundred thousand residents.

Concerning other prevailing conditions in the state of Pujacante, he was told it had been divided into more than sixty counties and its population according to the last census exceeded 2.5 million residents. Since the visitor had been very involved in politics in his own life, he asked how the parties were doing. He was told that the Republican and Democratic parties no longer existed. Both parties, he was told, had been dismantled, and the two new parties that had been organized where set apart by their position on capital and labor. The party that defended capitalism was called the Imperialist and the other Labor. And, he was informed, the former was in power and held a majority in Congress. There was now also a standing army of 2 million soldiers, the American navy was the most powerful in the world, and the United States also had an air force composed of flying machines that were potent instruments of war. In the past fifty years the nation had had several wars with powerful nations and had emerged the victor of each. He was told that Canada was now a part of the United States and three states of the Mexican Republic had been annexed only a short time before.

The visitor was not at all happy at learning of the changes that had occurred in what had once been New Mexico. He rejected the offer to see the reminder of the country and returned unhappy and full of woe to the land of shadows, resolving never to return, or seek to inform himself of what was happening in the land of the living, since he was certain that his feelings and memories would be trampled by all that was happening.

El Idioma Español

Jesús María Hilario Alarid

(El Independiente, *Las Vegas, New Mexico, 1905*)

Hermoso idioma español
¿Qué te quieran proscribir?
Yo creo que no hay razón
Que tú dejes de existir.

El idioma castellano
Fue orijinado en Castilla
Creencia que da al mejicano
Su gramática hoy en día
Pero quieren a porfía
Que quede un idioma muerto
No se declaran de cierto
Pero lo quieren quitar
Siendo un idioma tan lento
Y tan dulce para hablar.

Afirmo yo que el inglés
Como idioma nacional
No es de sumo interés
Que lo aprendamos hablar
Pues se debe de enseñar
Como patriotas amantes
Y no quedar ignorantes
Mas, no por eso dejar
Que el idioma de Cervantes
Se deje de practicar.

Cómo es posible señores
Que un nativo mejicano
Aprenda un idioma estraño
En las escuelas mayores
Dicen, "Vendrán profesores

Para enseñar el inglés
El alemán y el francés
Y toditas los idiomas"
Se me hace como maromas
Que voltean al revés.

¿Cómo podrá el corazón
Sentir otro idioma vivo?
Un lenguaje sensitivo,
Es muy fácil de entender
Para poder comprender
Lo que se estudia y se aprende
Pero si uno no lo entiende
Lo aprende nomás a leer.

Todavía en la ocación
Existe una mayoría
Que habla el idioma español
Y sostiene su hidalguía
Hablaremos a porfía
Nuestro idioma primitivo
Que siempre, siempre, esté vivo
Y exista en el corazón
Repito, que no hay razón
El dejar que quede aislado
Brille en la constitución
Del Estado Separado!

Cuando el mejicano entiende
Bien el idioma materno
Muy fácil será que aprenda
El idioma del gobierno
Rogaremos al eterno
Que nos dé sabiduria
Y que se nos llegue el día
De poder hablar inglés.

Pues señores justo es
Que lo aprendamos hablar
Y siempre darle lugar
Al idioma nacional
Es justo y es racional
Pero les hago un recuerdo
Para a San Pablo adorar
No desadoren a San Pedro.

Hoy los maestros mejicanos
Estamos muy atrazados
Pocos de nuestros paisanos
Obtienen certificados
Pues hemos sido educados
En el idioma español
Yo creo fuera mejor
Si se trata de igualdad
Que el tiempo de examinar
Fuera en español e inglés
Pues es de grande interés
Que el inglés y el castellano
Ambos reinen a la vez
En el suelo americano.

The Spanish Language

Jesús María Hilario Alarid
Translation by A. Gabriel Meléndez

Oh, lovely Spanish language,
What? They want to banish you?
I believe that no good reason can be had
For you to be removed.

Castilian has its origin in Castile,
A foundation that gives
The Mexican derivation its grammar to this day.
Oh, but they clamor that it should be a dead
    language.

They will not come out and say so,
But they would like to do away with you,
Any why, if the language is so sweet and soft on
    the palate?

I affirm that English
as the language of the nation
is of great importance to us
and thus it should be taught
so that if we are to become true patriots
we are not left in ignorance about the nation.
But, this should not cause us
To stop speaking the
language of Cervantes.

How will it come to pass, gentlemen?
In what way will the native Mexican
learn this foreign tongue?
Oh, they say, "Teachers will come
to give instruction in English, German, French
and all the languages."
But I see only high jinks tumbling back
    and forth.

How will the heart be able
To make another tongue come alive?
A language is full of meaning
And might prove easy to learn,
Enough to get by with what one
studies and learns,
But if one just doesn't get it
he will likely only learn enough to read it.

Today, the majority of the people
speaks the Spanish language and
keep its heritage.
Let's insist on keeping our
ancient language,

Señas falsas: Mickey´s Smile,
Zozobra's Embrace, 1977.

So that it will always remain alive
In our hearts.
I repeat there is no reason to
Leave it behind.
Let it shine in the Constitution
Of a different kind of statehood.

When the Mexican understands
The maternal tongue
It will be easy for him to learn
The language of the government.
We beseech the heavens above,
Grant us understanding
And grant us the day
We are able to speak English.

Gentlemen, it is only just
That we learn to speak it
And always reserve a place

For the language of the nation,
It is just and reasonable
But, I wish to remind you
That paying homage to Saint Paul,
Does not disgrace Saint Peter.

At present we Mexican teachers
lag behind
As so few of our fellow countrymen
Receive teaching credentials,
Because we have been formed in the
Spanish language.
I believe it would be better
That at the time of being examined
That it be done in English and
in Spanish,
Since it is of such great interest
that both Spanish and English
reign on American soil.

¡Viva la Fiesta!

Gloria Armenta Gonzales

(1999)

For hundreds of years, they came to worship the Sacred Cow. Beneath the turquoise skies and magenta sunrises, the many gave praise. They gave thanks for the beauty of the sacred, preserved mountains. They gave thanks for the pure water, clean air, and narrow streets. They gave thanks for the historically and culturally preserved plaza and neighborhoods.

It was a constant procession of admirers and visitors making pilgrimage, like those who go to Chimayó in Holy Week.

So frequent was the worship of the Sacred Cow by the multitudes that once a year a celebration of the townspeople was celebrated.

The burning of Zozobra. The Feast of La Conquistadora. Originally a celebration of the Spaniards' victory over the Indians in 1692, now an attempt to reconcile those differences and seek the harmony of the diverse triculture assembled here for some obvious reason.

Forgetting about the victory of war, it was the gathering of families, primos, and vecinos to celebrate and give thanks that they were honored to live in the midst of the Sacred Cow. It was similar to the original celebration though it was also an attempt to reclaim their city for their own pleasure from the multitudes of pilgrims coming to worship.

It seemed inevitable that after three hundred years, Hollywood would discover the Sacred Cow. First came the rebels and outcasts, claiming to be true disciples of worship. With each Star came the groupies. They were followers of the Stars and no longer followers of the Sacred Cow. Within the Groupies, came the promoters and developers. To survive, inasmuch as they were out of sacred blessings, they had to sell and promote. They invited the media (only the best) and attempted to capture the "Spirit." Yet, they never saw the Aura. So they attached neon to their view of this Sacred Land and the Sacred Cow. They made Fetishes. Coyotes that eat cows, and pottery that cooks the essence. They mined silver and Turquoise and even Gold, leaving the Ortiz Mountains barren. They sold art, paintings and posters, and buffaloes, and tea cups. Now the worshipers, as in all good religions, began worshiping the idol and no longer the "Spirit." So now, we had to house them. And they came in droves, creating a new system, a new government, electing their own officials. Their own officials who recognize their needs and catered to their comfort as though they belonged to the supreme race. They were more religious than the multitudes of pilgrims who had once worshiped here. They gave thanks for their wealth, for they were grateful to have the first and biggest house on the hilltop. And they were grateful they owned the unique and widely worshiped Market Places on the Plaza that promoted their neon fetishes.

The pilgrimage of worshipers of the Sacred Cow now worshiped its neon idol. The fiesta of Zozobra was no longer the coming together of vecinos and primos but the coming together of promoters sponsored by the patriarchal Mayor, elected by the masses of developers and promoters he brought in, to capture and tame the essence of "SPIRIT" of the barbaric people who once homesteaded this land. It was here, before fifty thousand foreigners and the very few locals left in this town with an overinflated economy, with a high cost of living and low wages, that I heard this Mayor announce, "We would like to invite all of you to join us on the Plaza after Zozobra for a FREE BARBECUE." This is the most Magical and Mystical beast that has ever lived, and after almost four hundred years, we, the select Few, will be immortalized by partaking in the last of such miracles known to man. ¡VIVA LA FIESTA!

The Spider & The Pants

G. Benito Córdova

(2006)

The curandera listened to Salvador's concerns before dictating her prescription. To set the proper ambience for the treatment, Salvador must light four Nuestra Señora de Guadalupe votive candles at her altar. Though Flaco was reluctant to follow the instructions, because of his mental condition, that night he was ready to do just about anything that the curandera ordered. Perhaps that's why gringos say, "No pain, no gain." For about twenty minutes they prayed together. First they recited his favorite prayer to Nuestra Señora de Guadalupe, Salve Reina—"To thee do we send up our sighs, mourning and weeping in this Valley of tears . . ." After the Catholic prayers, the curandera performed a special blessing—a barrida. The purpose for the spiritual sweeping was to cleanse his aura of toxins, which Blanca Flor used to tarnish his balance. On his head Doña Tonita placed a sleeping egg—symbolic of the Cosmic Egg—the shell that incubates night. The egg is the primordial orb where the daystar existed before the First Dawn. The egg, Doña Tonita explained, commemorates birth and rebirth—we are twice born. La mano santa went on to explain that humanity is begotten in ignorance: like a newborn chick, escaping from its shell. Breaking the egg, Doña Tonita said, is to flee, to go beyond time and space. All this was mumbo

jumbo to Salvador. But just in case he played along. With soft strokes that never touched his body, the curandera swept his head then brushed his upper torso and finally the rest of his body. With a focused solemnity she cracked open the egg, dropped it into a clear glass, and then showed him the toxins it had extracted from his body.

The second part of the ceremony was more involved. The patient was to recite a novena to the Morena Madonna at the Santuario of the Black Christ at Chimayó, and on the ninth and final day of the prayer, Flaco was to complete the most important part of the ceremony alone. "Weave a twelve-foot reata from da horse hair," the curandera ordered. She emphasized that the hair lasso should be cut in exact thirteen-inch strands, washed in yucca root lather, and made malleable with skunk tallow. "Finish da reata. Den take da black cord to da Cerro de los Broken Metates in da Sierra of Tsacoma, near da Tewa Pueblo of Santa Clara. Da're,' the curandera ordered. "Find an ocote da size of your wife. In da darkness of da morning, at exactly one hour before sunrise, place three pods of caña pistola at da foot of da standing dead tree. Den relieve yourself at its base."

Salvador knew that the caña pistola herb was used to assist in abortions. "After you pray da ninth and final novena, sprinkle da ocote with soil from el pocito. Carry da sweet cachana root with you at all times. Salvador thought that her spell had the scent of evil and ignorance, but he was too afraid to question or challenge her. The curandera's eyes were of dos vistas, and though blind, their color altered with her mood. People with dos vistas, like the Genízaros that don Wilberto B. C. Ferrán described, walk in two realities. Suddenly and without explanation, Doña Tonita became stern, secretive, and maternal. Speaking in a soft, barely audible Spanglish, she drew the weathered black shawl over her face. "Sal, mi hijo," she whispered from behind the night veil, "get da pitcher of your wedding. Tear it. Cut out da part where you're standing next to Blanca Flor." Salvador wondered how she knew his ex-wife's name. He was certain he hadn't told her. The thought of her power alarmed him. The curandera ordered the unhappy ex-husband to take his wedding photo to the high sierra and place it on the shadow side of the ocote. He must also carry a piedra iman along with the cachana root and, at the foot of the black tree, place the lodestone in water and feed it needles, thirteen steel spikes. The spears were his offering to the forest gods to help him thwart Blanca's power. After a brief silence, the curandera asked, "¿Entiendes? You do understand, don't you, hijo?" Salvador nodded before the blind healer. Again her temperament changed and turned deadly stern. The blind healer lifted her left hand, squeezed her fist, and with a thunderous crash banged the top of the rickety wooden table. "Drive da spike into her face," la mana santa hisses. "Chi dat hurt you, should feel your pain," the curandera seethed, and Flaco, too, felt anger and feared the sharpness of la curandera's emotional flames. "Leave da nail in da pitcher, and like da hombre dat you need to be, cry out, '¡Satanás, Satanás despídete! Satan, I rid myself of dis ugly curse.'" The curandera paused, caught her breath, and went on. "Say, 'I curse you Satanás.' Cry out dis words before da pitcher." The old woman instructed him on how to recite the mantra so that only he, the ocate, and the Forest Spirits would hear the incantation. The photograph, the curandera explained to Salvador, represented his attachment to Blanca Flor. A Chimayó knife, not a Zorro sword, would sever her charm, her powers, and terminate her possession over him.

The incantations, the curandera warned, would exhaust him. "Day'll make your strength leave you." It was to be expected. "Rest," the old woman advised. "Before da black eagle circles your heart four times, you will become empty of da old, da worn, and da sickness." She reminded him, "It's important dat you understand dis. Rest a while, hijo mío. After you empty yourself, you need to descansar." Doña Tonita instructed him to place his feet flat on the ground and walk backward seven paces. Then he was to sit on the north side of the tree and look westward toward the Pedernales. Only then would he free himself from the suffocating hurt and pain. The healer ordered Salvador to do exactly as she instructed. Only by following her instructions would time cease, and like the Águila Negra, Salvador would soar to the Mountain of the Black Eagle. Purification, the curandera reminded, is equally important. "Take da time to breathe slowly, deliberately," she cautioned. "Breathe in dat good air from da black sierra. It'll clean your poisons. Listen carefully," she warned, "dis is muy importante for da completion of your journey. Tie one end of da black reata to da dark ocote, and da other to your blacken self and cry, 'Satanás, ¡despídete!' On da fourth and final tug, cut da cord with one clean slash of your knife."

Her advice sounded simplistic, even stupid. Something sort of like the airy-fairy and hurry-scurry people from Santa Fe. The ones with piles of money who think that they can buy spirituality and old doors for their million-dollar fake-adobe houses, believing that old portals have intrinsic spirituality and are gateways to rare air and sacred space, similar to the pearly gates of Heaven. Their mere ownership of the old doors, they believe, will propel them to a multicultural spiritual dimension. The fact that Doña Sebastiana rides a horseless

Death Carriage doesn't mean she's getting better gas mileage with her dead-end carro. To satisfy the Santa Fe thirst for old puertas, so many doors have been unhinged from their frames that some traditional New Mexican houses are now exposed to the decadent drug winds that blow through the land of money-can-buy-anything except, of course, enough money. Ironically, there are now some Chimayosos who claim they can make a profit by selling their cultural underwear. As the Scriptures say, "It's easier for a burro to crawl through the opening of a cerveza can, than for a rich man to gain the gates of the Santuario de Chimayó": Salvador has heard this adage at his night catechism classes at the Broken Butt and has adopted the axiom as part of his Penitente creed.

Meanwhile, back at Alcalde, Doña Tonita ordered Salvador to do exactly as she ordered and assured him that by following her bidding, Salvador would rid himself of la embrujada—the web—Blanca Flor had on him.

Down and Out Along the Santa Fe Trail

Leo Romero

(2000)

He's not as friendly as you would expect him to be. Or would you expect an Indian to be friendly? Anyway, he's got red like a thin crust. It's blood that's hardened below his nose, over his lips, down his chin. Red like a red flannel shirt from 1846 except he doesn't have a shirt on. Doesn't remember where his shirt went to or if someone stole it. Or did he remove it when he thought he was going swimming? Only there wasn't a river there. Only asphalt. The parking lot in back of the bar reminded him of a pond of dark blue water out in Santa Rosa. The few parked cars with the setting sun shining on them reminded him of sharks. He had never seen a real shark though he had been over the ocean when he was sent to Vietnam in 1968. He had thought of the water way down

¡Qué Milagro!: Sundance on the Plaza, 1988.

below, all that eternity of water. It's like a desert in its own way, he had thought, like the New Mexico desert. As desolate as that road to Farmington. Or those roads leading out of Chaco. Pick any road. They all led to the same encircling desert. He was too drunk to realize where he was. Feeling dizzy. Seasick in the parking lot of Mi Amigo bar. What was this red water that carne out of him, over him? Tasting like the ocean.

He was "going home away." That's what he said when he was going out the door. "Like a good Indian," he said. "A good going home away Indian," he smiled drunkenly, the setting sun hurting his eyes as he opened the door. But he couldn't leave it at that. He had to turn back around, go to the table where someone was motioning to him, two men and two women. A full pitcher of beer in the middle of the table. Tempting him, I thought from where I sat at the bar nursing my beer, my money having run out. I knew he didn't have any money left. He had been asking me for a beer. I felt embarrassed I couldn't buy him a beer. I pretended like he had already had enough. I didn't want him to see how broke I was. "Go on home," I said. "We've been up since dawn. And then there was all last night drinking. What's your wife thinking? She's probably going crazy." I said that even though the day before we had found a note on his refrigerator saying she had left him for good but then she had added, "There's a pot of beans in the refrigerator." That's all we had eaten in two days. Several bowls of pinto beans each. Sprinkling powdered red chile over them for flavor. Some old hardened tortillas. He had been disgusted with me when he had pushed his heavy body away from the bar. It had been mostly his money we had been drinking on. But I had been drinking slowly so he would think I was taking advantage.

I couldn't believe it when he went up to that table and without a word lifted it up so the pitcher of beer came crashing down on one of the women. There was a terrible silence as the men glared at him. I was surprised they didn't rush at him right off. "I got no horse to ride," he said, dispelling that crowding silence. "If I did," he said, "I'd walk alongside it as if it were my buddy. Funny-faced buddy with big horse teeth and big horse ass. I walk on home always," he said, his words becoming more slurred. "And away," he added. And pensively, "Secure in my green cocoon blanket." Then looking in my direction he said, "Even if it were raining fire I'd walk on home and away."

We both ended up being pushed out the door and kicked a few times for good measure as we lay sprawled on the asphalt parking lot. When one of the men at the table had stood up and punched him in the face, I had rushed over to help but had ended up slipping on the spilled beer. The smell of beer was in my nostrils, my palms scraped from hitting the asphalt, my side and thighs aching from the hard kicks. He had gotten up as if nothing had happened and seemed to be swimming in the parking lot. Arm over arm, circling the parked cars. That red crust of blood down his face and on his naked breast. Where's his shirt gone to? I wondered. And as I stared at him swimming around the parking lot, I kept thinking, this Indian is mighty angry. He just looks friendly, kinda. But I can see it all coming out of him. Out of the deep blue of him. Into the red.

I went with him home once. He wanted me to see him dancing. He was dancing the Yellow Dance—that's what I called it—with several others. He had called it by its Indian name. When we'd be drinking and he'd start speaking in his native tongue, I'd start speaking Spanish. People hearing us talking would think we were understanding each other. But we weren't. He knew about five or six words of Spanish and that's about as much

Tewa as I knew. Like the word for grandfather if you wanted to insult an Apache or a Navajo.

The dancing went on all day and all night. I was surprised none of the dancers passed out on the hot day. All of them were wearing some yellow. I remembered him saying once, "Not too many people like to wear yellow anymore." At the time I hadn't given it much thought, but seeing all the yellow I was reminded of it. And watching them dancing I began thinking of prayer. It's like prayer, I thought, their dancing, like saying the rosary over and over, an endless cycle of praying but with your feet. I remembered when I was young and still sleeping in my mother's room, hearing her saying the rosary, bead after endless bead. I thought of a long road to a distant place as I fell asleep to her murmuring prayers, hearing the tiny sounds of the beads touching each other, or did I imagine hearing them touching?

Again I find him at the bar drinking a beer. Not at the Mi Amigo bar. They don't let us in there anymore. We now hang out at the Green Onion because it's the basketball playoffs, and neither of us has cable. "When did I see you last?" I say, plopping down on the stool next to him, the only empty seat in the bar. I'm feeling irritated that I've missed most of the first half of the game. He was supposed to have come by for me. There are four TVs scattered about the bar, hanging from the ceiling. Hard to hear with everyone shouting, cheering, groaning.

"Last was yesterday," he says indifferently, not offering an explanation or offering to buy me a beer as a peace offering.

"Was it only yesterday?" I say. I practically have to shout for him to hear me with all the noise going on. His eyes are on the nearest TV screen. I'm perplexed by his seeming indifference. I wait for him to say something, but he seems content not to say anything. He's just into drinking tonight, I think. All the other times I've seen him, he's offered to buy me a beer. And then I buy the next round. It's just the way of breaking the ice.

"I can see the purple talk is out of you," I shout. I don't know why I say that or what I mean by purple talk. It just slips out, my irritation at his coolness. But it doesn't get a reaction from him. I wonder if he hears me. He keeps staring straight ahead at the TV screen whether there's a commercial on or the game.

"Oh, hell," I find myself saying out loud. "I'll buy myself a beer."

"You cheap, son-of-a-bitch Mexican," he says turning slowly on his stool to face me for the first time. There seems to be real anger in his voice. I've noticed growing tension between us since he invited me to his home to watch him dance a few weeks back. Somehow I had insulted him, but I couldn't see what I had done. A couple times I had seen a dark look come across his face when we were among his family. It was as if he was expecting me to do something, but I couldn't figure out what it was I was supposed to do. Maybe I talked too much. Maybe I didn't talk enough.

"You acting like a Navajo now," I say angrily.

"Hell, we Pueblos could kill Mesicans, too!" he yells. "Like hell you could!" I yell back.

We grow quiet and brood. Our beers just a fist away. All the purple talk talked out of me. The basketball game is in the second half, and I still don't know what the score is.

His brother didn't like me the first time he saw me. He didn't see me a second time, but I knew he wouldn't have liked me a second time. He was on leave from the Marines and had his hair cut short.

Why you hanging out with this Mexican? I could see him thinking as he talked with his brother, hardly ever bothering to glance in my direction.

He seemed sore at his brother. Maybe it was because his brother wore long braids like an old-time Indian. He was a new-time Indian, sore as hell at everyone. Except his uniform and the Marines. That saved him.

Saved him from what? I thought. Then it dawned on me as he continued to ignore me except for an occasional contemptuous stare.

It saved him from hanging out with Mexicans and from looking like those Indians in those old-fashioned photos. Those Indians who were sent off to die in Florida and Oklahoma. Those Indians with long hair who could no longer wander freely and whose thin faces grew thinner as they waited for their rations.

"I had another one of those dreams last night," he said, still a little shaky from the thought of it. "It was 1856 or something like that. I think I saw that date on a calendar in my dream, or maybe somehow I just knew it was about that date, or maybe I figured it out by the way people were dressed. Anyhow, it didn't take long for my head to get blown off. It happened faster than in any other dream. It was a direct hit by a man shooting out of a train at the buffalo. I was dressed in war regalia, a one-man war party. But before I could put an arrow in my bow, the man on the train turned from aiming at the buffalo and aimed at me."

"If Marilyn Monroe had been an Indian," I said to him one night when we were at La Fonda for happy hour, "would she have still been considered sexy?"

"More so," he said filling up his plate with nachos at the free food table. "Much more so," he said as we sat down with full plates and ordered Mexican beers.

"Would her hair still have been as golden?" I said.

"Sure," he said. "You heard of those Seven Cities of Cíbola where all that gold was supposed to be. When those first Spaniards were out there by Zuni and they thought it was that gold they were seeing out in the distance, it was the hair of the women they were seeing, golden in the setting sun. There were lots of women back then looked like Marilyn Monroe, and even today there's some, but we keep those ones hid out. Out there around Zuni someplace. Otherwise white men would take them away just like they took away our land." It was all said with a straight face. I had been trying to be facetious, but he got the best of me that time.

As we ate our nachos and drank our beer, I thought of a Marilyn Monroe Indian every man in America would want to make love to when their wives weren't looking. A Marilyn Monroe Indian who would make teenage boys grow old with longing even if she spoke in a tongue no white man could understand. A Marilyn Monroe Indian with luscious cactus fruit lips, a tight sweater, and tight black pants. A Marilyn Monroe Indian who as a little girl had grown up barefoot on the reservation and who, by way of explaining her, other Indians would say, She belongs to the long lost tribe of albino Indians out by Zuni or someplace.

"Hey, you know what?" I said looking around the La Fonda bar and noticing most of the faces were Anglo. "This is the end of the Santa Fe Trail."

"What?" he said looking up from his empty plate.

"The Santa Fe Trail. It ended here, where this plaza is at, where this hotel is at. There's been a hotel here ever since then."

"And a bar no doubt," he said connecting with what I was talking about. "A few drinks after the long drive, huh?"

"More than few, I imagine," I said. He nodded knowingly. "You noticed all the Anglos in here?" I said looking around. "Uh huh," he said. "We're surrounded, huh."

"End of the trail," I mused.

"Huh?" he said. "It's still too early in the night for me. A lot more beers, then maybe." I nodded knowingly. We got up for more nachos.

Long after happy hour we got up to leave. Our table littered with killed bottles of beer. As we were leaving the bar, something in the gift shop caught his eye. A rubber tomahawk. He bought it, and we walked out to the plaza.

"I gotta stop drinking so much," I said. "The next day's awfully hard on me. My stomach's not what it used to be." I was feeling a little nauseous but not bad enough to throw up.

"You just start drinking in the morning again," he said starting to wave the tomahawk over his head. "Sometimes I only get an hour or two of sleep. Then I get going again where I left off. I don't feel so hung over that way. I got places I stash stuff. A small bottle of vodka, whiskey, gin, I hide them behind a rock, in a bush, behind a fence. Wherever. They're my emergency stash. Six or five in the morning it's not always easy to find something to drink. So I go to my secret places. They're lifesavers," he said smiling ironically, but the smile suddenly gave way to a mean look I've sometimes seen on his face when he's had way too much to drink. But that night he hadn't had near that much to drink. I wondered what was going on.

"Are you trying to kill yourself?" I said, keeping a wary eye on the toy tomahawk. With my blurry vision it looked more real than not.

"You'll understand someday," he said brusquely. "You're not such a serious drinker yet, but someday you'll understand."

I let it go. His mood seemed to be getting worse, and it frightened me to think of what I could become. It frightened me to think that he thought of himself as a lost cause. He was drinking himself to death.

"Hey, watch it with that tomahawk," I said as he swung it uncomfortably close to my skull.

"You would think a hundred mounted Apaches were behind you the way you're waving that thing."

"We're tired!" he yelled, still waving his tomahawk around crazily. I let him talk, sensing a dangerous situation even if it was just a rubber tomahawk. "We're tired!" he repeated in an angrier tone.

"Sure, sure," I said. The cool night air was sobering me up quick. "There's plenty to be tired about."

"You don't know what I'm talking about!" he said, getting angrier and meaner. He took a step toward me, and his unsteady, heavy body brushed against me. "You see that stone monument in the middle of the plaza?" he said as he lunged toward it, stopping short of the metal fence that surrounded it. His movements reminded me of a football player about to tackle the ball carrier. "It called us savages," he grimaced. "Someone's scraped it off, otherwise I'd do it right now."

"OK," I said, "I don't know what you're talking about. Lower that tomahawk and tell me what you're tired about."

He didn't lower it. He was on the warpath. I thought of 1680 and the Pueblo Indian Revolt. A lot of those Indians must have had the same terrible, vengeful look he had on his face.

"Scalping a Mexican isn't gonna make things better!" I said feeling cold, sober, and angrier than I had been in a long time.

"Scalp!" he yelled indignantly. "You white people started the scalping business." He slowly lowered the tomahawk. The cold night air had been sobering him up as well. "I tell you what. I want you out of my land pronto! You and all them foreigners in the La Fonda. I want you to go over there and tell them. I want you all out of my land. You hear me?"

He didn't have to tell me twice. I was getting pretty tired myself, but I wasn't sure of what.

I walked toward the La Fonda. I walked past it. I headed for home, musing about the uneasiness of what had been our friendship. I felt saddened and thought about all our drinking, how that had ruined our friendship. But then I thought, if not for the drinking, we wouldn't have been hanging out together. It was too much for me to try to think about. I walked along Old Santa Fe Trail for a few blocks and took a right at Paseo de Peralta. I was swearing to myself that I wouldn't drink anymore, and I wished he'd stop too. The end of our friendship had been building up for weeks. But even if we weren't friends anymore I wished him a straighter road than the one our drinking had led us on.

As I approached Cerrillos Road, I thought about the people I had called Anglos in the La Fonda bar. They're not Anglos, I thought. They're people. I remembered a great-grandfather who was German. There was French blood and who knows what else during the hundreds of years my ancestors had been in New Mexico. Many of the mountain men and traders married the local women. It was like a sudden insight. The lights on Cerrillos Road seemed brighter than I had ever noticed them before. People are always putting Cerrillos Road down because of the crazy traffic and the density of businesses, but I had a vision there past midnight. No more excuses in life. I smiled to myself, and then a car pulled over. A car full of *vatos* I hadn't seen in some time.

"Hey bro, what's happening?"

"The foot mobile," I said. "The car's busted."

"Where's that Indio friend of yours?"

"Oh, he's around."

"That dude's crazy, huh? Mean mother. But he can sure drink."

"Yeah," I said. "So what you vatos up to?"

"*Aquí*, cruisin' around. Con el chorizo up, like they say." Laughter from everyone in the car. "Why don't you come around with us? There's room. We'll kick somebody out. Like Fred. He's so feo the *rucas* won't talk to us when he's in the car."

"Kick your sorry butt out is more *like* it," Fred said from the back seat. "*¡Qué cabrón!*"

But it was all said in fun.

"You coming with us man? *Como dicen*, the night's still young."

I squeezed into the back seat with three others. Nobody got kicked out.

"Let's try La Bamba." I said. "Those rucas from Mexico are pretty hot. Those guys from Mexico are always getting our women. We'll even up the score with some of their babes." Everyone laughed. "Besides, they got that Tex-Mex group. They play loud and long."

We got going. The car barely clearing the street, being a lowrider and so full of people. "They check for *cuetes*," I reminded everyone. "Leave it in the car. It's like a strip search to get in that place."

As we made our unhurried way down Cerrillos Road, I noticed the Indian School, and I thought of what I had left behind on the plaza. I wondered if we would ever be friends again. And I realized the car was heading south, the same direction the Spaniards headed when they were chased out of New Mexico during the Pueblo Indian Revolt of 1680. And here it was 1980. Three hundred years later, and the Indians still wanted us out. I looked around at my friends. At least half of them could have passed for Indians. The blood's too mixed, I thought recalling some Indians who looked less Indian than some of my friends. We're in this land to stay, I insisted to myself. And then I stared thinking of the refrain of the country-and-western song, The women all get prettier at closing time. And I hoped it was the case for men, too, that we'd show up at La Bamba and look like shining stars and get lucky.

Juxtaposition

Levi Romero

(2009)

Throughout the years I have designed
high-end custom homes
crafting spatial poetics with vigas and latillas
hand peeled by mojados
whose sweat translates into profit for developers
working at a nifty rate

sometimes I go visit these homes
as they are being finished

"may I help you?"
I am asked by the realtor
standing at the door,
thinking that I may be the guy
who mixed the mud and pushed the wheelbarrow

I introduce myself as the designer

"oh, well, it's so nice to meet you,
what a wonderful job!
please, come in."

I once was asked by a home magazine journalist
if I felt insulted by such incidents

"well, no," I said, my mind mixing for an answer
"a good batch of cement is never accidental"

last year on my way up through Santa Fe
I made a detour and drove by a house of my
    design
the season's first snow on the ground,
smoke rising out of the fireplace chimney

inch by inch
I know that house
through its X, Y and Z axis

but, I cannot approach the front door
knock and expect to be invited in
to sit in the corner of my pleasing
and lounge around with the owner
as we sip on cups of hot herbal tea
making small talk about the weather
or discussing a reading
by the latest author to come through
as the sun's last light
streams in gallantly
through the window
just where I placed it
and for that reason

I take a handful of snow to my mouth
toss another into the air
my blessing upon the inhabitants
"que Dios los bendiga y les dé más"
my grandfather would have said

I turn my car toward home
to my mother's house
a place near and far to me

she, my mother, is bedridden
and my brother is the self-appointed caretaker

Judas en llamas: The Agony of Zozobra, 1977.

proclaiming my brother's spray-painted inscription
Jesus Saves
on the opposite side it reads
Keep Out!

"I guess it just depends on
what kind of day he's having,"
someone once remarked
like a rattlesnake
it's a fair warning
years ago I accepted this madness
and called it not my own
"it's better that he be drunk on Christ," said my
       mother
"than on what he used to drink"

we all agreed

Las dos Lloronas de Santa Fe

Enrique R. Lamadrid
(2008)

> She roams all around, but never too far
> from the arroyos, Acequia Madre or the
> Santa Fe River; wherever the water flows,
> when there is any.
> —Francisco Mateo Ángel

¡¡*Ay, mis hijos* . . . !! A woman's voice. She cries in
the dead of night. Unmistakable sobs of deepest
grief. Convulsive sobbing, inconsolable, the kind
heard in emergency rooms or funerals of young
people. Then the high wails sometimes confused
with sirens in the city or coyote howls at the edge
of town. La gente knows about her. Very few have
seen her. Most who have heard her never realize
it—Mothers waiting up for their children to get
home. Battered wives. Kids who play too long

to bathe her and feed her
bring her morsels of conversation

it is their own world now

ruled by a juxtaposition of understanding
against what I have come to know, now
here, so far and away

I am greeted at her front yard
by an old, propped up, truck hood

outside after dark. People driving home in a snow-storm. *Tecatos* who wake up in their cars strung out. Adolescents out on the town way past curfew. Stalkers of young women (and men). Men and women who have drunk too much to drive home. Lost fishermen. Lost hikers. Lost hunters. Parents whose children are missing.

La Llorona is a female soul in deep mourning. Everyone knows why. Her crime of infanticide is unfathomable, unpardonable. Who are her children? Where did she drown them? How could she do it? The people feel a compelling sympathy for her. A feeling bordering on kinship, some say. Who is she? they ask. Which Llorona lives closest to you? Are there really more than one? How do you really know if you have seen or heard her?

Stories about the wailing woman are woven deep into the history and folklore of greater Mexico. It seems she has been in New Mexico since the beginning and in Santa Fe since its founding. Tears flow easily in such a dry land, so many times conquered. As in the old Salve María prayer, we inhabit *un valle de lágrimas*, a valley of tears. In our fragile mortality, if we succeed in surviving our restless youth, humans realize we are destined to lose everything. Religion teaches how to deal with loss, how to die in grace. The people pray to San José for *una buena muerte*, a good death after a life well lived, with some idea of what it might be for.

But what of violence, war, and plagues? There is something sinister about untimely death, mass death, the kind caused by smallpox, which carried away eight out of ten Native Americans within a century of the first encounters. What about deaths caused in warfare? The 1599 siege of Ácoma is remembered and mourned, as are all the victims of the 1680 Pueblo Revolt. Tears from the Comanche and Apache wars still salt the ground. Footsteps from the Long Walk of the Navajo and the soldiers of the Bataan Death March can still be heard. And what of lesser tragedies as huge as the loss of land and water, the erosion of culture and language? There is much to lament in Nuevo México.

The first documentation of La Llorona in Mexico is in the Aztec account of their defeat, the *Cantares Mexicanos*. Before the coming of Cortés, there were many presages of the coming disaster, a comet, fires in the lake, and a woman crying for her children night after night in the streets of Tenochtitlán. Fray Bernardino de Sahagún, the first student of Aztec culture, recorded testimonials about the goddess Ciuacóatl, who appears at night near crossroads, crying for her children. In the mestizo, *mexicano* story of La Llorona, both Europe and Mesoamerica provided motifs and narrative threads. All the weeping woman of Europe are represented in one, Medea, the wife of Jason, who kills her children in a fit of jealous rage. Her anguish is total, and we have little sympathy for her. In Mexico, she becomes an Indian or mestiza woman, usually wearing a white dress, who confronts and terrifies people. The most important new ingredient, though, is water. La Llorona is doomed to roam the scene of her crime forever. Since she drowns her children, her spirit frequents local water sources: rivers, beaches, lakes, and in the deserts of the north, irrigation ditches or even wells. Water is a deep and ambivalent symbol that signifies both destruction and creation, leading ultimately to birth and redemption. It is the wellspring of our sympathy for her.

But the longevity and ubiquity of the story are part of the aftermath of the Spanish conquest, centuries of painful resistance and accommodation. The Weeping Woman was thus assured a prominent place in the cultural history of Mexico. She has a powerful hold on imagination and collective memory. Unlike the Virgen de Guadalupe, no institution or hierarchy has tried or even wanted to appropriate her. She roams every region, every valley, every lake and river in her tearful dialogue with the people. People share her pain even as they are repulsed by her crime. She reciprocates by taking care of her own.

As Santa Fe activist and storyteller Gloria Mendoza claims:

> She has served us well. Some have feared her, but she is not a horrible person. It's a friendly fear. You'd better be good, you'd better be in by dark. I was fearful my children would be harmed at the river. La Llorona has put a limit. She has been a part of my life.

With her own testimonials and those of her family and neighbors in La Cieneguilla, west and south of Santa Fe, Gloria speaks with authority and belief in her Llorona stories. The Weeping Woman is more than a cultural icon to her; she is a cultural repository of values, respect, and pedagogy for the next generation.

There are two Lloronas in Santa Fe. Both wander near the Santa Fe River along its path through the city. One lingers on the exclusive east side of town, where the original Nuevomexicano inhabitants of the quaint barrios were forced out by sky rocketing real estate values and the taxes they could no longer afford to pay. The other Llorona has rejoined her people on the west side, where they were banished to trailer courts and low income housing. Downstream, the only flow left in the narrow channel is the effluent from the municipal sewage treatment plant in La Cieneguilla.

With the flight of her people, the East Side Llorona stories have become desiccated and breathless, largely existing as vivid recollections of past performances, journalistic references, or literary inventions. Many of the original motif and structural elements of the story are still present, but this Llorona is a shell of herself, like east Santa Fe itself. She is a captive of pen and ink, a prisoner of writing. Here are the outlines of her story, its common places and themes, a synopticon of dozens of textual treatments:

La Llorona del East Side

The events surrounding La Llorona take place in a mythic historical past, invariably during Spanish colonial times. She is a beautiful mestiza or even Indian woman, usually named María, much darker and of lower caste and social class than her lover. Her beauty makes her proud and haughty. She knows she can attract men beyond her social or cultural standing.

A strapping young man of fair complexion comes into Santa Fe. He may be a *peninsular*, or at least a *criollo* in caste. He is sometimes a wealthy ranchero from the south. Otherwise he may be a dashing new officer in the Santa Fe *presidio*. He is entranced by her beauty. They fall in love at first sight. They become domestic and sexual partners, sometimes blessed, sometimes not, by the sacrament of marriage. They have children, usually two. He leaves Santa Fe and abandons the family. Sometimes he is assigned to another military post. Sometimes he returns to his business or ranching interests in the south. He betrays María with a woman of his own social class and caste. She learns of her betrayal and in a blind rage, kills her children, usually by drowning them in the Santa Fe

River or one of its acequias. In alternate versions, she becomes despondent and haunts the gambling parlors, cantinas, and fandangos of Santa Fe, and her children die of neglect. In any case their bodies are thrown into the river. She realizes the magnitude of her crime and suffers extreme remorse and grief.

She either dies of grief, or by her own hand, or is found on the banks of the river. Or she jumps into the river and drowns as well. If her body or her children's are found, they are buried in the Campo Santo de San Miguel, a condemned cemetery that now lies under the PERA (Public Employee's Retirement Association) Building and parking lot, near the river and across the street from the New Mexico state capitol.

Buried or not, her spirit haunts the Santa Fe River and its acequia system. She roams the night looking for her children and crying. She may approach and challenge anyone, even tourists, who read about her in brochures and web sites.

The written sources for the Santa Fe East Side Llorona are legion. She and her children float on rivers of ink. One of the first published accounts appeared in New Mexico's premier Spanish language newspaper, *El Nuevo Mexicano*, in 1917. Mexican writer Luis González enhanced the suspense of the story by serializing it over three issues. His piece, "La Llorona de la Época," traces the deep history of the story, setting it at the time of conquest in the Aztec capital of Tenochtitlán. Then he related the story to modern times. By publishing it in Santa Fe, the editors of *El Nuevo Mexicano* link its implications to New Mexico, sixty years after the American invasion and five years after statehood.

Poco a poco, al través de los tiempos,
la vieja tradición de la Llorona ha ido,
como decíamos, borrándose del recuerdo popular. Sólo queda memoria de ella en los fastos mitológicos de los aztecas, en las páginas de antiguas crónicas, en los pueblecillos lejanos o en los labios de las viejas abuelitas que intentan asustar a sus nietezuelos, diciéndoles-Ahí viene La Llorona!

Pero La Llorona se va, porque los niños de hoy no se espantan con los fantasmas del pasado y se encaran muchas veces con las realidades del presente.

(Bit by bit through time, the old tradition of La Llorona has been, as we have said, erasing itself from popular recollection. She is only remembered in the mythology of the Aztecs, in the pages of ancient chronicles, in far-off towns, or on the lips of the old grandmothers, who attempt to scare their little grand children, telling them, There comes La Llorona!

But La Llorona is going away, because the children of today do not take fright with the phantoms of the past when so many times they have to face the realities of the present.) [Author's translation]

Since Luis González, the list of New Mexican Llorona writers are like a *Who's Who* of New Mexican letters. Fabiola Cabeza de Baca, Nina Otero Warren, Cleofas Jaramillo, Pedro Rivera Ortega, Sabine Ulibarrí, Rudolfo Anaya, Emma Moya, Ray John Aragón, Rosalía Aragón de Pacheco, Edmundo Delgado, Kathy and Arsenio Córdova, Larry Torres, and Anselmo Arellano are some of the names toward the top of the list. Like González, they have faced the phantoms of their past. And they remember. Only two write in Spanish. Then follows a lengthy list of Anglo pulp writers, none worthy of mention, enchanted with the exotic cultures of New Mexico and their marketability. The exceptional case is the talented storyteller, Joe Hayes, who uses some Spanish, but not after cleansing it and washing away its colorful regionalisms and archaisms. Already deprived of her voice, the East Side Llorona becomes a "brand" emblazoned on tourist brochures, web sites, and souvenirs such as dolls, T-shirts, bumper stickers, and mugs. She is even billed as the city's "most infamous ghost" and star of a local "Santa Fe Ghost and History Tour," which includes a guided walk by the river across from the infamous PERA Building. For the English monolingual, directly from one of many web sites, here is a synopsis, translation, and pronunciation guide (*my emphasis*, no pun intended):

> . . . from Spanish the crying female ghost. Llorona = *your-own-ah*.
>
> The ghost lived in Santa Fe during Spanish colonial days. She had two kids out of wedlock, eventually she fell in love with a Spanish noble man. After a en fuego [*sic*] affair, she was rejected, crazed she drowned her two children in a Santa Fe acequia. She later commited [*sic*] suicide in the Santa Fe River. Her ghost has been haunting the area for centuries, her cries pierce through the night as she searches for her kids. On a tour as I [the tour leader] tell the group about where the old cemetery used to be. Under and by the PERA building. Legend has it, La Llorona's two murdered children were buried in what is now the parking lot.http://www.santafeghostandhistorytours.com/LLORONA.html 5/1/2008

"En fuego" is left untranslated. The tourist presumably knows about the fiery salsas and temperaments of local women, especially *Your-own-ah*. The question is, has this Llorona been appropriated, along with everything else on the East Side? Is she complicit in this transformation? Or has she simply fled to the other side of town?

La Llorona del West Side

To approach the Llorona stories from the Chicano and Mexicano side of Santa Fe requires an understanding of the dynamics of oral performance. These legends live on the lips of tellers who literally breathe life into them. New Mexican folklorists like Aurelio and Manuel Espinosa, Juan B. Rael, Aurora Lucero White, and Arthur Campa listened intently to storytellers for the purpose of collecting, studying of phonology or diffusion, and analyzing motifs. Others like Paulette Atencio, Teresa Pijoan, and Don Usner Ortega retell the cuentos they learned from their grandmothers. Charles Briggs and Enrique R. Lamadrid have utilized performance theory to appreciate the full resonance and localized meaning of these stories as told in the context of specific communities.

Again, we follow the Río de Santa Fe downstream to La Cieneguilla and the passionate performances of Gloria Mendoza. Her account of La Llorona is stripped of the romanticism and Spanish colonial fantasy and starkly framed in a domestic setting of spousal abuse and the challenge of parenting.

> Her husband was an alcoholic. He beat her, and she feared for her children. She took her children and took off, she followed the river. She was very, very depressed. She didn't know where she was going. They got up one morning, and

she went out to look for firewood. When she got back, her children had not taken her advice and drowned in the river.

Most of an electrifying two-hour performance her nephew Francisco Mateo Ángel recorded in 1995 is dedicated to specific sightings of La Llorona by family and friends and the implications of the encounters. There is no nostalgia in this narrative, only the negotiation of credibility and the implications of belief. The encounters cause a kind of personal and cultural awakening, as in the case of her sons, both of whom have seen La Llorona and no longer doubt her.

My son Adán was driving home at night with his cousin Eric on State Road 56 a couple of years ago. It was summer, and they had been out late. Eric was falling asleep, it was a long drive. He saw something coming up over where the Santa Fe River borders the waste water treatment center. He saw something come around the corner. She had very long black hair. She had her head held down. She was all dressed in white.

Adán saw her and immediately recognized her. He made a U–turn, and he went back up, and she was still walking. Sure enough, Eric saw her too. They hauled to the house. My son was crying,

"Mom, wake up, wake up, Mom, we saw the Llorona."

They couldn't believe that at the age of twenty they had encountered her. Her hair was all, just real long hair. You couldn't see her face. She had just come up from the side of the sewage plant, right at the side of the river. I says,

"You saw her!"

They took me over there, but of course she was gone. I never believed in her. She wanted us to believe in her. She wants us to pass on that story.

Mendoza's own account of La Llorona is direct and unembellished, brimming with what she calls "good fear."

I lived on Highway 14. I would miss my grandchildren; I would go over to spend the night. I was driving, but there was a big storm, it was raining, pouring really bad. I took 599, and about a quarter mile up from the bridge at the sewer plant, on the embankment I saw something. I slowed down and saw a shadow movement. I stayed looking, and sure enough somebody walks up. Black hair, cream sweater, black skirt. There was no question, there was no panic. She never stopped, just kept walking. I smiled, I thought it was wonderful, I smiled, made a U-turn. She was totally gone as if nobody had been there, maybe she's playing hide and seek. She went back down to the river; she does follow the river.

Using the classic metanarrative devices of topography and genealogy, the use of verifiable places and people, Mendoza is convinced and convincing in her delivery. She frames her Llorona stories as a kind of cultural pedagogy, a counterideology that advocates for cultural survival in a hostile environment. In her career as political activist, one of Gloria's many projects was a proposal to the State Department of Education for more Spanish and regionally based curriculum public schools in

Santa Fe and across New Mexico. Her advocacy for the values of teaching culture is deeply grounded. Her story continues:

> She's been around a lot in the bringing up of our children from generation to generation. The Llorona has been used to getting your kids to behave, to getting your kids to not go out at night, to getting your kids to get potty trained or not to cry at night, you know. It has been used for many different things. She is so much a part of our culture that we could never do her justice for the things that she has helped us do in the day-to-day life of our children . . . She was part of our value system, of knowing right from wrong, because if you did something bad, the Llorona might come to seek you out . . .

> Without her tributes, she would die off. She is upset at language loss. Our children are not learning our history. It's a way of killing off our culture. That's why we need to bring back Chicano culture and New Mexico history.

La Llorona is alive and well on Santa Fe's west side, where she is assigned the role of icon of cultural resistance and activism. She cries for her lost and displaced children. She finds, confronts, and challenges them. The young learn respect and obedience. Adults learn to defend and believe in their culture. In 1917 Luis González thought La Llorona might be going away, since the youth no longer fear the phantoms of the past. In Nuevo México's oral tradition, however, she continues to lurk around the edges of Santa Fe, hoping to awaken her people. ☀

BIRD'S EYE VIEW OF THE CITY OF

SANTA FÉ, N.M.
1882.

Copyright 1882 by J. J. Storer, Madison, Wis.

1. Palace.
2. H'd Qrs. Dist. N. M.
3. Post of Fort Marcy.
4. Government Corral.
5. First National Bank of Santa-Fe.
6. Second National Bank of New Mexico.
7. Cathedral.
8. St. Vincent Hospital.
9. Academy,
10. Chapel,   } Sisters of Loretto.
12. Convent,
13. St. Michaels College.
14. San Miguel Church. Erected in 1582, destroyed by
      Indians 1680, rebuilt 1710 by the Marquis de la Penuela
15. Congregational Church.

16. Guadalupe Church.
17. M. E. Church.
18. Presbyterian Church.
19. Episcopal Church.
20. Oldest Building in Santa-Fe.
21. Palace Hotel, P. Rumsey & Son.
22. Exchange Hotel, Read & Bishop.
23. Capitol Hotel, Gray & Bailey.
24. Herlow's Hotel, P. F. Herlow.
25. Santa-Fe Planing Mill, F. Hesch.
26. Cracker Factory, D. L. Miller & Co
27. Post Office.
28. Depot.
29. Gas Works.
30. Fisher Brewing Co.'s Brewery.

Bird's eye view of the city of Santa Fé, N.M. 1882.
[Drawn by] H. Wellge. Beck & Pauli, lithographers.
Library of Congress, Geography and Map Division.

Before the War

Excerpted interview with Anita Gonzales Thomas
(2004)

You didn't see as many fresh vegetables in the winter as you see now. There would be lettuce and celery. You relied a lot on canned goods for green things. And of course, people here used to dry an awful lot of stuff. People dried fruit. Apples, apricots, peaches (you'd save them for the winter, to make pies), then squash, what we call "calabacitas Mexicanas," which are little and round, those were sliced real thin and dried. The Indians, I think, in the pueblos still do this—take the cantaloupes and melons and just cut them into a long, thin strip and dry them. And then in the winter soak them and cook them a little. Most people had gardens, anybody that was on a ditch. In fact, the year we built this house was the last year that any water ran down the ditch.

That was 1950. Well, we built the house in '49. And that was the summer that it was so dry that the town was divided into watering over there on one day and on this side of the river on the other day. Everybody was saving bath water, trying to just save the bushes. In those days, piñon nuts were a pretty big business.[1] The years that there was a lot of piñon, families would actually take the kids out of school, go in their wagons (because most of them didn't have cars), and camp out for a week in areas where there were a lot of piñon nuts, and bring it in to sell. That was their cash for the winter. With that, they could buy sugar, coffee, and the things that they didn't raise themselves, and clothes for the kids. And in those days, they had to buy their schoolbooks.

Gormley's Store on Canyon Road used to buy the piñon. I have a picture somewhere: it's this big wagon, and I bet you there's fifty or more big gunnysackfuls of piñon, and then the Raels, and, I think, one of the Moyas are sitting on top. They were taking them down to the depot to ship them out. They shipped them to New York, I think. You know, piñon nut is used a lot by Italians. The peoples from the Middle East like piñon in a lot of their dishes. The time I remember (because my dad and Uncle Manuel thought they had really made a killing) was the year they decided to start buying piñon at—I think it was ten or fifteen cents a pound. And they stored it in the basement of Uncle Manuel's house there at the bottom of García Street on Canyon Road where that Tibetan art place is. Then they sold it for like a quarter a pound. Anyhow, they doubled their investment, and they thought, boy, that was really making easy money. If you had a place to store the stuff, well, then, you could hold it until you could get the price you wanted. In the years when there wasn't piñon, well, I guess these families found some kind of little jobs. Of course, piñon from New Mexico evidently has long been a trade item because Don Gaspar Ortiz (for whom Don Gaspar Street is named) was called the "piñon king" because he used to ship them to Chihuahua. This practice stopped as soon as a lot of these places began to be fenced. See, you used to be able to go out past Sunmount, there was nothing, no houses, no anything. You just went out there and started picking. None of that was fenced.

Mom and Dad and we would all pile up in the car on Sundays ('cause everybody worked on Saturdays, then) with a lunch, and go to early mass, and then go out to that part that's called Piedras Negras, close to the Lamy Road. There are some biggish black rock formations. That always had good piñon. There were big trees [laughing], so you didn't have to get down on your hands and knees and get pitch all over your head. We'd pick all day long, then come home keep it for the winter. But some families would go out and camp for a whole week, and all the kids would be picking. So they would bring in several hundred pounds. I would say this lasted until the late '50s. After that the town started to spread, and people began to fence in their yards. So now, a lot of the piñon goes unpicked. I think a lot of the people now go up on Rowe Mesa. Of course, that's a good place to pick because trees are big enough.

Gormley's used to buy hides also. In those days, so many people had relatives out in the country. We had Uncle José Gonzales, my father's oldest brother. He was married to Aunt Manuelita, who was one of the Ortiz y Pinos. She was a sister of Concha Klevin's father, from Galisteo.

Uncle José had a ranch called El Chaquaco. It's between Cerrillos and Galisteo. He had a big sheep ranch there. We used to go in the summers. And Mother and Aunt Manuelita would make cheese and dry it for the winter. You know the regular fresh-milk kind of cheese, the kind that was giving everybody troubles because the milk was unpasteurized. *Queso blanco*. They'd make the cheese, and then set it out in a cool place to dry. Nearly everybody had cows. In those days, you could keep a cow in Santa Fe. Anyway, Uncle José would bring a lamb, or maybe a calf, to Grandmother. Then Dad would kill it, and they would take the hide and peg it out to dry. Then you could take the hide up here to Gormley's and sell it.

Another place that used to buy hides was where Tito's Market used to be on the corner of Acequia Madre and García Street. Then I suppose they shipped them, probably to someplace that had shoe factories. I know Missouri and Arkansas had a lot of small-town shoe factories because that's where Mr. Thomas comes from. The price depended on the size of the hide, but I remember getting seventy-five cents for one. Gormley's then

was a general merchandise store with groceries on one side, meat in the back, and on the right-hand side was dry goods. They had clothing and shoes and even yard goods. Then in the back, in that big old barnlike building, that's where they kept the hides, and hay, and grain, and bales of alfalfa. They also had a delivery wagon.

Before the war, you certainly didn't have to go picking your groceries off the shelf and everything. You didn't do all the work. They had clerks who did the work. And if it wasn't too much, you hauled them home. But if it was a lot, well, you had it delivered. Life was more self-sufficient then. Acequia Madre and Canyon Road used to be mostly cornfields and alfalfa fields. San Antonio Street wasn't there when we were kids. Neither were all those other little streets across from Acequia Madre School. Those were fields and some orchard. In fact, some of the old fruit trees are still there. This was all alfalfa—this street, Camino Escondido. Then where all those new apartments are up on Canyon Road that belongs to the Vigils. That was all cornfields. They were farmed until the 1950s when there was no more irrigation water. That was a source of income for people, because a lot of them would sell some of the corn, and then, if they had a horse, they used some to feed the animals. A lot of people had chickens then. The economy was more at home. You didn't run to the market every whipstitch [laughs].

Music and Entertainment

Dr. John D. Robb of the University of New Mexico claimed that a lot of the Spanish American people just had natural musicality and that you have it in people that have not been in contact with much organized music. They had a natural ability to do what we call in Spanish *darle segunda*. In other words, to sing harmony to the basic tune. And you still see that. We sang the other night for Carla Aragón's wedding. Carla used to be on *P.M. Magazine*, and she got married up here at Cristo Rey Church. We sang some of the old Spanish hymns, besides singing the mass. I noticed George Gonzales, who was our leader and playing the guitar, we had three other guitars, and he'd say, "OK, delen segunda," for some of the boys to take either an alto or a tenor part. And that just came naturally to a lot of people.

One of the really nice things of Santa Fe when I was growing up was that there were very few cars, and of course the plaza was the center of everything. I remember summer evenings, some of these boys in their late teens and early twenties from way up all Canyon Road, after supper, just to have something to do, would walk down to the plaza and mill around. They probably didn't have a dime to spend. And then, walking back, they would sing all those beautiful old songs like "Cielito Lindo"—and always in harmony, like a chord. This lasted till about the war. And then, see, after the war, people all began to get cars. You didn't walk to places. And I think there was a lot of other music available. Life was not as simple as it had been. These guys probably had other means of entertaining themselves.

Well, of course, some of these people have that Protestant idea, you know, that church and that God is real grim. But Spanish people don't have that idea of God [laughs]. They think God is good, and God is happy. If people are happy and enjoying themselves, they don't think dancing is wrong per se, so it shocked Josiah Gregg and the rest to think that the same violin and guitar that had played for the baile were playing for church. Well, there's an old Spanish saying, "Some with their big loud voice, and some with their little voice, but we all praise God." "Unos con su grande voz y otras con su chica voz, todos alaban a Dios."

Music must have been very important to the people back then, because there was no other entertainment. But it had to be something you could carry—violins and guitars, maybe accordions. The traditional music was kind of dying out by my youth. Because jazz was the big thing when I was growing up. We learned to dance to jazz music. I didn't learn to dance to those old Spanish things until in 1930 that the Unión Protectiva took an active part in fiesta, and we had lessons up there at the hall across from the new Unión Protectiva on Camino del Monte Sol. That's where we learned all those polkas and schottisches and *cunas*. Then we danced on the plaza. Those were the traditional tunes that had been handed down from musician to musician. From comments that I found in Gregg's book about the Santa Fe Trail,[2] and in that book by Susan Magoffin, they mentioned how much the people enjoyed dancing, and that that was their favorite pastime.[3]

It's disappeared under the weight of television and radios. Then we used to get these shows that came up from Mexico—*maromeros*. The Spanish word *maroma* is when you tumble over. They had dogs that could do tricks, and they had singers and dancers, but they were mostly trapeze artists and tumblers. And they had a lot of music in them, all the latest songs that were being played down there. They'd set up a tent out—well, anything west of the railroad tracks on Hickox Street was just empty fields where corn had been raised. That's where the circuses and the carnivals used to stop because they'd come in by rail and could unload right there. Then they'd go around in a wagon announcing their show. Sometimes they were a small group, and they would rent a place in town. I remember going to performances at

Loretto Academy because the sisters would rent the place to them. There was singing, dancing.

I remember going down in the 1960s to a convention with my husband at Ruidoso. As part of the entertainment for the ladies, we were taken to visit Peter Hurd's studio. He was showing us all his paintings, and here was this painting of all this dance and everything. He said, "This is one of those traveling companies that used to come up from Mexico." I said, "Oh, yes, los maromeros." And he was so excited! He was real excited to find somebody who knew about the maromeros because when he was young he had gone to a lot of performances.

The maromeros came up at least once a year, maybe twice. There was more than one group. And I guess they would make most of the towns of any size. And I remember twice that orchestras came up from Mexico. I was still at Loretto. They had performances at the Old Paris Theater, which is now El Paseo Theater [today, 123 W. San Francisco St.]. That was the only movie house that Santa Fe had. Sometimes they would rent it out to something like the Mexican traveling orchestras 'cause the seats were more comfortable than the hall at Loretto or the gymnasium at the public school. Ooh, I remember what a time we'd have selling community concert tickets to people back in the days when they had to sit at Seth Hall in those hard, folding chairs. No, no, they weren't about to sit there for two and a half or three hours, no matter what it was. So I always feel now that, well, one reason the opera is so popular is because it's also a social event; it isn't that they like the music that much. 'Cause I think if you really care for music, you don't care if it's a hard seat . . . [laughs] . . . as long as you can hear something good! So the maromeros would play the newest music from Mexico. And then we had the Mexican orchestras—marimba bands of thirty

to forty players. They also played a lot of classical music. But we'd learn all the latest songs: "Cielito Lindo," "Adelita," "Pena."

And then, at school, the sisters saw to it that whenever there was a play or a pageant, there would also be musical numbers, and all the music pupils would give recitals of pieces that were classical or semiclassical. So we were acquainted with the kind of things that everybody knows.

We didn't hear what we now call mariachi music until the late 1920s, when Martin Gardesky went fishing in Guaymas. And then I guess he went to Guadalajara because that's where the mariachis were supposed to have gotten started. He saw these wandering groups of musicians, and he thought it'd be great to bring them for fiesta, so he did. Well, that's the first time we had ever heard music like that. What we were used to was like the Música de los Viejitos. But the songs we were singing in the sociedad were the songs that we sang for fiesta. We'd sing "El Venadito" ["The Little Deer"]. That's got thirty or forty verses, I think. "El Zapatero"— "The Shoemaker." "Tecolotito" ["Little Owl"], and "Paloma Blanca" ["White Dove"]. But it wasn't the "Paloma Blanca" that came up recently from Mexico. "Yo soy tú paloma blanca, tu eres mi pichón azúl"—"I'm your white dove, and you're my blue pigeon"—is the first line. And sometimes we'd sing that Mexican song of the Pancho Villa revolution, "Adelita." That was real popular when I was a kid.

In church we sang the "Panis Angelicus," the "Ave Maria," Schubert's, the Gounod, music written by classical composers, besides the Gregorian chant. We sang a lot of hymns. We had a hymnbook that was called St. Basil's Hymn Book. Certainly they sounded a lot better than some of these hymns that they try to sing now, and the congregation doesn't join in because they are so icky. They don't have much tune. Well, the traditional music has been tunes brought here from Mexico and, I suppose, from Spain. Certainly, a lot of the old hymns I'm sure have Spanish origin, like "Salve, Salve" that we sing to the Blessed Mother. We don't happen to sing that many verses when we sing it here, but some of the verses of "Salve, Salve" mention the Battle of Lepanto and some of the great Spanish battles that were helped by praying to the Blessed Mother.

Gosh, I remember that old phonograph we had with those thick records . . . oh, boy, I used to love to play the record of Caruso singing "O Sole Mio." I wish now that we had kept that old thing. People were exposed to many kinds of music then. But the modern stuff has taken over. I think there's fewer music pupils now compared to when I was growing up. In those days, people wanted their kids to learn how to play the piano, violin, and so on. There was less in the way of entertainment. Occasionally there were the orchestras and groups that came through town, and the old Elks' theater used to be there next to the Ugly Building [First Interstate Bank Building, now Wells Fargo] next to what are now the museum offices. I remember attending musical events there, and plays.

Well, everybody had a phonograph. That was what you had instead of a TV and a radio, you had a phonograph. Then some people had player pianos. Uncle Manuel had a player piano. [With enthusiasm] Oh, I used to just envy them having that player piano because I used to think it would be so much fun to just pump the thing and hear the music.

One of the things that was so nice in the old days was the custom of serenading people on the eve of their saint's day. You'd wake up all of a sudden with these people singing with the guitar outside the door. They'd come over to our house on the twenty-sixth of July, because that's the eve of St. Anne's feast day. And they'd also come in June.

My father's name—although he was called Paul, his name was actually Leopoldo. But from Leopoldo they called him Pol and then people thought it was Paul. And the feast of St. Peter and St. Paul is in June. Well, they'd come playing then. Then Frank, my brother, of course, the feast of St. Francis. So they'd come to our house three times a year. And to other places they'd go for the eve of their saint especially if it was one of those big saints, like St. John, St. Paul, St. Peter, St. Francis, and St. Joseph. And St. Anne, she's one of the big saints. And of course any Mary—any of the feasts of the Blessed Virgin—any María.

Big bands or big-band-type orchestras would come after the Lensic was built in 1931. It offered a larger place and was new and everything. Now, I guess it's offices. But that staircase that's on the west side of the theater entrance led to a big dance hall up on the second floor. People went dancing, it seems to me, more than they dance now. Well, maybe the young do a lot of this rock-and-rolling kind of dancing, which to me is just gyrations, but that was real ballroom dancing [laughing] that we were doing at the Lensic and then, later on, at La Fonda after they brought the Mexican orchestra. Boy, if you had a real date, he'd take you to the movies and then to dance at La Fonda to the Mexican orchestra. And everybody . . . everybody danced!

They'd build a platform down there on the plaza, and that's where we sang. We never sang on the roof of La Fonda Hotel, except maybe Oskenonton did (that Indian, the Mohawk that used to come and sing) or Tsianina, that Cherokee Indian princess, although my remembrance of her singing was her singing down in front of the Palace of the Governors.[4] Maida López used to sing and dance up on La Fonda roof, and of course Jacques Cartier. That's where he started all his fiesta dancing.

When I was a kid we called it the pagoda, but it was the bandstand. But then they got rid of that when they remodeled the plaza. That's where they had the Sunday band concerts. It was pretty good music—or anyhow, it was pretty good to us. We didn't have anything to compare it with. And it was fun going down there to the plaza and milling around and around while your folks sat on the parapet: the plaza used to have around it this little wall about two feet high. In fact, during the fiesta, that was a very handy place to sit—until the booths were built around the plaza. See, now the sidewalk is practically level with the street. The band was called Los Conquistadores, and Mr. McKenzie was the leader.

Mr. McKenzie—like so many of the Anglo names you hear here, Catanach is one, Dalton is another—they're fourth generation down from the original Anglo, and all the rest is Spanish. Well, McKenzie was the director. There must have been about twenty men in the band. They played not only for the band concerts but at the Fourth of July or when there was any parade. Memorial Day and also for Corpus Christi, they walked in the procession and played, and for the processions for the Conquistadora.[5]

The Reservoir

I think there's always been a certain amount of resentment toward the power company [which included the water company and owned the city reservoir]: these days, I don't know that the power company does many civic-minded things. In the very early days, when it was the Santa Fe Water and Light, they used to do some very nice things. For fiesta, they would crisscross wires with colored lights from one side of the plaza to the other so that there was a whole network of colored lights overhead.

Two Santa Fe tragedies happened at the reservoir. Two men committed suicide by drowning. We were at school and saw the ambulance and the whole bit. In fact, when George Mignardot jumped in there—he was a businessman. Mr. Mignardot had lived right here on Delgado Street. The Mignardot home . . . well, it's that house that's on the corner of Delgado by the bridge, on the right-hand side as you're coming towards Canyon Road. So he'd been a neighbor for a long time, and that was a big shock! Mignardot's was one of the big hardware stores here. Anyhow, he jumped in, and then when they started looking for him and found his truck parked by the basin, they came over to our school because there was no phone at that little power company building. Later on, we saw the ambulance; they had pulled him out. The other one, I can't even remember his name. But he had worked for years and years at the White House, which was the original name of what was later the Guarantee [today, Santa Fe Dry Goods, 56 Old Santa Fe Trail]. It was run by Mrs. Blatt, who was Gene Pachesky's grandmother. It used to carry men's things and yard goods. This man went up to the reservoir and jumped in. Now, George was only there a few hours. But this man— nobody knew what had happened; he lived alone. It wasn't till two or three days after that that he floated up. So then, when they emptied the settling basin, the kids said, "We don't want to catch the fish this time!" They were in there with that dead man.

Religion and Ethnicity

In the 1920s and 1930s, Catholics and Protestants socialized very little. For one thing, of the earlier Anglos that came here, quite a few were Masons. And you know, the church used to be very leery of the Masons . . . well, it still is. Just the other day I saw in the paper that the pope doesn't want any

Catholics becoming Masons. Tommy's not anything [referring to her husband], but his uncle was a big wheel in Chickasha, Oklahoma, in the Masonic group. After we were married he thought, "Well, maybe if I were a Mason," it would help him. Maybe, you know, the brothers would help out. So he wrote to his Uncle Raymond and asked, what did he think of the idea? And Raymond's answer was, "Remember, your wife is a Catholic." So there is something there.

There was not nearly as much intermarriage then as now. But there was some. My mother's father was John Fayette, and he came here from New Orleans. He was Irish and French, and Grandma and he were married in 1878, I guess. He knew some Spanish, because of course in New Orleans—it being a tricultural city. But Grandma wouldn't talk in English to any of us. Now, she knew enough English that she could get along. She'd take the train and go to California to visit Aunt Lottie. But you couldn't get her to speak English here. You had to speak Spanish to her. And Grandpa John, as long as he lived, he had to speak Spanish because she wouldn't learn English.

However, there has been intermarriage since the Anglos first started coming out here! You take the Deans, the Daltons, the Catanachs, the Muliers that by now are five generations down, and all that's left is the Anglo name.

Social Mores

By the time I started to grow up and go dancing, well . . . remember where the Canton Cafe [known locally as the Chinaman's] used to be? Upstairs was the American Legion Hall. They had dances there. We'd go dancing, and then Father Leonard—when the Franciscans first came (that was in 1918 because before that we had the old French priests),

he started a young ladies' sodality and a young boys' club, and we'd have dances and so on. A sodality is a Children-of-Mary kind of thing. We'd put on plays. The boys would be the male characters in the play, and we'd be the females, and so on. And then we'd have the dances.

Then as we got a little older, Sierra Vista Dance Hall was built. That was over close to the School for the Deaf, about where Sierra Vista Street is now. It had a swimming pool, and it seems to me there must have been a motel connected with it. Of course, all of that was during Prohibition, so you weren't supposed to be drinking. And I can say I never did because the only time I ever tried it, it tasted so horrible I couldn't stand it.

What would happen is, these boys would take you to the dance. And then they'd go outside and have a drink. The Digneos had a real good orchestra, and of course jazz was at its height!

As we got a little older, it was Sunset Inn. Sunset Inn used to be over there about the corner of Osage Avenue and Cerrillos Road. That was out of town. The town ended at the Indian School. But you always had to be home by one o'clock in the morning. If not, boy, you didn't go next time.

Sometimes you'd go clear to Lamy if the boy had a car.[6] If it was in any shape, you went to have a piece of pie and a cup of coffee at the Harvey House. That took a little time. So there were the usual problems with parents not understanding their children, and vice versa, which is still going on.

Of course, after La Fonda brought the Mexican orchestra that was the big thing. If you got taken to La Fonda to dance, oh boy—you had a big date then! They played in what used to be the big dining room, the New Mexican Room. It had all those murals by Olive Rush.

As for speakeasies, most of the time they were ignored. Claude's Bar: people used to go and gawk at all the people that were supposed to be of that persuasion [homosexual] that used to congregate there because Santa Fe (which has always attracted artists) is the kind of place that people like that come to. Certainly they weren't as open as they are now, but I know that that was a place. When my brother Gonzo, Edward, was growing up, he got to the age where he was going to nightclubs, and they used to think it was great fun to go there. It had a great reputation here, and I guess people had a good time there. I think Claude James was a good old soul. You know, he treated the people well, and that's why it was so popular.

The bar in town that used to have the fights (of course we were absolutely forbidden to go there) was a dance hall on lower Water Street. Well, when they did that urban renewal, Water Street, where it goes into what is now called Sandoval Street, is entirely different. Water Street used to go down to what was then called Jefferson, then angled off because it connected Water Street with Guadalupe Church. The railroad tracks of D&RG [Denver and Rio Grande Railroad] used to go right in front of the church, what is now the *santuario*. The bridge across was at an angle, not like now. Anyhow, down there at the bottom, close to the bridge, was this dance hall. It had a bad reputation for fights. Of course, this was in Prohibition days, see? And boys from out of town (let's say, from Pojoaque) would come in and go to dance there. And since an awful lot of White Mule was being manufactured up there, they had some, and maybe the locals didn't have any or couldn't afford it. So boy, every Saturday there would be a fight there at the Bucket of Blood they used to call it. I don't remember what the name of the dance hall really was.

Most everybody would drive up to Pojoaque, but also the moonshiners would bring it to their regular customers. Then [laughs] I remember one family telling that somebody tipped them off the revenuers were coming. They put the liquor in some buckets, and then let them down into the well. So when they came, they looked around and couldn't find any evidence.

I remember Delia Baca, from Las Vegas (her father was don Antonio Lucero, who was the first secretary of state under statehood), telling me that in Las Vegas, the gals that lived in those houses [brothels] would go out in their carriages with their fancy boas and their big hats for a ride in the afternoon around the plaza. I don't ever remember hearing any talk like that here, but I do remember them saying that all those houses on the plaza side of the Hilton, there used to be a long old house, a one-story house, and those were the *congales*. That's where the ladies of ill repute were. It was considered a scandal, but I can't remember any raids. It was "live and let live."

Ethnic and Racial Relations

[Author's note: In the 1930s the paper ran a story about Carl McGee, a man from Albuquerque, who was supporting more school aid for Spanish Americans. This was considered a tremendous surprise because the urging came after years of his characterizing Spanish Americans as "ignorant, degraded, un-American vote-sellers."] Well, he was quite a character. That's how come he finally was shot to death. There's plenty of them that talk like that now! It's those people that don't know any Spanish Americans, see? They just have that, inside of them, that hatred. It's there in the east side of the state, the southeast side, and the northeast.

I can't say that I ever felt any tension, but I've always been kind of aggressive. But it was there. I remember friends telling me their little brothers would go over to play with a kid they had met in school, and the mother would come out and say, "I don't want you playing with those little Mexicans!" That kind of thing. But I think I've always felt, "Well, hell, I know who I am. I don't have to have them tell me." I always felt anybody that acted like that wasn't very sure who they were, that they acted like that in order to be superior. There has to be a pecking order, so pick on the poor Mexicans. Oh, joy!

But sometimes I think the Hispanics were at fault because they start talking in Spanish when they know the person doesn't understand. Little things like that. But I think any tension was always within tolerable levels and never carried to the extremes that it seems to be carried right now.

Then the Chinese at the Chinaman's, well, they didn't mix with anybody, see?

When those kids grew up, they brought more Chinese over. So if any of those Chinese kids had any notions of intermarrying with anybody else, they didn't get a chance because they all stayed pretty much in the family. Then—I never knew how come, but for some reason, they were Episcopalians. Well, I suppose they were whatever they were in China, but here, the Episcopalians kind of took them under their wing. But everybody liked them. My dad was a good friend of Henry Park. Twice a week during World War II, I used to help as a translator at the Red Cross office because so many families would come in with regard to their sons. Some of them didn't speak any English. Then Phyllis Mayne and I would go down to the Canton and eat lunch. They had the businessman's blue-plate special. It wasn't very good.

You know, Chinese cooking is considered some of the best in the world. But they didn't play that up. They just had the good old meat and potatoes and vegetable routine like the Greek restaurants here. Most of those restaurants downtown were Greek, then. The Plaza, the Mayflower, the Faith on the corner of Galisteo and San Francisco. They all had Greek owners, but the food was plain old American not-very-good restaurant [laughs].

With the Chinese, there was no racial animosity. Even during the war, you know, Chuzo Tomatsu [a Japanese artist] lived here in the neighborhood. Everybody knew Chuzo and thought he was such a nice, kindly old man. Nobody that I know of was ever mean to him after Pearl Harbor. I don't know why he wasn't interned. They interned those from California because California had always been a bit neurotic on the subject.

I went to summer school in Berkeley in 1932. I didn't stay at the International House, but Marie Sena and another gal from here, they stayed at the International House. The big talk was that half of the Japanese men students were not really students—they were grown men with their hair dyed, here to study all the American military secrets.

Anyhow, in '32, already California thought that they were going to be invaded by the Japanese. So when something did happen, they just kind of went berserk, put all those poor Japanese in . . . some of them actually citizens.

You know, before the war, Franklin Roosevelt had to do all kinds of little tricks in order to get aid to Europe. I remember when the Selective Service Act went through. It won by about two votes. My husband was a reserve officer, and he was called up right away for training at Fort Bliss, in El Paso, on how to run these induction stations. That was just a year before Pearl Harbor. Then he came back here and worked at the induction station. Pearl Harbor was the following year. I think it took the war to teach Americans about the outside world. Of course, World War I had to have taught them a little bit. But World War II really did. I think all the boys who came back had a very different idea of the world.

Before that, I think people were so busy with their own little lives. See, we didn't have the world right at our doorstep! Sure, maybe they were fighting in France. Maybe they were having strikes. But by the time you opened the paper and read it, well, it wasn't right there every minute, like it is nowadays. Of course, maybe the wars would have ended sooner if we could have seen all that was going on, like we did with Vietnam. People wouldn't have stood for some of what was going on.

Santa Fe always attracted people from everywhere, even before it became part of the United States. I remember one time . . . it was back in days when the maharajas in India were still the big thing, and I've never forgotten the name. It was the Gakewar of Boroda; I saw him at La Fonda and his wife—beautiful, in a sari with a diamond in her nose [laughs]. Because they were dressed a little differently, you would notice them. And of course, it came out in the paper. Other than that, I don't remember a big to-do was made out of foreigners.

There were very few blacks back then. When I was growing up, there were just two families. The Slaughters were one; Ernie was a mailman. They were real nice. His brother was a porter on the trains. The other family, the mother was a seamstress. I suppose they attended some one of the churches here; they were not Catholics. But everybody was real nice to them, treated them real well. And of course, the Millers. He was a mulatto and had been a cook at the Palace Hotel, the one that burnt. Then he married a Spanish woman, I think she was a Lovato. The grandchildren and great-grandchildren are still living on Alameda where the Lovatos always lived—across from Cristo Rey and the school.

Well, those Millers, see, since the mother had been Spanish, they were just part of the Hispanic world here. I remember Mother saying . . . see,

Mother grew up on Otero Street. And of course, going to Loretto and going downtown, they passed by the Palace Hotel, and she'd say that Miller was such a nice-looking man—real tall. And since he was a mulatto, he wasn't as black as some of them are, a very handsome black man.

Manners

I remember well. In those days, men all wore hats. Well, for that matter, women all wore hats. I remember walking to school from Delgado Street. Lots of times Uncle Francisco Delgado, my grandmother's brother, would walk along with us. He'd meet other men, they'd take their hats off [imitating them], "Caballero . . . Buenos días." Always, and then always (you still sometimes see it) when they'd go past the cathedral, always tip their hats. I feel so good when I see that: someone driving in a truck, maybe they've got a baseball cap on. But the minute they drive in front of the cathedral, off comes the cap. The greeting was always, "Buenos días, le dé Dios"—may God give you a good day. Or "Buenas tardes, le dé Dios" [in the afternoon].

There was a great deal more formality, always. There was a courtesy that I find missing today because, of course, you were taught to respect your elders. That's something that is not being taught to the young.

When company came (and the company was usually a relative because the families were so close-knit), you were called from playing outside, "Come and speak to your Aunt So-and-so" or whoever it was. We'd come in and shake hands and stand there, and then Mother would say, "All right, you can go out to play." We went out to play; we didn't stay in the room monopolizing everybody's attention. And this is something that really burns me! Young couples come with a little kid, and what happens? The kid is all over the place, and the parents sit there real calm, never say, "OK—shut up! Go on outside."

You see, to the people raised here, whether they had any money or not didn't matter. And then, in those days, we weren't as conscious of social distinctions because all of us had relatives who were richer than we were and relatives that were poorer. Everybody was in that situation. You didn't judge people by what they had or anything like that. You judged them by what kind of person they were.

Education and Teaching

I would say 85 percent of the kids at Manderfield were Hispanic, and just a handful were Anglo. We had the McCrossen kids, who were children of the weaver—back in the days when those woven ties were in style. Eric McCrossen of the *Journal*, he's one of those McCrossen kids. The Anglos and the Spanish got along just fine. In fact, some of those McCrossen kids got so they spoke English with a Spanish accent [laughs]. I tell you, one reason they got along fine is because they came from families that themselves got along. You know, showed no discrimination. They were just kids in school.

The Spanish children went to parochial school because as long as a Catholic can afford to pay for a Catholic education, he's going to do it. I think the public schools in the earlier years were just not as good as the Catholic schools. And then, it didn't cost what it costs now. For one thing, there were more nuns and brothers. You know how much the nuns got a month? Fifty dollars! Yet a lot of the boarders at Loretto, from ranches, the parents would pay with cattle, which was eaten at the convent. And I'm sure the brothers did this.

Generally, the Anglos went further in their education. The Spanish children, they would go to St. Francis School or the public school, but most of them went to the Catholic schools. Then many had to go to work. And there were jobs that you could go into after the eighth grade. The rest, of course, would finish. Not too many went to college. For one thing, college wasn't such a requirement in those days. In a way, when we got out of high school, we knew as much as college graduates do now. We had taken Latin and all that that the kids don't have anymore.

Also, you didn't have to have as much money then because, certainly, you didn't have to be paying for a car. The town was small enough that you could walk. Then, you didn't have to be paying all these high bills for electricity, for having the TV and videos and all that. The refrigerator didn't run on electricity because you bought ice in summer from the iceman. And it cost less to live because you weren't so tied to machines that take money to run.

This changed after the war. Before that, kids would work at the post office, the capitol—you know, as long as they'd had typing and stenography. And there wasn't the competition for jobs from people that had just arrived.

And when I started teaching, you didn't have to have a degree. I happened to start teaching with one year of college, but a lot of the other girls started with just a certificate. Then that following summer, they went to summer school. They'd come up from Albuquerque and give extension classes, and that's the way many of us got our degrees, finally.

Customs and Culture

A lot of the old customs have just gone by the board. For example, the custom of the father or the godfather of the groom coming to ask for the hand of the bride. Often they brought a letter in fancy, flowery language. Later was the *prendorio*, where the answer was given—yes or no.

The word *prenda* is jewel. The reason the party was called a prendorio was they brought the bride-to-be out and said, "Esta es la prenda que usted busca" (This is the jewel you are seeking). But when they were gonna say no, they would write a letter. And that was known as *darle calabaza*—to give them a pumpkin, which is an old Spanish expression that can mean being turned down for lots of things, not just that.

I have seen a copy of a letter of refusal. Pete Olivas and Gracie Olivas have a copy of the letter written to their great-grandfather. It's addressed to the father of the groom and said they have nothing against his son, but they feel that their daughter is too young. Eventually, he asked for her hand again, and they did get married.

Weddings nowadays, the reception is in a hotel, some public place. In the old days, it was always in the home of the bride. Of course, it was the groom who furnished the fiesta, not the bride's parents. He saw to all of it. He would send a load of groceries and somebody to cook them to the bride's home. Sometimes they would rent a hall for the dancing, but for everything else, that was always in the bride's home.

The feast itself was more or less a sit-down dinner in relays because you didn't have much table space. Sometimes all the guests wouldn't be invited to eat, maybe it'd be just the immediate family. But then, in the afternoon the rest of the relations and friends would come. I can remember, they'd pass dishes full of raisins, and dishes full of peanuts, and then cookies, and cake, and some kind of a cold drink or maybe chocolate.

In the old days, they danced the dances that the Coloniales are doing now. Also the newer dances: the two-step, the fox-trot, waltzes, and polkas.

As far as the funerals go, you didn't have the body in a mortuary. You had the body at home.

Then the wake would take place that evening, and usually there was a supper served about midnight for the people that were going to stay up with the family.

My goodness! They used to really cry in those days. They didn't hold it in. The family would be seated around the coffin. People would view the remains and sympathize with the family. If they were close, they would stay all night. If they'd been embalmed, well, maybe they could keep 'em a couple of days, but if they hadn't been, they'd bury them the next day. Santa Fe had only the two parishes, the cathedral and Guadalupe. And always, the bell at the cathedral tolled all during mass. In fact, when the family went to the cathedral to make arrangements, the bells would toll once for every year of the person's life. So you'd hear the tolling bell, and if you happened to know somebody that had been very sick, you thought, well, that person died. But after a while, there were complaints from St. Vincent's. The patients didn't want to hear the tolling, so that was discontinued [laughs].

Last I saw a coffin kept at home was when Anita Bergere, my *tocaya* [namesake], died. They asked me if I would pray the rosary in Spanish because she loved to hear the rosary in Spanish.

When my great-grandmother died—she died in 1916—she had never been in a car. Cars were very scarce, but Watts had a hearse, an automobile. She said she didn't want to be taken in that. So they had to drag out this old thing and horses covered with those heavy—[laughs] it wasn't a cloth, it was like a net, except it was beautiful black silk, then woven in squares and big tassels on it.

And the men walked all the way behind the hearse, all the way to the cathedral, and then all the way to Rosario. The women did not go; they stayed home.

Today, the reception has gotten to be a regular old party time! Tommy thinks that's terrible [laughs]. Then, only the immediate members of the family would come back. I've been to funerals lately where the after-funeral business was at a hotel [disgusted]. You know, it's like a party.

Religious Observances

We didn't eat meat on Fridays. We actually didn't have to abstain because this had been part of Spain. And after the Battle of Lepanto, the pope said that Spain and all its colonies didn't have to observe Friday abstinence because Spain had saved Europe from the Moslems.

We always had the rogation days in the spring and the fall, to pray in the spring for the crops, and in the fall is thanksgiving. Those are hardly observed, now. And Corpus Christi isn't the big feast it used to be, although some of us are trying to bring it back. I think the reason it was such a big event here was that all the Catholics in Santa Fe participated in the cathedral procession. But after the war, Archbishop Byrne decided that since there were several parishes, each parish would set up its own altar. After Vatican II, each parish would do its own little thing. Well, it makes for a very skimpy Corpus Christi procession. It isn't like it was when everybody came to the cathedral, and this long procession wound up here to Delgado Street, and the Delgado altar was on the corner, and then it went across to Palace Avenue and down to Sena Plaza.

During Lent, after the Franciscans came back to Santa Fe (they returned to the cathedral in 1920), they started having that beautiful, beautiful service on the Wednesday of Holy Week called tenebrae. The chanting by all these Franciscans was so beautiful. Well, they don't do it anymore. Lent is just not observed the way it was: those penances and practices. It's a shame because you were doing all these penances, then when Easter came—and you didn't have to do the penances anymore—Easter was a big celebration.

Oh, my goodness, we anticipated the liturgical feasts! Like in the spring, boy, you looked forward to Corpus Christi procession because you usually had a new dress. Then the processions of the Virgin, those were important. Then in the fall, the feast of Saint Francis at the cathedral on the fourth of October. You had your first winter dress then. Then, May devotions were very important. During the month of May, an altar would be set up in the right-hand side of the sanctuary of the cathedral. It was a series of steps which were tapered and so formed a triangle next to the main altar but on the side. It had about seven, eight steps. Then they put a statue of the Blessed Mother at the top. This altar was intended to receive flowers.

So the sisters would have the children choose seventh- and eighth-grade girls. Francis Parochial School just went to the eighth grade. It used to be where La Fonda Hotel parking lot is now. Then that girl who was chosen to be a *reina*; she chose ten little girls from the first, second, and third grades to go with her. They'd make a whole rosary that way. At the end it'd be a fifteen-decade rosary because there would be boys who were caballeros, with ten little boys behind them.

The queen carried a tin pan that had three candle holders. It was filled with flowers and covered with crepe paper. Then these ten kids trotting behind were the Hail Marys of the rosary, each one with a little vase, or maybe a jelly glass, with flowers in it. The girls were dressed in white with little white wreaths on their heads. And for the first of May, and for the last, the boys would participate, and they wore navy-blue suits with a sash across their chests—blue for the Blessed Mother. Each little boy with a big bow of blue on his arm, carrying a vase with flowers.

They marched up into the sanctuary in two rows, then they would separate and line up in front of the altar with the queen in the middle and five on each side. You genuflected there, then you walked over to the temporary altar, and the flowers and the baskets were put on the steps, until the whole thing was filled. And the baskets would be arranged in such a way that the candles spelled the letter "M." Then every day of the week there'd be two or three, sometimes even four queens, or maybe two queens and two boys, taking fresh flowers. Mr. Sena and the janitor of the cathedral would take out all the faded flowers and make space for the fresh ones, so that the whole altar was filled all the time. That went on every night until the end of May.

And once inside the cathedral, the rosary was recited, the whole congregation because the church would be packed with the families. Then there was benediction of the Blessed Sacrament.

In those days there wasn't any boob tube. So that was something to do in the evenings. That was another World War II casualty. [Laughing] Oh, I'll never forget. I was in the fifth grade, and I considered myself too big to be one of those "little kids" 'cause I was always tall. Maggie Cortínez was going to be one of the queens; she was in the eighth grade. Her niece, Carmen Hunter, was in my grade and was about the same size as I. Maggie's mother insisted she ask her niece to be one of the maids, and Carmen told her to ask me to be one of the *damas* [laughing]. I went home, and I told mother, "I don't want to be the dama! I'm too big!" Mother said, "When they ask you, you have to accept. That's something you cannot turn down."

So here we go. All these little damas, and then Carmen and I. So we decided the best thing to do,

so we wouldn't look so tall, was to walk like this, scrunching down at the knees [laughs].

We traipsed up . . . My mother was beside herself! When we got out, she said, "What was the big idea!" I said, "Well, Momma, I told you we were too tall. We were just trying to look shorter!" "Well," she said, "you made an exhibition of yourselves! People noticed you more for doing that."

Then, when a child was to be baptized, there were customs related to the godparent. Usually it was the parents of the groom for the first child, the parents of the bride for the second child. Then uncles, aunts, cousins. The godparents always bought the clothes the baby wore for the baptism. Something as fancy as they could afford. Usually the godparents lived close by, so when the child went to confession, he went to ask the godparents' blessing. Then, always, if you were going on a trip, you'd ask your parents' blessing, and you'd also ask your godparents' blessing. And should your parents die, very often the godparents took the child and raised it as their own. I don't know that anybody does that anymore.

Once the child had made his first communion the godparents saw to it the child had proper clothes. As he grew older, if he wasn't sent to a Catholic school, they saw to it he went to instructions. They took their responsibilities seriously. Another of the old customs, if somebody had a party and there was dancing (they'd just shove the furniture into another room), then the people would tie together some couple. They called it *amarrarlos*. They would take a neckerchief or something and tie their arms together. And then they had to *desempeñar*—promise that they'd give another party. Then they'd untie them.

The religious plays that we saw as children were the *pastores* and also the apparition of Our Lady of Guadalupe. That was put on nearly every year by people from Guadalupe Parish, and it was the story of the little Indian, Juan Diego, going to the hill of Tepeyac and the Virgin appearing to him—the whole story. The last time I saw that was in the 1930s, by a group from Agua Fría. La Fonda had them put it on in the Santa Fe Room.

Culture Loss

During the war, so many of the young boys were gone. People left to go to California to work in those big airplane factories and everything. A lot of people went. I suppose people got to feeling that, well, there just wasn't the time and so the devotion died out.

You see, the young men had seen other ways of doing things, other countries, and they had a different view of life than before they went. They wanted more than they had had before because they saw what was available. They began to think that maybe some of our things were not worth saving. They didn't realize the richness of the cultural patrimony here. They found they needed to speak English better. Many were not interested in their kids speaking Spanish. Instead of being bilingual, like we were, they only spoke English, and so the language gradually has gotten lost.

That, to me, is a terrible loss. And what's so sad is that they didn't want the child speaking Spanish because they thought the child would speak English with an accent. Well, if they themselves had an accent, the kid would speak with an accent. You speak the way of the people around you. I remember when my brothers went to St. Michael's, the brothers were all Frenchmen, and they spoke English with a French accent, so my brothers learned to speak English with a French accent!

Well, there's a Spanish joke that two old Spanish ladies had been listening to two Anglo carpenters. And the carpenters were son-of-a-bitching and son-of-a-gunning all the time. So one of the old ladies said to the other, "You know, they're so religious. I don't know who those saints are, but they keep saying, 'San Ovabitch, San Ovagun'" [laughs heartily].

Funny things happened when there was no communication. I remember a story a teacher in Pojoaque told. It was a history class. Part of the problem was his fault because he spoke English with a Spanish accent. He was teaching about the Missouri Compromise, when they were trying to make the states one slave and one free. But, of course, with his accent, he pronounced the word "come-pro-mice." And the kids were just laughing away, and he couldn't figure out why. They were hearing, "Compro maiz"—I buy corn [laughs].

1. The piñon tree, *Pinus cembroides edulis*, is a small evergreen, native to the Southwest, that has edible seeds much like nuts. The nuts are virtually indistinguishable in taste from the pignola nuts used in Europe and Asia Minor.

2. In 1844, Gregg wrote *Commerce of the Prairies*, about the trade along the Santa Fe Trail and the people of New Mexico. The book is considered a classic.

3. Susan Shelby Magoffin, eighteen years old and newly wed, was taken by her husband on a trading expedition out of Independence, Missouri, in the years 1846–47. She kept a diary, which has been published as *Down the Santa Fe Trail and into Mexico*.

4. As my father pointed out when I was a child, la fonda mean "the hotel." So "the La Fonda Hotel," as it is commonly called, means "the the Hotel Hotel." Another common mistake is to refer to the Alameda, the street that runs along the Santa Fe River, as "Alameda Street." "Alameda"

is not a street name, per se; the main street that runs along a river or park in a Spanish town is known as la alameda, as is the park.

5. La Conquistadora is the statuette of the Blessed Virgin that accompanied the Spaniards in the reconquest of New Mexico in 1692. She is credited with a bloodless victory.

6. Lamy is the passenger-train station for Santa Fe, about twenty miles south of town. It is named after Santa Fe's first archbishop, Jean Baptiste Lamy. Lamy town is now pronounced "lay-me." Archbishop Lamy is pronounced "lah-MEE," no matter how often it is mispronounced.

A Night of Horror

Cleofas Jaramillo

(1955/2000)

Destiny, still not satisfied, seemed bent on crushing me down to the very last of my endurance. Now it dealt me the hardest blow a mother may suffer. Three weeks after parting with my dear mother, a most heartbreaking tragedy, one that horrified every citizen not only in this city of Santa Fe, but throughout the state, fell upon me like a piercing dagger, cutting through the very core of my heart and soul.

After seventeen years of praying for strength and resignation, I am now finding the courage to tell about this most terrible tragedy—not for the curious, but to let the truth be known and dispel suspicion on some other person. There were some false stories told by ignorant people, always ready to invent lies. Those who knew my daughter and my family knew better than to believe them. When I read the story someone told me was published in a detective magazine, I was so shocked. Who had dared to give them such information? I was the only one who knew the truth of what had happened. My family tried to keep me from hearing about the newspapers and all the publicity, but others were not so considerate. Years after, people were still telling me, "I have the magazine with your daughter's picture," or "I have a daughter named for her." Yes, the name I thought I had invented to please Sister Angélica was now a favorite one. They told me it means virgin and martyr, but my heart would sink every time someone came up to me in a public place and mentioned her name.

I have said before how Angie had skipped locking the screen and window in the dressing room. Like myself, I suppose she thought no one could come through it, as it was so well blocked. But it was through this least suspected window, so full of obstacles, that the one who had been seen lurking around windows in the vicinity, since he had been freed from the penitentiary, crawled in and smothered the life out of my beloved daughter.

What can still the hand of fate? Not even prayer for protection, as we had prayed for this, night and morning. It is something one cannot understand nor escape, but must endure.

I had been so careful every night when I awakened about 11:30 to look in Angie's room. This Sunday night, tired from my walks to church and to blind Leandra's home. I slept soundly until a flash of bright light on my eyes awakened me. "Angie!" I called, opening my eyes but seeing nothing but darkness. That seemed so strange. Had not someone just now lit the light in the kitchen? I lit the candle on the little table by my bed, slipped on my slippers, took the candle and stepped into the kitchen, finding the dining room door still swinging. Someone had just gone through it. Slowly I pushed the door open. Seeing no one, I placed the candle on the table and, then, noticed the light in Angie's room. Cautiously I walked through the living room, held back the portiere, which someone had drawn over the opening between that room and her bedroom. A horrified scream escaped me as I saw before me, standing by Angie's bed the broad shoulders of a man in a black and white shirt (not coveralls they showed at the court trial). Startled by my scream, his shoulders gave a quick shrug. I imagine he sprang at me and caught me by the throat, for my throat later felt sore all night. Fortunately, as I screamed, my eyes closed in a faint and I was spared the terrible fright of seeing his face, which like those black and white stripes, would have been impressed upon my mind, making me shudder every time I see a dark face.

The next thing I saw, as my eyes opened for just a second, was the corner of the dining room wall. My eyes must have been dilated with fright: the wall looked glaringly white. I screamed in a horrible voice, "Marie!" and knew nothing more. I had fallen in a faint by the dining room table. The man must have released his grasp my throat, to run after Marie, as he caught sight of her running out the kitchen door to tell Mrs. Clark, my neighbor.

How long I lay there I don't know. As I began coming to, I felt something rough on my cheek, and felt around with my hand, wondering why I was lying on the rug at my bedside. Then, like a flash, there came to me the thought of what I had seen in my daughter's room, and I sprang up and ran to her room. From the opening I turned back, horrified at the ghastly sight which met my glance. There was my daughter stretched across the bed, her face covered with a pillow. Mute with fright, I ran back to my room. At the door I discovered that Marie's bed was empty. Grabbing the door and the little blanket at the foot of my bed to wrap around me, I stepped back into the kitchen and saw that the back door was ajar, "They took her out through here," I thought. I closed the door with a feeling of

terrible horror, afraid someone would push it back in my face. Through the other door of the kitchen, I ran out on the front porch, at the end of which I met two men turning in. I stopped, calling, "Hurry! My daughter!"

"What! Have they taken her?" one of the men asked as we went into the kitchen.

"No, she is in there," I said, pointing to the dining room door.

One of the men went in and the other took me by the arm into my room and sat by me, holding me on my bed. I was crying so much that I did not notice when the man left. My brother and sister were now sitting on each side of me, holding me. "Call a doctor," someone said in the kitchen. "What doctor shall I call, Doctor Ward Livingston?" Mrs. Clark asked me. I saw her standing against the door frame, Marie, still in her night gown and with bare feet, standing by her, looking extremely pale. "Livingston or anyone," I answered. "Why didn't you come sooner?" I asked her. She only hung her head and left.

Very soon, Dr. Livingston was standing in front of me, asking for a towel. I looked in the mirror of my dressing table, and shook with fright at the sight of my bloody face and gown. I had not even felt that I was hurt until the doctor started to bandage the cut on my head. "Wrap her up and take her to the hospital. My car is out in front," he said to my brother. Some strong arms carried me out to the car and into the hospital, laying me on the bed. All through the rest of the night I had nausea and choking spells, feeling as if I could not get my breath or swallow even water.

The sad day dawned. My sincere old friend, Marguerite, came in and relieved my sister from her watch at my bedside. Later, my three brothers from Taos came in. My good neighbors, the Martínez, from El Rito, were there earlier. No one seemed to know what to say, and I could only cry. Marguerite stayed with me all night and all the next day. In the evening of the second day, when my brothers came in to see me again, Marguerite said, "Mr. Sayer says he will come in the morning and take you to see Angelina, if you wish." I hesitated.

"Yes, you had better see her. She looks so beautiful. I have already prayed to her," my brother Tom said to me.

I replied, "I shall let you know in the morning. Stay with me tonight, Tom, and Comadre Margarita, you go and take a rest."

The next morning Marguerite was back. I told her, "You may tell Mr. Sayer to come for me." I had prayed for strength all night. Lying on a cot, I was wheeled into the living room at my father's home. The room was like a floral shop, filled with perfume from the floral tributes banked all around the room.

"You have many friends, Mrs. Jaramillo," Mr. Sayer said as he led me to the casket. For a moment I looked down at my dear Angie. Yes, she looked sweet and so natural, as if in a happy dream. She was dressed in the pale pink chiffon dress, all of which I had made by hand for her for the junior-senior banquet. As I looked down at her pale hands, I realized that she was not just asleep, but that she was now leaving me, and that this was my last look at my dear one. I felt faint. Mr. Sayer and Marguerite led me to my cot and then took me back to the hospital.

After five days I was longing to be with my family. The doctor said I could be taken home. My brother, Ben, and my sister came for me, taking me and placing me in a bed by my father's bed. For more than a week I lay there, too weak and disheartened to care to live. I tried to pray, but my heart was too grieved. All I could do was to ask our God to forgive me and to accept my tears as a prayer. Shock and desolation had come upon me. I was about to give up when I received a letter from a dear friend, saying, "Dear friend, no matter what this cruel world does to us, it cannot take the love of God from us." Yes, I still had the love of God and this counted more than everything else. He did not send me this trial, he only permitted it, perhaps, to open my eyes that I might become better, more humble and forgiving.

So many kind letters, prayers and verses composed by friends were sent to me, that they made me think the world was full of good people. My heart grew more resigned. Had this great grief not come into my life I would never have known that great reservoir of kindness, which has grown into the wide friendship I meet on every side, not only in my home town but in every place I visit.

And now came the awful court trial of the accused. I was summoned to appear as a witness and my cousin, Blanch, came and took my sister and me to the courthouse. District Attorney Kenney led me by the arm to the witness chair. I could only testify that I had not seen the man's face. A man's life was at stake; I could not lie. Some people thought I could have said that I had seen his face. Marie also said she had only seen the figure of man, as his arm brushed the candle off the dining table. It extinguished as it fell on the rug, or it would have set me on fire.

Our testimonies of not having seen his face encouraged the criminal to deny his guilt and to carry on his fight for freedom, but there was strong evidence against him. On the base of my beautiful gold inlaid Venetian vase that he grabbed from the piano to hit me on the head, he had left his fingerprints. After the policemen and detectives gathered the evidence they could find at my house, they went to the nearest garage to get gas in their car. There they found the night watchman lying on the floor half unconscious from blows he had received on his head by a man who had come in and stolen a car. The injured man was sent to the hospital, and the police followed the tracks of the thief who had stolen the car. They found him having an early breakfast in a restaurant in Albuquerque. They brought him back by a different road and placed him in safekeeping at the penitentiary.

Men friends of my father's came and offered to do whatever he said, but my father was a peaceful man and told them to let the law take care of the case.

During the trial, the attorney for the defense tried to introduce the point that I could not have seen the light in my daughter's room five rooms away. That was the light which hit my eyes like a flash of lightning, awakening me that awful, eventful night. I thought it had come from the kitchen, but then I opened by eyes everything was dark. This puzzled me.

It was some years after when the mystery was cleared up. One night when the light had been lit in the dining room and the door to the kitchen was open, I went into my bedroom. As I bent to get something out of the dresser drawer, the bright ray of light hit my eyes. Looking up, I saw a bright reflection from the glass on a picture of little Virginia that hung over the radiator by the corner wall where I had fallen on the rug. The glass was catching the light from the open door into the kitchen, and reflecting it to the mirror of my dresser, where it was reflected again in a slant to my face! This had to be seen to be believed. Both attorneys had passed away before the puzzle solved itself. The intruder had come into the dining room, lit the light before closing the door, turned the light out immediately and gone back to stand by the bed where I had seen his back. How strangely things had worked out.

Promptly, the New Work Life Insurance Company agent came to pay me Angie's policy. I left the money with the company. I could not force myself to touch what I had sacrificed to save for my daughter. In October I had told her there were only two more premiums to pay. "When the policy matures, I am going to leave the money in escrow so you will get an allowance of just so much a month."

"Fine idea—so I won't blow it all at once," she said.

A few months after the culprit was sent to the electric chair, his attorney, who had conscientiously defended him, send a communication to the editor of our leading newspaper. It read in part as follows:

Santa Fe, N.M. Jan. 26, 1931

Mr. Editor:

I am not at all satisfied with the aftermath of the Johnson case, referring to the little publicity given to a most striking instance of public self control—one, I am inclined to think, of the most remarkable in the history of crime and its prosecution in this country.

The crime was most fiendish and horrifying—none could be more so, committed in the center of the capital city of the state, in the early part of the night, in proximity to houses of several neighbors still awake. This devilish boldness of the criminal added force to the public shock, and yet the people of the city, under a nervous tension that generally superinduces an irresistible impulse to immediately convene the court of Judge Lynch, contained themselves, kept their heads, permitted the alleged criminal to remain safely under custody, accorded him every right under the law, both by the court and the district attorney. The counsel for the defense was courteously given every opportunity to present his case. Under the circumstances, the people of Santa Fe and the surrounding country are justly entitled to have their self-control and observance of law published to the world in blazing headlines, and to be congratulated on their steadiness under circumstances more grievous than any that have occurred, or likely to occur again, in the history of New Mexico.

As a citizen, I for one am patting myself on the back because I live in a town of such levelheaded, law-abiding people. We of this capital city are abundantly entitled to paraphrase Little Jack Horner as we pull a plum out of the pie and say, "Oh, what great people we are."

On Thanksgiving Day, my cousin Blanche came to take me to have dinner with her. "Wrap up and come; only Gonzalo will be there," she told me. She could not have chosen a brighter day to bring me out of my dark confinement. For a month I had seen only sad faces come to my bedside to offer sympathy.

We rode along Hillside Avenue. Just the night before winter set in, leaving the world clad in a blanket of glittering snow from the high Sangre de Cristo Mountains to the evergreen-covered hills and the city's streets. New Mexico sunshine from a spotless blue heaven blinded us with its brilliancy. It was a scene to which not even an anguished heart like mine could shut its sense of feeling.

My cousin's home reflected her simple good taste. It was bright and cheerful, and her sweet boy, who had cried, "No, I don't want to see her with her head cut up," was now happy to see me. I had a nice, silk scarf draped over my head, and I tried to be cheerful and enjoy my cousin's good cooking. Tears must be shed in the heart, in secret, and like St. Monica, we must meet the world with smile.

From that day forward a change began coming over me. I again felt my love for that pure beauty which fills the world and like a tonic injected into me, it lifted my spirits. For the day I forgot my bitter cup.

Some weeks after, when I took courage to go out for a walk, the sun seemed to have lost its bright rays and the whole world to be in an eclipse. I could not lift my head until some kind person passing me would speak to me.

My little four-year-old niece Virginia was the only cheering tonic at home. Every night before going to bed, she would come to my door and ask, "Shall I dance for you?" Looking like a beautiful angel in her flowing white nightie, her dimpled arms outspread like wings, her long golden curls like a golden halo framing her beautiful face, she would flit gracefully all around the room, singing and dancing until she bowed herself out at the door and disappeared like a beautiful apparition, leaving my mind in a state of relaxation.

Gradually I started going back to my home, although the first time I want to Angie's room and saw her things everywhere, the pain was almost unbearable. Horror crept through me every time I passed the dressing room door, or saw the window, even from across the street. "Take that room out," my sister advised. "No, I need it," I answered. I had faced things which were much harder to face than the presence of this room. I could bear this.

The hardest task now was to part with my daughter's things. The piano, the Edison phonograph and her ukulele went first, for music brings

Nietos de Vargas: Conquest of the Barcodes, 2005.

more tears when the heart is sorrowing, especially when associated with the dear ones who have departed from us.

Fifteen years have passed and I still hold on to some of the books and things she loved the most. Gathering our personal possessions to pack them away, clearing the closets and drawers, so as to rent the house, for I could not stay in it for more than a few hours at a time, I found Angie's bulging memory book, full of clever writings, pictures, letters. There was one letter addressed to herself as "Sister???—Mrs.??—or Miss 16??" The letter was sealed. It is a long letter and reads partly:

Are you still Miss, nun, or Mrs.? I hope still Miss at home with Mumsy. Lonesome? I never dream. Has Mother kept you as she used to? You are supporting her nicely, I hope. Don't forget your dear school chum, friend Margaret Ortiz. Keep praying to her to help you. You need it. Please be true to dear Loretto and your Alma Mater. Best of all for you.

Among the clippings cut out of newspapers and glued in her book was one which reads partly "*El Jaramillo* is the name plastered on the side of one of the Santa Fe's newest all-steel Pullman observation cars, which passed through Albuquerque on the California Limited for the first time today. *El Jaramillo* is a beauty, finished in the most exquisite of polished woods and with about every device for safety and comfort. It is the first of a series of cars which will be named for famous families in the Southwest. This particular car has the name of former Colonel Venceslao Jaramillo, the successor of one of the most noted Spanish families in the Southwest," etc.

This and other newspaper articles written and published about her father fired in her family pride. She had kept them. Consoling herself about her small stature, she had another article: "Small stature is no detriment to great achievements," mentioning Napoleon and other great men not much over four feet high.

What Goes Around Comes Around

Robert Himmerich y Valencia

(1991)

Only a part of my formative years were spent in New Mexico, but perhaps this was an advantage because I had a basis for comparison that both natives and newcomers lack. My dad, you see, was a railroader who was not content to stay in the place where he was last laid off and responded to any opening his seniority entitled him to fill, regardless of where it was. He was a boilermaker in the era that saw diesel-electric power replace steam engines on the main railroad lines and he felt that he had to go where the work was. The alternative was to revert to the labor gang and lose the pay and prestige that accrued to a boilermaker. Even so, he spent enough time on the waiting list to farm actively wherever he could. When that was neither feasible nor possible, he would work as a carpenter, a truck driver, or whatever was available to support his family of seven. He'd drop everything when the call came for railroad work, though.

My family returned to New Mexico and Santa Fe in August 1949 and I entered my fifth high school as a junior. We moved into a place off Cerrillos Road, across from the old Bruns Army Hospital. Beside our place there was a motel, a service station and a few other houses. We were really beyond the edge of town, but we did have an unobstructed view of the Jemez Mountains.

I don't remember registration at Santa Fe High School—I do remember the first day of football practice. Our last home was in Southern California and the physical adjustment from sea level to Magers Field was a painful one. it took more than a couple of days to comfortably get around the goalpost once, let alone the mandatory four times after each afternoon practice. it was almost Thanksgiving before breathing was under control. Playing in Albuquerque or Belén was a piece of cake!

Even with the active participation in football, the band, and Mrs. Carr's Thespian Club, I think I was pretty much of a loner. Being the perennial new kid has a way of developing socializing callouses. (By this time—at age sixteen—I had already attended almost twenty different schools in a number of states and some of them I had attended more than once.) I feel that these experiences did develop in me a greater sensitivity to the personality of the town, the school, and the neighborhood. I learned later that those of us with similar backgrounds can almost instinctively recognize who could be trusted and who had best be left alone. About half the teachers that I took classes from at Santa Fe High School just did not have time to deal with yet another transient ethnic. Others, though, more than made up for their colleagues by making it clear to me that my education was important and this was a new experience to me. Perhaps the most significant part of living in Santa Fe was that for once I was part of the majority and that did not go unnoticed. The only other place we had lived that was even remotely similar was with my father's German-Russian people in rural north-central South Dakota.

It was necessary for me to work and fortunately I got a job in the circulation department of the *New Mexican*. It seems that my schedule fit their requirements nicely. After football practice I would deliver papers that the regular carriers had missed. This was an excellent way to learn the town, and learn it I did with the help of the Cantú brothers. In short order my duties increased to include a motor route north of town, assisting Mr. García in the mailroom and working with the gang who assemble the Sunday paper. For a while in the autumn of 1949, the *New Mexican* was central to my life and my grades reflected this inattention to schoolwork.

Not many of the guys at Santa Fe High had a car of their own and some did not even have access to a family car. My pride and joy was a 1931 Model A Ford with a 1927 Model T roadster body that I drove from Southern California. It was the result of a summer job irrigating orange groves in Orange County. Looking back, it was not much of a car, but it did provide transportation to school, the *New Mexican*, and back home again during the week. Saturday mornings and Sundays were often spent cruising the trails west and south of Santa Fe. It seems most of these dirt roads are buried under subdivisions or closed for one reason or another today. The really fun trip was across the mesa to the west and down the old La Bajada road and then on to Peña Blanca. My companion on this outing was usually Jesse Longacre. Among the fantasies I had then was to have a farm in that little community someday.

Perhaps the point of this essay is to prove that what goes around comes around. Even as a sixteen-year-old wanderer, I knew that I was at home in Santa Fe and that wherever I went that Santa Fe was home—for all the reasons I have touched on here and many others that are yet impossible for me to articulate. During my twenty-three years in the Marine Corps, thoughts of green chile, the mountains, Santa Fe, and things New Mexican were constantly being reinforced. I brought my wife Eva here after I retired from the Corps in 1973 and she sensed what I had been talking about for over twenty years (we were married in 1953). We got the farm in Peña Blanca in 1981, I finished graduate school in 1984, and the following August—almost thirty-six years to the day, we returned to New Mexico and Santa Fe. There has been physical change, not necessarily for the better. The spirit of the place, though, is much the same. This is what has kept so many here, this is what has drawn so many back, and most important to me is that I am home for good. ☼

PART VIII

Cuentos

STORY TELLING

Mi abuela cobraba interés

Sabine Ulibarrí

(1988)

Mis recuerdos de mi abuela materna se extienden por viente y tres años, desde que yo nací hasta que ella murió. No creo que cambiara mucho en todo ese tiempo. Ella siempre fue lo que fue sin dejar de serlo una sola vez. Ahora, al escribir esto, la memoria se me inunda y me rebosa de ternura. Es que nunca me escatimo su cariño y su tiempo cuando yo era niño mocoso, cuando era adolescente receloso y cuando primero quise ser hombre.

Me acuerdo que ella se sonreía cuando yo, niño de seis años, les decia "santafeos" a la gente de Santa Fe, lo que hacía rabiar a mis primos. Me escuchaba con atención cuando yo le decía que allá en las sierras de Tierra Amarilla era tan alto que andando a caballo yo podía tocar las nubes.

Lacasa solariega de mis abuelos en Santa Fe estaba situada en las últimas alturas de la calle Cerro Gordo. En ese entonces, no era calle, era un triste camino tortuoso que trepaba laderas y cruzaba un arroyo. Cuando llovía o nevaba lo mejor era quedarse en casa. A lo largo del camino vivían unos cuantos vecinos. Terrenos agrícolas a ambos lados.

La casa era grande. Tenía que serlo. Además de sus dos hijas y un hijo, mi abuela había criado a cuatro sobrinos que se habían quedado huérfanos desde niños. Cuando yo aparecí en la escena toda esta prole se había multiplicado. De modo que a cualquier momento la casa estaba llena de nietos, tíos y metabolismo.

Los muebles eran de los más finos de la epoca y demostraban el exquisito buen gusto de mi abuela. Yo conservo dos de esas piezas con máximo orgullo y cariño. Claro está que la sala y el comedor eran sitios vedados para nosotros los chicos, o, al parecer, para todos, excepto para pasar a los dormitorios que estaban al fondo. Allí se entraba para ocasiones grandes y solemnes como Navidades, Pascuas Floridas y Thanksgiving, o, una primera comunión, una boda o un entierro. La vida familiar se hacía en la enorme cocina con su estufa de leña y su mesa de Última Cena.

Al lado de la casa corría una acequia con agua cristalina. En su fondo había una arena rojiza salpicada con flecos de talco que despedían brillos. Corría por una arboleda bordada con flores de todo color. Allí nos pasábamos los días enteros, mojándosnos en la acequia, trepando los árboles, metiéndonos en la hamaca o en el columpio, comiendo fruta. Los duraznos, albaricoques, manzanas y peras verdes son bien buenos con sal y galletas. Se creería que la casa grande, el familión, la fruta, y todos los quehaceres que todo esto implica tendrían a mi abuela agitadamente ocupada todo el día. No era nada así. Bien temprano por la mañana empezaba a arreglarse y pronto salía a la calle bien plantada de compras y de ventas. No volvía hasta rayar el sol. El cocinar, lavar y planchar nunca fueron dignos de su atención. Fue mujer emancipada sin necesidad de movimiento social o árbitrio legal. Así mismo el abuelo. El también salía por la mañana a administrar sus terrenos, a jugar a las cartas con los amigos, a politiquear. Llegó a ser Asesor del Condado de Santa Fe. No sé cómo se las arregló ya que no hablaba nada de inglés. Un travieso dijo que se había presentado el primer día en la oficina y la había dicho a alguien, "Me Asisor" y que la habían contestado, "So what? Mine is sore too, but I don't brag about it." En todas partes se le conocía por "don Anastacio."

Nunca supe de ningún conflicto entre los dos. Mi abuela lo adoraba y le regalaba. El se dejaba adorar. Eso lo dice todo. Curiousa pareja. El era tieso y duro como un palo. Ella era blanda y suave como una gamuza. Se veían de noche. No hacía falta que se vieran de día.

Todas las mañanas traían a mi abuela a la plaza. Primero en carro de caballos, después, cuando hubo automóviles en la familia, en coche. Debajo del tapalo negro llevaba un sinfín de envoltorios y, claro, un bolso bien gordo. Repartía su dinero, solo ella sabía con qué motivo, en diferentes cantidades y las envolvía en diferentes pañuelos con sus respectivos nudos. Por las tardes tarde volvía en taxi.

Tenía crédito en todos los mejores almacenes de ropas de señoras, y como ella era su mejor cliente, en todos le daban descuentos. Compraba de las prendas más caras, cada una destinada a alguna dama de su elección que en ese momento no tenía la menor intención de comprarse un vestido o un abrigo nuevo. Después se presentaba en la casa de la dama elegida, vencía su resistencia y le vendía la prenda.

Primero compraba la prenda a descuento. Luego le subía el precio. Después le cobraba exagerado interés a la compradora por haberle vendido a plazos. Es que mi abuela supo resolver el problema aritmético de la sociedad.

Más tarde, ya hombrecito, vi la maestría de la mañas de mi abuela. Cuando se murió mi padre en Tierra Amarilla nos mudamos a Santa Fe. Mi madre hizo construir una casa en Cerro Gordo Road en un terreno que mi abuelo le regaló. En un dado día, de buenas a primeras, llegaba mi abuela. Se sentaban las dos mujeres a tomar cafe o chocolate con bizcochitos. Charlaban de esto y aquello. De pronto:

"Hijita, quiero que te pruebes un vestido que te he traído," desatando un paquete. "Mamá, yo no necesito vestido nuevo." Ya sabía a donde iba.

"No lo compres si no te gusta. Solo pruébatelo."

"Ay, ¡qué lindo!" Se le escapaba un suspiro al ver la elegancia y buen gusto de la pieza. "El momenta

que lo vi me dije: Este tiene que ser de mi hijita. No puede ser de otra. Y ya vez que tenía razón."

Mi madre no tenía más remedio que probarse el vestido. Y por supuesto le quedaba las mil maravillas. Conocer los talles, medidas, colores y gustos de cada una de sus clientes era la primera parte de su éxito. Conocer las flaquezas humanas, saber halagar el egoísmo, narcismo o amor propio de cada quien era la segunda parte. La tenacidad, perseverancia y paciencia (todo con tono personal, confidencial y discreto) era la tercera parte. No tuvo más suave tiento, más imponente talento, la Celestina de Rojas. Mi madre terminaba con comprar el vestido, como ya se lo sabía la astuta dama de Cerro Gordo. De la misma manera atrapaba a las demás. Muy pocas se le escapaban.

No se limitaba a ventas y compras. También se dedicaba a prestamista. Las maestras de las escuelas públicas, oficinistas, casadas con maridos tacaños, todas aquellas a quienes se les acababa la plata antes del día del pago, contribuían al bien estar y a la renta de mi abuela. Los intereses que cobraba eran de otro mundo. Pero también lo eran los servicios: entrega a domicilio, discreción, personalismo.

Había una bodega en la casa que siempre estaba bajo llave. Nosotros lo llamábamos "el cuarto del tesoro." Estaba llenos de bultos, envoltorios y cajas. Allí tenía mi abuela su mercancía.

Había de todo, hasta abrigos y capas de pieles. Joyas, reliquias, cachivaches, antigüedades, cosas que le daban en pago, en garantía, o que le vendían en un aprieto pecuniario.

Cuando yo tuve coche llevaba a mi abuela en su ronda de cobranzas una vez por semana. Sus clientes vivían en cada rincón de la ciudad. Era cosa de admirar cómo se movilizaba esa mujer porque iba a todas partes a pie. Otra cosa de maravillar era la calidad de las familias que le debían dinero. Jueces, abogados, políticos, negociantes. Yo sumamente impresionado. ¡Mi abuela vestía o subversionaba a medio Santa Fe! ¡Medio Santa Fe le debía dinero! Quizás por eso mi abuelo llegó a ser Asesor.

Mi abuela sabía muy bien a quién prestarle dinero. "No he cobrado los cheques (siempre en plural)," decía cuando no quería o no podía hacer el préstamo. Admitir que no tenía dinero era algo que su orgullo no le permitía. Sus limosnas, obras de caridad y regalos eran eso. Su negocio era otra cosa.

Vino la guerra. Mis dos hermanos y yo nos alistamos en el servicio militar y resultamos los tres en ultramar. Los tres le escribíamos a la abuela con regularidad y le contabamos el lado alegre de nuestras aventuras. Ella también, a través de una nieta, nos escribía a nosotros y nos tenía al día respecto a la familia.

Murió mi abuela. Vinimos los tres hermanos de sitios muy remotos de Cerro Gordo al entierro. El pesar fue hondo y doloroso. La pérdida enorme. No obstante, había entre todos nosotros un aire de paz y sosiego. Su memoria fue harto consuelo.

En el camposanto, mientras las oraciones y plegarias se repetían en la rutina de rigor, mi mente visitaba las flores y frutales que ella sembró en la vida. Recordé uno por uno, con sumo cariño, muchos bellos momentos, y, luego, todos en conjunto.

Yo no sé cuando, pero fue buen temprano, atrapó su vida y la hizo suya. La adiestró a que hiciera lo que ella exigía. Hizo siempre lo que quiso porque quiso sin agraviar nunca a nadie. Le gustaba el dinero, y le gustaba gastarlo. Supo ganárselo primero e invertirlo después. La encantaban las cosas finas y elegantes y se pasó la vida gozándolas. Le atrajo el reto del comercio y ganó y venció en ese ruedo. Necesitaba el trajín social, la comadrería y disfruto. Sobre todo, odiaba el que hacer casero y rutinario y no se dejó esclavizar. En todo esto se ganó el afecto y el respeto de cuantos la conocieron, y fueron muchos. Estoy seguro que murió contenta. Fue libre, fue alegre, fue suya.

Después del entierro mi tía nos repartió a todos los nietos un bultito que mi abuela nos había dejado, cada uno con el nombre de cada quien. Era un pañuelo anudado. Dentro había una cantidad respetable de efectivo. Su último gesto fue típico, todo suyo. No, no hay que lamentar su muerte. Hay que celebrar su vida. Se llamaba Gertruditas Armijo de Gonzales y era de Cerro Gordo.

My Grandmother Charged Interest

Sabine Ulibarrí
Translated by the author

My memories of my maternal grandmother stretch over a period of twenty-three years, from the time that I was born until she died. I don't think she changed very much during that time. She always was what she was without ever ceasing to be just that. Now as I write this my memory overflows with tenderness. She never deprived me of her affection and her attention when I was a sniveling kid, when I was a resentful adolescent, or when I entered manhood.

I remember that she smiled when I, a child of six, mischievous and spoiled, called the people of Santa Fe santafeos, something that made my cousins very angry. She listened intently when I told her that in the sierras of Tierra Amarilla it was so high that on horseback I could reach out and touch the clouds.

My grandparents' big house in Santa Fe was located at the end and highest part of Cerro Gordo Road. At that time it wasn't a street, it was a wretched, winding road that climbed hills and crossed an arroyo. When it rained or snowed, the best thing was to stay home. A few people lived along the road with farmlands on either side.

The house was big. It had to be. Besides her two daughters and one son, my grandmother had raised four children [her sister's] who had been orphaned in childhood. When I appeared on the scene these offspring were grown, and at any moment the house was full of grandchildren.

The furniture was the finest of the time, evidence of my grandmother's exquisite good taste. I still have two of those pieces which I look upon with great pride and affection. The living room and the dining room were forbidden areas for us children, or, it seemed, for everyone, except as a passage to the bedrooms in back. One went in there on solemn occasions, like Christmas, Easter, and Thanksgiving, or a first communion, a wedding, or a wake. Family life was carried on in the enormous kitchen with its wood stove and its Last Supper table.

Along the back of the house ran a ditch with crystal-clear water. Its bottom held reddish sand with flakes of talc that flashed in the sunlight. It ran through an orchard embroidered with flowers in the spring. We spent many spring and summer days there, wading in the ditch, climbing the trees, swinging on the hammock or the swing, eating fruit. Green apricots, peaches, apples, and pears are quite good with salt and cookies.

One would think that the big house, the large family, the fruit, and all the work this implies, would have kept my grandmother extraordinarily busy all day. Not so. Quite early each morning she got ready and very soon she hit the streets all dressed up, ready to go shopping or selling. She didn't come back till the sun set. Cooking, washing, and iron-ing were never worthy of her attention. She was an emancipated woman without the benefit of a social movement.

My grandfather was the same way. He, too, left in the morning to administer his property, to play cards with his friends, and to engage in politics. Everywhere he was known as "Don Anastacio." He got to be assessor of the County of Santa Fe. I don't know how he managed since he didn't speak a word of English. One wag said that he showed up at the office the first day and announced, "Me assisor," and that somebody had answered, "So what? Mine is sore, too, but I don't brag about it."

I never knew of a single conflict between my grandparents. My grandmother adored my grandfather and waited on him. He let himself be adored. That says it all. A strange couple. He had red hair and green eyes, a big moustache, white, somewhat freckled skin, and he was tall and slim. She was dark with dark eyes, plump, and small. He was as stiff and hard as a pole. She was as soft and smooth as a chamois cloth. They saw each other only at night. There was no need for them to see each other during the day.

Every morning someone took my grandmother to the plaza. In the early days it was in a wagon; later, when there were automobiles in the family, by car. Under her black shawl she carried all kinds of bundles, and, of course, a voluminous purse. She divided her money, only she knew why, in different amounts and wrapped it in different handkerchiefs with their respective knots. Late in the afternoon she came home in a taxi.

She had charge accounts in the best ladies' apparel stores, and since she was their best customer, they all gave her a discount. She bought the most expensive garments, each one destined for some lady of her choice who at that moment didn't have the least intention of buying a new dress or a coat. She then showed up at the home of the chosen lady, overcame her resistance, and sold her the garment.

She bought the garment at a discount, and when she sold it, she raised the price. Afterward, she charged the buyer interest for buying on the installment plan. My grandmother worked out the economic problem of her society.

Later, when I was older, I saw the mastery of my grandmother's ways and means. When my father died in Tierra Amarilla we moved to Santa Fe. My mother built a home on Cerro Gordo Road on a piece of land my grandfather gave her. On certain days, unexpectedly, my grandmother would show up. The two women sat down for a cup of coffee or chocolate with biscochitos. They talked about this and that.

"Dear, I want you to try on a dress I've brought you," my grandmother would say suddenly as she untied a package.

"Mother, I don't need a new dress," mother complained. She already knew where this was going.

"How lovely it is!" She gasped on seeing the elegance of the garment.

"The moment I saw it, I said to myself, this has to belong to my daughter. No other woman should have it! And, as you see, I was right."

My mother had no choice but to try on the dress. And of course, it fit her perfectly. Knowing the sizes, shapes, colors, and tastes of her clients was the first part of my grandmother's success. Understanding human weaknesses, knowing how to flatter the ego, narcissism, and self-respect of everyone was the second part. Tenacity, perseverance, and patience (all of this in a personal, confidential, and discreet tone) was the third part. Roja Celestina didn't have a softer

touch or a more imposing talent. Mother had to buy the dress, as the astute lady of Cerro Gordo very well knew. She trapped others in the same way. Very few got away.

She didn't limit herself to buying and selling. She was also a moneylender. Schoolteachers, office workers, married women with stingy husbands, all of those who ran out of money before payday, contributed to the well-being and to the income of my grandmother. The interest she charged was out of this world, but so was the service: home delivery, discretion, the personal touch.

There was a room in her house that was always locked. We called it the "treasure room." It was full of bundles, packages, and boxes. That's where my grandmother kept her merchandise. She had everything there, even fur coats and capes. Jewelry, relics, knickknacks, antiques, things given to her in payment or as a guarantee, or things that were sold to her in an economic squeeze. There were also toys, candy, chocolates, and cookies. Many of these things she forgot. When she gave us goodies, they were often hard and dry.

When I got to have a car, I would take my grandmother on her collection rounds once a week. Her clients were scattered all over the city. I was amazed at how that woman moved around since she went everywhere on foot. Another thing I marveled at was the quality of the families who owed her money. Judges, lawyers, politicians, business people. I was extremely impressed. My grandmother was dressing and financing half of Santa Fe! Half of Santa Fe owed her money! Perhaps that is why my grandfather got to be assessor.

My grandmother knew very well who deserved a loan. "I don't have any money," she said when she didn't want to lend the money. "I haven't cashed the checks" (always in the plural). Admitting

Veteranos del infierno:
Survivors of Bataan, 2004.

that she didn't have any money was something that her pride didn't allow her to do. Her alms, works of charity, and gifts were one thing; her business was something else.

The war came. My two brothers and I enlisted in the military, and the three of us ended up overseas. We wrote to our grandmother regularly and told her the bright side of our adventures. She wrote too, through a granddaughter, and kept us up-to-date on the family.

When my grandmother died, my brothers and I came to the funeral from overseas. The sorrow was deep and painful. The loss was enormous. However, there was among all of us an air of peace and tranquility. Her memory was more than sufficient consolation. At the cemetery, as the prayers and supplications followed the usual routine, my mind wandered through the flowers and orchards she had planted throughout her life. I remembered, one by one, with deep affection, many lovely

moments, and, then, all of them together. I don't know when, but it was quite early that she took possession of her life and made it hers. She trained herself to do what she demanded. She always did what she pleased, without ever offending anyone. She liked money, and she liked to spend it. She knew how to earn it first and how to invest it next. She loved fine and elegant things, and she spent her life enjoying them. She was attracted by the challenge of business, and she triumphed and conquered in that arena. She needed the social whirl, and the gossip that entailed, and she indulged in it. Above all, she hated housework and its routine and did not allow it to enslave her. In all of this she earned the affection and respect of all who knew her, and there were many. I am certain she died happy. She was free, alive, and her own person.

After the burial my aunt handed all the grandchildren little bundles my grandmother had left us, each one with its appropriate name. Each was a knotted handkerchief. Inside there was a respectable amount of cash. Her last gesture was typical, all her own. No, we mustn't lament her death, we must celebrate her life!

Her name was Gertruditas Armijo de Gonzales, and she was from Cerro Gordo Road.

The Colonel and the Santo

Fray Angélico Chávez
(1957)

The Colonel had said little since the drive up to Los Alamos and the return ride down its orange cliff approaches, when the Santa Clara Valley opens up like a panoramic canvas of endless blue sky and bluer sierras, the river course below like a string of emeralds set in silver and displayed on the ruffled fabric of ochre deserts. These ruffles were bluffs and mesas of every shape and hue scattered about for miles and ages.

The Colonel was a landscape painter of sorts as well as an amateur geologist and therefore interested in bits of history connected with each phase of the landscape. The driver of the car was keeping him supplied with such items, as though he knew the intimate story of each rock and every turn of the river. He, too, was in military uniform, but wearing the small crosses of a chaplain. His rank was lower as were, decidedly, his age and weight. The olive-drab caps and blouses, and the many-hued campaign ribbons over their hearts, were the single point of resemblance between the two men.

But though they had met for the first time in Santa Fe that morning, they understood each other; that is, the younger man knew what words to use in pointing out a cliff or basalt, or naming the color of a sandstone fault, and finally, after they reached bottom and crossed the river, in recounting the strategy used by a Spanish Captain-General of long ago in dislodging the Tewa Indians from the Black Mesa of San Ildefonso to their left.

This mesa looked like the gray-blue uneven pate of some gigantic elephant, and the Colonel spoke for the first time in twenty minutes. It reminded him, he said, of another bluff on a far Pacific island as well as the one purpose of this his first visit to New Mexico. He had forgotten the soldier boy all this while, but now the scape and sky, triggered by the sight of that bluff, brought him back to Cash, especially the unbelievably wide and blue sky. For Cash had always talked with a touch of homesickness about his blue sky back home. He believed the lad now.

"Are you quite sure where Cash's mother lives?" he finally asked, swiveling his big weight toward the driver.

His companion nodded and said they had to go on for several more miles to the east, to the foothills of the great sierras, which now were a deep velvet green. What had appeared like a short skip, when he pointed out the place from Los Alamos, was actually a distance of twelve miles or so.

"If they had dropped that thing a couple of months before they did, Cash wouldn't have died," the Colonel said, after the driver had mentioned Los Alamos. "Poor kid. He would have seen this place, this sky, again."

"You must have really liked the fellow, Colonel, to come all the way out here. He must have been a top soldier."

"Well, yes and no. In fact, he was a poor soldier when you come to think of it, and still he was the best, the very best. And he was a likeable character. You couldn't stay mad at Cash for long."

"Cash? That's a strange name for a boy from these parts. Was it a nickname?"

"Not that I know of, Padre. That was the name in his file—Cash Atencio. Well, he was in my battalion since the division was activated at the start of the war. He started training with us and was with us until the day he died. You know how one gets to know and like the men who have been with the outfit for years."

The chaplain nodded.

"And Cash was no ordinary soldier, in the sense that he'd fade in the ranks of a company, or even a whole battalion. From the start I noticed Cash. Besides, he showed signs of leadership and quick judgment in field problems. He got to be a sergeant several times."

"Several times?"

"Yes. I had to bust him down to a buck private on different occasions, and each time he climbed up to corporal, and at last to top sergeant. But then he would get busted again. in fact, he was a private, and I had him for my jeep driver, when they got him."

"Colonel, how could he have been a born leader, a likeable character, and still be such a sad sack?"

"Well, let's put it this way. He had brains and other qualities, but didn't realize it. He had all the makings of a good non-com, and let me say that he had no basically grave faults that would call for court-martial. And he was a very religious guy. Never missed chapel on Sundays, and he used to wear a big five-inch cross, you know—yes, crucifix—on the same chain with his dog tags. Its weight made it drop out of his fatigue jacket while at work, but I never heard of any soldier kidding him about it.

"But all of a sudden Cash would take off without leave, or he would overstay his furlough without notifying his captain.

"Or he would get drunk downtown on a couple of beers and wreck up the joint, and then resist arrest when the MP's nabbed him. Each time it was a formal military police charge, and so I had to discipline him. But Cash never got mad or sulked. In fact, it was I who got raving mad when I lectured him and pleaded with him like a father, only to see that he could not grasp what I was driving at. I could not drive into his head the idea of responsibility—that's it, responsibility. And that's what most of these Mexican boys lacked."

The driver colored a trifle but grinned to himself. "Pardon me, Colonel," he said, "But let me inform you that Cash and your other boys from these parts were not Mexican."

The older officer's jaw fell at the unexpected remark.

"New Mexico was a Spanish colony long before New England, and existed for two centuries and a quarter before there ever was a Republic of Mexico. Hence, 'Old Mexico' is a misstatement. And she belonged to the Mexican Republic for only twenty-five years, while she has been a part of the United States now for a hundred years."

"But the people are part Indian, aren't they? Cash looked a little bit Indian."

"One cannot go by looks alone, sir, especially with the Latin races. But even if Cash did have a remote strain of Indian, which is no disgrace, this does not make him an Indian. The famed Will Rogers, whom you mentioned this morning as a distant kin of yours, was a quarter Indian. Does this make him a Mexican? Of course not. This is because the word 'Mexican' denotes a nationality and a culture, and a very superior one. A citizen of Mexico, whether he be white, red, black, or mixed, is a true Mexican and proud of it. he might make social distinctions, but not racial ones. It is we reputedly democratic Americans who make them, and incorrect ones at that."

"I'm sorry," the Colonel apologized. "You see, that's what I have always heard. Only this morning, at the hotel, a Santa Fe gentleman referred to these people as Mexicans."

The chaplain was laughing. "I am not blaming you, sir, just explaining, just as we were discussing geology, history, and art a while back."

As the Colonel remained gloomily silent, the driver chuckled and spoke again.

"Let's get in a bit of psychology also. It is only here in New Mexico that some people can think the word 'Mexican' and at the same time pronounce the altogether distinct word 'Spanish.' It's a hard trick with many a slip. And do you know that we priests are the worst offenders?"

"No!" the Colonel started. "That's strange."

The chaplain could feel that his companion had regained his composure, now that he shared his faux pas with others.

The Colonel did feel more at ease now, but at the same time he began wondering if Cash had resented the term. He could not recall a single instance, but it might go some way towards explaining his irresponsible outbursts. The last time was at Seattle, when he almost missed the boat for the islands. Not that he was afraid to go. Cash was afraid of nothing. he simply went off the restricted area, wrecked a small bar and restaurant downtown, and was dragged up the gangplank by the military police at the last moment. From then on Sergeant Cash was a private until the day he died. That day was a dark and muggy one, just like most days in the topics during the rainy season, and especially during action. It seemed as though constant artillery barrages and aerial bombings tended to shake the heavens loose. The regiment had been detailed to take the northern tip of the big island and had done so after almost a week of heavy fighting and mopping up. The regimental commander was killed by a sniper's bullet on the second day, and the Colonel, then a light Colonel, was removed from his battalion to take his place. After the main action was over, he remembered Cash down in the battalion and had him transferred up to regimental headquarters.

"He was a wonderful driver in all kinds of bad roads, including axle-deep mud. Besides, he knew what I wanted without having to say much. That's the advantage of working and training together for a long time. Cash had done well during combat, his captain told me, and was on the list of those to be recommended for decoration. My intention was to use his driving abilities for the time being and then restore his sergeant's stripes when the medals were dished out.

"Well, it was one of those muggy days, as I was saying, when I decided to inspect some forward gun positions on the other side of Elephant Butte, a lone mountain bluff on our end of the island. This was the name the men gave it, only they mispronounced the second word. Which made no difference as far as looks were concerned? It appeared very much like that Black Mesa we passed, except that it was all green, the bits of steep ground with grass and bush, and the bare rock with lichen. Between us and the bluff lay a couple miles of dense swampy jungle, not open country like this where you can see a jackrabbit leap and hop for a mile. And the sky was a heavy gray, like lead.

"I was kidding Cash about missing his blue skies as the jeep roared and squirmed over the narrow raised road of black muck, always managing to keep from slipping down among the thick stands of dripping palm and bamboo on either side, when more than a dozen enemy soldiers broke out of concealment and blocked the road ahead. I was sitting in front next to Cash, my adjutant on the seat in back.

"Before either of us could say a word, Cash threw the jeep in reverse and roared madly backward for several yards, while those monkeys began shooting at us. The adjutant and I just got our guns out of their holsters when we were catapulted head over heels into a murky trench of mud and reeds. Then the jeep roared back on the roadbed and made angrily for the roadblock ahead. It was then that I realized that Cash had purposely dumped us off to carry out a plan of his.

"How he got that jeep to clamber back on the road was miracle enough. How he went through that ambush and past it without getting hit was another wonder. Of course, they leaped aside when he rushed past them. Once beyond them, he stopped the vehicle astride the road, took off the rifle strapped to the jeep's side, and began peppering them, using the jeep as a bunker. The adjutant and I wanted to do our part, but the two pistols were in deep water beyond retrieving.

"I saw them toss grenades at the jeep, and suddenly it blew up with a couple of explosions. By the time the smoke cleared away they had slunk back into the jungle.

"We didn't dare move, without weapons, and we lay still in the reeds and palmettos. One of our patrols had started our way on hearing the shooting, but when they reached us the heavens opened up with bucketfuls. When the storm was over we went cautiously to examine the wrecked jeep. But Cash was not there."

The chaplain's car slowed down, veered off the main road, and rolled down a short distance among some clumps of bluish-green sagebrush, to stop before a small adobe house dozing cool and quiet under the glossy umbrella of a giant cottonwood.

"Is this the place?" the Colonel asked, shocked out of the reverie which his narrative had conjured up.

"That's what it said on the mailbox by the roadside." the chaplain answered, going over to knock on the low blue door.

For a spell there was no answer, nor any noise, only the very slight but sharp rustle of big leaves overhead. It was like being in a painting, the Colonel felt. Then the door opened quietly, to frame a young mother with a baby on her arm.

Her long black hair and plain dress were disheveled, and the light skin of her bare arms and face glowed with the clean flush that comes from working over hot water. The child and its dress were spotless. When the chaplain spoke to her in Spanish asking for Cash's mother, she replied in English, first excusing her appearance, then bidding them come into the house. She was Cash's sister. Her husband was up in the mountains getting wood. Her mother was at the neighbor's down the road. While they made themselves at home she would run down and fetch the old lady. The Colonel began to feel a strange comfort in the room. He soon found the answer in the wavy floor, which felt like packed earth that was padded over with neat rag-rugs of every size and shape—and in the uneven flow of the whitewashed walls from floor to equally uneven cloth ceiling. He had felt the same comfort in a campaign tent; it was the round touch of mother earth, of one's own mother. He was about to expound to his companion about the true functionality and hominess of rounded uneven surfaces, as against inorganic modernistic angles, when an old picture on the wall caught and held his eye.

"Say! That's the strangest way of dressing Christ on the Cross!" he almost shouted, getting up and pacing over to examine it more closely.

It was a two-foot wooden panel, uneven like the walls, with a few thin cracks running up and down the grain, which was almost visible underneath the age-darkened pigments. The main figure stood out because of the simple black outlines, without depth, like a child's effort or one of those modernistic French paintings—only not so impudent and glaring. At the foot of the cross were painted six miniature soldiers. The first had a drum, the rest stood at dress parade with their little muskets.

But the main crucified figure, in military uniform like the tiny soldiers beneath, still clamored for an explanation.

The padre was laughing quietly to himself, and finally began to explain.

"That is not Christ on the Cross, sir, but the figure of a once very popular saint in New Mexico, by the name of San Acacio. Acacio! That explains Cash's name. I'll bet you anything it was his grandfather's name and his father's also."

The Colonel's face went suddenly drawn and colorless as he leaned for a moment against a rug-covered chest that stood below the picture. When he spoke again his voice was hoarse and trembling.

"This is a most uncanny thing, Padre. I hadn't finished telling you about Cash's death. I said we didn't find his body by the wrecked jeep after the rainstorm was over. But hours later some of our men did find him—like this." And he pointed to the saint.

"He lay faceup on a steep slope of Elephant Hill with arms stretched out, a bayonet through each hand pinning him to the ground. That crucifix he always wore was hanging off his open denim jacket. Perhaps it gave those demons the idea. My theory is that they dragged him over to the hill during the storm. I only hope that he was already dead."

He contemplated the painting before speaking again. "This 'San Cashio' must have been a Spanish officer. He's wearing a colonel's uniform of Spanish troops in the early 1800s—epaulets, black sailor hat of the period, scarlet sash over light blue blouse, and long white trousers stuck in campaign boots. Only the boots are more like a cowboy's."

"They were military boots originally, sir," the chaplain offered, pointing out where a much later hand had drawn curved tops on each boot and added the curlicue decorations affected by western footwear. No, he further explained to the Colonel, San Acacio was not a colonel in the Spanish army of the nineteenth century, but his uniform did date the painting itself. It must have been in this Atencio family for three generations or more. San Acacio himself, or St. Achatius, was a Roman army officer of the fourth century, serving in Asia Minor. Because he and his men had become Christians, they were all crucified like their Master. The little soldiers could represent his executioners, or even his own soldiers before they themselves were nailed to crosses.

"And Cash was one of his little soldiers," the Colonel said, pounding his fist forcefully. Just then they heard footsteps at the door and turned around to see the young woman with her child. In front of them was a tiny wisp of an old lady in a long black dress. Her small round face, netted with wrinkles, and the clasped hands in front of her small bodice, were browned by thousands of sunlit days. Her white hair was swept back tightly into a neat ball of cotton on the back of her neck. Her large brown yes were guilelessly clear, like a little girl's, yet rich with the sweet pains of a lifetime bravely borne.

Jesusita de Chihuahua: Mariachis in the Plaza, 2004.

This was what the Colonel saw while the chaplain made the usual introductions and explained the unusual visit and then proceeded to tell the old woman (all in Spanish) about her son's death in the islands. Meanwhile, the sister in the background was crying softly to herself.

At one moment, when some invisible light suffused the aged mother's features as a quiet smile formed on her lips, the Colonel put his hand on the chaplain's shoulder and interrupted him.

"Padre, be sure not to tell how we found him."

"But I just did, sir."

The old lady looked up at the Colonel but spoke to the chaplain: "Tell the gentleman how proud I am to know that my son died like the Lord and his patron saint."

With this she took the hand of the Colonel, who had taken out a ribbed medal to pin on her dress, and kissed it reverently. Then she took the decoration from his helpless fingers, glided over to the santo, and stuck the open pin in a crack over San Acacio's heart. It covered most of his blue blouse.

The Santa Fe Dress

Rosalie C. Otero

(2008)

Grandmother was prim, almost starched, some might say. She used her full name for even the most ordinary occasions, Miranda Verónica Carabajal Fernández de Peralta. I knew her as Nana Minda. She had been widowed for more than twenty years but still wore her mourning clothes and pulled out her lacy handkerchief to wipe tears every time someone mentioned her once popular and famous husband. Most afternoons when I came home from school she would be crocheting or sewing.

She had a passion for cutting scraps of the family finery, hoarded for years, into squares and strips and fitting them together again in careful patchwork patterns, outlining each bit of velvet or satin or taffeta with a running briar stitch. She had assembled enough quilts to have furnished several households. Her crochet pieces were intricate and rivaled the most beautiful needlework one could find anywhere. She liked to embroider as well, so that our pillowcases, kitchen towels, napkins, and handkerchiefs were decorated and bordered with Nana's handiwork. Some had elaborate flowers ranging from tiny baby's breath to roses and carnations while other items had whimsical fairies or beatific angels.

When my mother suggested that Nana should modify my new dress, though, I was apprehensive. For the rest of that week, I'd rush home from school to check on the progress. Nana just put me off in her prim manner and said she would show me when she was finished.

"Do not be so anxious, *mi'ja*. The dress will be ready in time, and it will be beautiful."

"But, Nana, why can't I see how it's coming along?" I pleaded.

"Selena, leave your grandma be," my mother shouted from the kitchen.

"Ah, you young people, se les cae el cielo encima," Nana stated, looking up at the ceiling as if in prayer.

I gave up, knowing Nana would show me when she was good and ready and not one second before.

The preceding Saturday, Mom and I had gone to Santa Fe to find the perfect dress for the prom. Santa Fe was the place to shop for very special occasions. It was always a treat to take a trip to the capital. There was a distinctive ambience about the city so that even the air seemed different. You could feel the history. The people seemed more sophisticated and worldly, and there were certainly more things to do in Santa Fe.

As we neared the center of town I pointed to various sites as if I were a tour guide and we were tourists seeing Santa Fe for the first time. "Mom, there's Fort Marcy Park where they burn Zozobra! Remember when I used to hide under the picnic blanket? He was so scary and loud, but I did like the fireworks. Are we going to come this year?" Sometimes our drive would take us to other areas of the city where I kept up a stream of trivia, rhetoric, and gossip. "That's where Saint Joseph built the staircase without a single nail! Grandma went to school there, at Loretto, right? It's where she learned to play the piano. Isn't San Miguel the oldest church in the United States? There's the capital! Why is it round? Have you and Dad ever stayed at La Fonda? That's the cathedral!"

Mom, too, had some insightful tidbit of history or current gossip she would add as we circled the plaza or drove down narrow streets.

This day, mother took the street into the main part of the city, down Burro Alley and around the plaza. The Indians had staked out a spot on the long veranda at the Palace of Governors, spread out their blankets, and set out their jewelry—bracelets, earrings, necklaces, belts—to sell mostly to the tourists who had taken early vacations. They looked like little blanketed dolls lined up on a shelf.

Mother parked the car behind Sears—plenty of roomy spaces, which is not true in most of the city—and close to everything. We walked through Sears toward the plaza. Our first stop was going to be Dunlap's, right on the corner facing the plaza. We went upstairs where the better dresses were located and began looking through the racks in my size. "May I help you?" a saleslady asked in a self-important, high-pitched voice. We both looked at her. She was a strained, unhappy-looking woman with a pinched nose and a large mouth. She wore a brown nondescript dress with a small white collar from which hung a filigreed gold crucifix. "No," mother answered, "we're just looking." We rounded the dress rack and began pushing one hanger after the other, taking a quick look at each dress. "May I help you?" that annoying voice again. "No, thank you," my mother's less patient voice answered. I moved to a group of dresses that caught my eye, pulled a blue shift, and was about to get my mother's attention when I heard, "May I help you?" My mother and I looked at each other. Since the saleslady's back was to my mother, she had the freedom to snigger quietly. I, by contrast, had to keep a straight face and answer politely, "No, thank you. I'm just looking." I placed the shift back on the rack and giggled. By the fifth time the persistent woman asked us if we needed help, we both burst out laughing right in her face. She harrumphed and walked away from us, her black heels clicking an off-rhythm beat on the hard floor. We quickly left the store tittering and snickering. Still laughing we walked to La Tienda, a trendy shop on García Street.

We made a direct line to the fancier dresses on one of the back racks. My mother pulled out a pink taffeta, but the series of small, shocking-pink bows down the front were too loud for my taste. I pulled out a lemon chiffon dress and decided to try it on. Mom and I crowded into the dressing room. After she zipped up the back and I stepped out to look at myself in the large three-way mirror, I found myself staring at what looked like a large canary with very strange feathers. The saleslady was being helpful, pulling out this dress and that. Finally, there it was—the perfect dress. It was made of white satin with a bow in front. The bodice was plain with a low neckline and short puffed sleeves. When I stepped in front of the mirror, I was transformed except for the socks and penny

loafers on my feet. I spun around, and the skirt flared and settled back down in a most elegant ballet of its own.

"Oh, Mom. This is it! Can I have it? It's beautiful!"

Across the street on the corner we found a pair of white satin pumps. I wanted more of a sandal, with high heels, of course, but my mother said the plainer shoes would show up the dress better.

We walked along the west side of the plaza to Woolworth's. It was our favorite rest stop after a long morning of shopping. I liked to browse through the merchandise, especially since I could afford many items for a nickel or a dime. We ordered banana splits. I smiled appreciatively at the enormous pile of ice cream, bananas, strawberries, chocolate syrup, and whipped cream. It was a very rare treat, and I ate the whole thing.

"What's showing at the Lensic?" mother asked. We still had the whole afternoon, and she thought we could take in a movie. The best ones always came to Santa Fe before they ever got to Taos.

On Monday, my best friend, Luz, told me she had found the perfect dress for the prom in Santa Fe. That's why she had missed school on Friday. She had gone shopping with her older sister, Miriam. During third period we chatted in our not-so-secret pig Latin.

"Legets yogo togoo magy hogouse agat lugunch!"

"Yeges! Agi wagant togoo seegee yogour dregess."

At lunchtime a light rain had started, so we ran to Luz's house, shielding our hair with our lunch bags. I sat on her bed while she pulled out a beautiful white satin dress with puffy sleeves and a satin bow in front—an exact replica of mine. I was speechless. I didn't know what to say. She kept asking me what I thought. Finally, in a very small voice, trying not to cry, I said, "It's very beautiful, Luz." She was so excited and thrilled by her purchase that she didn't notice my restraint and despondency. On our way back to school, Luz chatted the whole way about how she would have the prettiest dress at the prom, next to me, of course, and how her boyfriend, Mikey (all the boys in school seemed to have diminutive nicknames—Eddie, Louie, Tony, Bobby, Johnny, and my boyfriend, Joey) would absolutely drool all night. I just nodded, and when she asked me to describe my dress, I shook my head.

"Why? Tell me, Selena. Pleeeeeze! Come on, I showed you mine. Tell me what your dress looks like."

"You'll see it on Saturday night, Luz."

"I know, but I want you to describe it anyway."

"No, I'm not sure I will wear it anyway."

"What do you mean? You didn't buy two?"

"No, I didn't buy two. Are you kidding, one dress like that is all my folks can afford."

"Then tell me."

"I just want it to be a surprise."

"That's not fair—I shoulda kept mine a secret, too."

I trembled visibly at the thought, but Luz didn't notice. She was busy trying to stay out of the puddles.

That afternoon when I got home, I went immediately to my room, took the dress out of the closet. I didn't need to be reminded of the details; it was exactly the same as Luz's. It was beautiful, but I couldn't wear it. I started crying when my mother walked in.

"What's the matter, Selena?"

"Oh, Mom, something awful," I sobbed.

"Well, what in the world happened?"

"Luz has a prom dress exactly like mine," I blurted out between sobs.

"Well, that's nice, dear. Obviously your best friend has similar taste to yours. You two will be the prettiest girls there."

"Oh, Mom! You don't understand. Nobody wears identical dresses to the prom. We'll be laughed at and called *twins*. I know some of those guys. They'll spend the night calling me Luz and her Selena or worse. I can't wear it. Please can't we go back to Santa Fe and exchange it before Saturday?"

"No, you know we can't do that. It's a long way, and you have to go to school all week."

"¿Qué pasa? ¿Por qué está llorando mi'jita?" Grandma entered the room with worry lines deepening her wrinkles.

"She says Luz bought the same dress as Selena's for the prom," my mother answered. "And now she wants to go back to Santa Fe to get another one."

"Mi'ja," grandma said, "do you think that your mama has *el bolsón de Mana Cruz*?"

I didn't know who Mana Cruz might be, but grandma always said that whenever anyone wanted to spend beyond their means. I guessed Mana Cruz was wealthy and carried her money in a big purse.

Nana picked up the dress. "We'll just have to make some modifications."

"Oh, grandma, what can we do? It's perfect the way it is. It's beautiful. I don't want another one."

"Selena, you just told me you wanted to go back to Santa Fe to exchange it. Maybe grandma and I can do something to make it different."

"But then it will be ugly and homemade," I cried even harder, tears streaming down my cheeks and landing on my lap.

"Selena, you know your grandma is the best seamstress in the whole of Taos. She's even made that beautiful wedding dress for your cousin Clarita, and I'm not half bad myself. You liked the turquoise fiesta dress I made for you last year out of that crepe material, and Nana sewed all those miles of silver and white rickrack."

"But, what would you do?"

"Vamos a ver, hija," grandma said as she turned the dress on its hanger slowly. "Hmmmm, this dress has lots of possibilities. And, *mira aquí*, tsk tsk, they didn't even sew on the bow, just pinned it. *¡Qué porquería!* Some seamstresses these days put things together with *babas*."

"Selena, dry your eyes and help with supper. Tomorrow grandma and I will put our heads together and come up with something even more beautiful."

"It will be more fashionable than anything you could find even in Santa Fe. You'll see." Nana put her hands on my shoulder to comfort me, but when I saw her arthritic hands, I was moved to hysteria and panic and cried even harder.

That night I dreamed that I was at the prom in a quilted dress. Nana had sewn on patches using various pieces from her quilting bag. She had crocheted the sleeves and the bottom of the skirt. On the bodice she had embroidered an image of Our Lady of Guadalupe with a great deal of gold and red thread. Nana hadn't known what to do with the bow, so they placed it on my head and sent me to the prom.

The rest of the week was terrible. I couldn't think about anything except the dress. I was fearful that my dream would come true. That, regardless of my Nana's reputation and skills or those of my mother, the dress would be ruined, and I wouldn't be able to go to the prom.

Joey, my date, asked me what kind of corsage I wanted. I didn't know what to say. Maybe a large floral arrangement, like the kind they use in church or at funerals, so I could hide behind it all night. He said he was going to get me a white gardenia or pink miniature roses with baby's breath, unless pink would clash with the color of my dress. I felt like telling him to get me lilacs and large peonies and maybe an orange and green bird-of-paradise or sunflowers. With a huge, ugly corsage, nobody would pay attention to the dress.

Nana and Mom knew I had been fretting all week, so on Saturday morning, they let me try on the new creation. I could not believe the modifications. The dress was unlike anything I had ever seen. I knew I would be the only one at the prom with such a dress, the only one anywhere in the state, in the nation, in the world. I couldn't speak, and my dark eyes got enormous as I stood looking at my prom dress.

"*Anda, hija*, try it on. You can't stand there all day. Let's see how you look," Nana laughed and took the dress off the hanger, ready to place it over my head.

I looked in the mirror and couldn't believe it was really me. The dress was still white satin, but the skirt now had a soft chiffon layer that was pulled up a few inches at several intervals and held there with tiny white silk roses. The puffy satin sleeves were gone and in their place were soft chiffon sleeves with small pearl buttons at the wrist. The neckline had been widened and rounded so that part of my shoulder was exposed and the tops of my breasts were just barely visible. The bow was gone, replaced by a pleated pink sash that fit like a cummerbund.

"So, what do you think?" Mom asked, obviously flushed with their success.

"*¡Qué linda*, my hijita! You'll be the belle of the ball!" Nana cooed, as she patted this down and fluffed that up.

"Oh, Nana. Oh, Mom! It's the most beautiful dress in the whole wide world. Thank you. Thank you. Thank you!" I hugged both of them in turn.

Reluctantly, I took off the dress until it was time to get ready for the prom. I felt sheepish that I had doubted the abilities of the two women who loved me the most and who were, after all, the best seamstresses in the whole county. Although Miranda with her quaint, old-fashioned ways sometimes caused me acute discomfort, more often than not, she surprised me.

And One for John Coffee

E. A. Mares

(2008)

The following is a novel in progress by E. A. Mares. It is set in the Santa Fe of the early 1970s. The protagonist, Roque Smith, is a veteran student organizer and political revolutionary who has become disillusioned with many aspects of his own life.

Roque stepped out of brilliant blue Santa Fe light on Canyon Road and into the shadows of his basement apartment. The floor was cement and cold in mid-November, the walls rock lined, and the three windows were barely at street level.

"Get out! Out! Out! And take your damned motorcycle with you!" Jocelyn, she of the hypnotic thighs, had unceremoniously kicked him out of her home this way.

He surveyed his little kingdom: the efficient but sad and ancient kitchen with its quaint circa 1920 gas stove mounted on bowed iron piano legs. The squeaky rope bed rumored to have once belonged to Witter Bynner. Like Bynner, Roque aspired to write, but he doubted he would ever achieve the heights of Santa Fe glory and be invited to the Witter Bynner Dinner. Roque looked down at his tree trunk stool and at the brick bookcases and the chest of drawers he had paid five bucks for.

He sat down and contemplated his telephone wire spool coffee table he had rescued from a junk-yard. The wire spool table sent his mind back to his protest years. He remembered looking up at the telephone wires crisscrossing through the oak trees when the noise at the demonstration became unbearable. Those wires seemed to carry the promise of escape to a better world, one populated by a more evolved species than the one to which he belonged.

"Mr. Roque, that is your name?"

"Yes, sir. Just call me Roque."

"Well, Mr. Roque, you have got to tell that student to come out of that tree, or we are going to have to move in and forcibly remove him. Now, we don't want to do that. Do you understand?"

The accent was Arkansas. The intent clear.

A student had climbed into a tree on campus to protest the war in Vietnam and many other things. It was an intensely beautiful day, but gradually, as angry students began to gather around the tree, some in support of the demonstrator, many in opposition, clouds also began to gather above and to darken.

"Yes, sir. I do understand. But I wouldn't do that if I were you."

"And why not, Mr. Roque?"

"Well, you see, officer. We have this plan."

"Yes?" Arkansas eyes searching for meaning.

"If you attack this guy in the tree, we've asked all the SDSers to climb into every tree on campus."

It was the University of Arkansas in Fayetteville. Hundreds of easy to climb trees on campus.

"Now, you wouldn't do that?" Arkansas turned pale as the impossibility of the logistics hit him.

"Oh yes, sir. And the newspapers will be here to cover the story. You know, all you cops chasing students up and down all these trees. But don't worry about me. I just want to sell popcorn to the spectators."

Roque leaned forward on his primitive cedar stool. He recalled with pleasure the discomfort of the campus cops. In the end, a fierce thunderstorm broke up the demonstration. The man in the tree, who was protesting everything from war to death and taxes, came down with the rain, and everyone went home.

After all the marches, the beatings and the burnings, after the failed marriage and the children, after the divorce and the sobering need to earn money, it had come to this. He had put aside, temporarily he thought, his politics, his fascination with history and philosophy, and his writing, to settle in as a low-profile bureaucrat in Santa Fe. A "health planner," a little bureaucratic turd in a bowl full of certified medical turds, doctors who padded their own incomes with meaningless health programs that diverted public attention from urgent health issues. Doctors would do anything, he discovered, to avoid socialized medicine.

"Roque, we want you to draw up plans to move children from Jémez Pueblo to the docks on Fenton Lake."

"Docks on Fenton Lake?"

"Yes. They haven't been built yet, of course, but Congress will appropriate the funds." Mr. Buckles's eyes gleamed. "Just think, Roque, those wonderful kids from Jémez being able to experience a submarine before they are ten years old. Oh, don't look so blank, Roque. The submarine will become a learning tool for the kids. Filled with info they need on hygiene and health care."

Something didn't register with Roque. "Excuse me, Mr. Buckles, but won't a submarine get stuck in the mud at Fenton Lake?"

"Well, yes, but who cares! It's a great health adventure!"

"But I thought Jémez needed good roads and health clinics, not submarines."

"Right, Roque, and that's where you come in!" Buckles beamed with pride. "You will be in charge of setting up all the lecture programs inside the submarine! This is your chance to grow, Roque!"

Santa Fe was filled with painters who didn't paint, poets who didn't write, and politicians who didn't, who couldn't, who wouldn't, think. So a submarine in a small, land-locked mountain lake made good sense in the inner circles of medicine and health planning in Santa Fe.

Oh well, mused Roque, what cared he about Santa Fe being a Marxist textbook town divided by wealth and poverty, by social class and race? What cared he about the revolution now? He looked at his books by Rilke and Neruda, by Whitman and Machado, by Williams, and yes, by that old bigot, that *sinvergüenzaputo*, Pound. And he felt empty. The revolution had failed, his life had failed, and most recently, his affair with Jocelyn, she of the inimitable thighs.

There had always been a pragmatic streak in Roque. He preferred girlfriends who were beautiful and could cook, or who were at least reasonably attractive and had some literary interests and some useful domestic skills. But it was hard to come by these desired attributes, or so it seemed to him. Of course, he knew he was a kind of macho pig, but like all good pigs, he loved to wallow in what he was.

So it was quite understandable that he had been swept off his feet by the lovely Jocelyn, she of the ever-ascending thighs. Jocelyn was well read, an outgoing bon vivant, and a hard-working chef, well aware of her powers both in the bedroom and in the kitchen.

It was good for lazybones Roque that Jocelyn lived and worked across the street from him, but there was a problem. Both had fierce tempers. One day they argued over her cat, Chuckles. He, who was allergic to cats and avoided them, made the casual remark that Chuckles would make a good meal for a coyote. Jocelyn's lovely face turned bright red, and she exploded. And she threw him out. It was somewhat melodramatic as he only had to travel across the street.

But now he was lonely. Santa Fe was a town of cliques. He, being a near-penniless alien from the south, didn't fit into any of them. He preferred the Chicanos, but his southern accent was a little off-putting. Roque wasn't from the "South" south. He was from south of Santa Fe, and it didn't help even when he pronounced his own last name as "Esmith."

"Roque Esmith. That's my name, bro. Así me llamo."

"Roque Esmith? Where do you live, ese?"

"On Canyon Road."

"Uhu. *Con todos los gavachos*."

"*Nel ese*. I just rent there. From Mr. Cisneros."

"Oh, that's good, bro. Bueno, listen. Come see us sometime, man. *Bato firme*."

"Bato firme." But it didn't matter that he was a bato firme, a good, reliable, half-assed Chicano dude. He knew he didn't quite fit in the Santa Fe world. Deep down, he wanted to organize the west side batos, but they were doing a good job of those themselves.

Mr. Buckles, head of the Health Planning Authority, regarded Roque with a mixture of awe, respect, and fear. Not fear in the physical sense, but Roque did make people uncomfortable without meaning to do so.

The first day Roque roared up on his fire-engine red Ducati, Mr. Buckles almost freaked. When Roque decided to make his own working and eating schedule, Mr. Buckles could only give him more work to do, hoping this tactic would straighten out the young man. But Roque marched to his own tune. He lived the way he wanted to live. Yet the work was always done. Not sloppy work but Rolls-Royce work. Data analysis with no mistakes. Position papers that rivaled what the academy could produce. Buckles liked this, and so he tolerated Roque. Barely.

All this and much more ran through Roque's head as he sat in his little kingdom of an apartment. Following his primitive survival instincts, he prepared what for him was a bachelor's gourmet meal. No Mozzarella in Carrozza sandwich for him, with a layer of capers, such as the wondrous Jocelyn would have prepared. No, he had to settle for a can of heated Dinty Moore stew. Lukewarm and he ate right out of the can. With saltine crackers.

His late grandmother would have scorned this fine cuisine. His Chicana grandmother. Or, as she would say, his Spanish grandma. An army of ancestors loomed before him. Small farmers, herdsmen, musicians. Poor folk up from Mexico a long time ago. Long enough to call themselves Spanish rather than Mexican. Roque didn't buy it. He could not see any sense in calling yourself Spanish, or worse, Hispanic, as Mexicans and gringos alike preferred in New Mexico. There was also an Irish branch to the family, the wandering Smiths who had left nary a trace of themselves except for the name deposited by an unsung great-grandfather more than a century ago. They were all Mexican as far as Roque was concerned.

In honor of his forebears, he improved his humble evening meal by dumping a small can of El Paso green chile into the Dinty Moore. A quantum leap forward. No tortillas but the bread from the Santa Fe Bakery was good. He went to the refrigerator. Inside was a wizened apple and a bottle of Bud. No lattice-crust peach pie for dessert. Not even a lousy Hershey bar. He settled for a glass of water. Now Roque had a meal fit for a king. A wretched meal for a wretched king in a miserable kingdom utterly devoid of any kind of holy faith.

A vision of Jocelyn flashed through his mind. She of the exquisite thighs. She of the English accent and haughty demeanor. She of the incredible cuisine that transformed her sandwich shop into one of the star attractions of Canyon Road. And he had lost her. Through his own mulishness, through his gross insensitivity. So here he sat with his water, his Dinty Moore stew, and his canned green chile. He chewed. And chewed. And remembered.

Once done eating, Roque's options radically narrowed. He could read. He could go to bed. But it was only seven o'clock. He could go to Maude's Bar and risk a fight, or a hangover the next day, or worse. He could take a hit from his flask of Jack D., but he would only want more and end up sliding into a deep depression. He longed for Jocelyn across the street, but he knew it was over. Downtown his last option, he walked outside and hopped on his Ducati. There was still time to visit the Santa Fe Connoisseur Bookstore before it closed.

Coles groaned under the weight of yet one more box of books. He had been fetching and toting boxes of books all day, and now he was looking forward to closing the store. He fancied himself a book expert, a man of great culture. Alas, he had to deal with filthy lucre because he had only a very small trust fund. Nevertheless, he was very proud of his Santa Fe Connoisseur Bookstore. He depended on the tourist trade and on the gays to survive. Especially the gays. They bought books. Lots of books. At times he thought it might help business to have a few Santa Fe literary types hang around. Like the artists down at the La Fonda. They would add color to the store. To attract as many literary types as he could, he stocked the large presses but also the smaller ones that specialized in poetry. Bait for the local poets.

Unfortunately, the local poets didn't look anything like the idealized Romantics of Cole's imagination. They came in extremes. Either they looked too ordinary, like insurance salesmen, or they were scruffy, evil smelling, and bad tempered. Aloof in a world of their own. Often not quite sober. And worst of all, their appearance and sometimes-bizarre behavior tended to frighten away the tourists. Sadly, Coles observed to himself that poets were shits.

Huffing and puffing from his heavy lifting, Coles decided to sit down and rest for a minute behind his dusty desk before closing the store. He plumped his ample rear down into the comfortable armchair, reached to his desk for his favored Whitehall briar, and lit a bowl of Virginia burley. The soothing smoke had started to curl down though his nostrils when he heard a motorcycle pull up outside. He glanced out the window, and his shoulders slumped. Oh, shit, he thought. He recognized Roque, and he sighed the sigh of the damned.

Cole saw a slightly disheveled little man getting off a bright red Ducati. The man was paunchy, had long dark hair, and a dark beard. Coles knew this person, and he knew his kind. He was one of the local poets. He would come into the bookstore once every so often, say hello, and head straight for the literary section or the used-books shelves. He would select a book, read it for a few minutes, put the book back on the shelf, and then leave. He rarely bought a book. Coles had seen this fellow about a week ago standing in front of some recent arrivals. Old books of little value. He stood and stared for what seemed like hours, and then he left. Coles figured the dumpy little man was a fast reader who tried to save money by reading a book in the store and never actually having to pay for it. If he could only do it in someone else's bookstore, Coles thought to himself.

"Hello," Roque said. He walked straight to the old-book section. The slim volume was still there. It had an elegant and rich cream-colored cover, like vellum. *An Early Martyr*, by William Carlos Williams. Roque had first seen it there months ago but on his low income was reluctant to pay the required fifteen dollars for it. The poems were laden with luminous objects, the things without which, according to Williams, there could be no poetry. Even though he still couldn't afford it, Roque reached for the volume and went up front to Coles.

"That'll be fifteen dollars."

Coles barely glanced at the book. He was relieved to see that the little man was leaving. As soon as Roque left, Coles locked the door and put up the "Closed" sign. He slumped back into his chair to have a good smoke, but the roar of the Ducati grated on his nerves. If only he could find a poet who looked like Rilke in the photographs. Tragic eyes and all. No such luck in Santa Fe. Coles sucked on his Whitehall and enjoyed the burley.

Roque secured his Ducati with a heavy chain inside his landlord's garage. Like a condemned man, he reluctantly entered his apartment. He tossed the Williams book on a chair and found that he couldn't stop thinking about it. His eyes drifted to *An Early Martyr*. He picked up the book and examined it carefully. The stitch binding of the five folios was superb, as was the stark simplicity of the cover. The print was dark and clear. Obviously a work of love. He saw there was a dedication: To John Coffee. The publisher was the Alcestis Press in New York. Book by a major poet. The major poet for many. And an obscure press.

Something began to rumble deep in the interior of Roque's mind. John Coffee. The Alcestis Press. Published 1935. William Carlos Williams. Medical doctor and poet. *Coyote* poet. Not Chicano but Spanish on his mother's side. The poet who did what Roque seemed unable to do. Combine a

profession with writing poetry. Lead a stable life. Roque had read Williams's *Autobiography*, and he remembered how the poet would write until a patient entered his office. Williams would slam his poetry notebook shut, tend to his patient's needs, and the moment the patient was out the door and out of sight, out would come the poetry notebook.

At least tonight, with *An Early Martyr*, Roque did not feel it necessary to flee to Claude's Bar. He was beginning to think he had stumbled on a kind of detective story. Who was John Coffee? What ever happened to the Alcestis Press?

Try as he would to remain upbeat, Roque succumbed to a gathering depression.

His mind wandered away from the poems. He glanced around the apartment and saw the dust, the cobwebs. He noticed the desiccated body of a roach behind the photo of his young daughter in California. He was past master at feeling sorry for himself.

There was a knock on the door.

"Whoever it is, come in."

Jocelyn pushed the door open. She was holding a package in her hands. "May I come in?"

"Yes, of course."

"Mrs. Valdez canceled her party, so I had this lemon pie left over. I thought you might like it."

"Well, yes. Uhh, thank you. Would you like some?"

"No. I'll just stay a minute. I saw you getting off your bike. You looked so down. I thought this might cheer you up a bit."

"I don't think so."

"Roque, I'm sorry about what happened a while back. You know it's been hard on me. I have another friend now. Just a friend but—"

"Yeah. Well, thanks for the pie. Tell the other guy I liked it. And while you're at it—"

"Good-bye, Roque. Come see me when you can be more civil. I want to talk with you. I do want to be friends."

"Yeah. Like I said in a civil way, thanks for the pie! And as for friendship, you know where you can take—" She was already outside the door and gone.

Gall. Bitter gall. Back to his silent walls, his books that were the coldest of comforts and the thinnest of gruels for the hungry heart. He surveyed his dismal kingdom once again. Then he sat down and unwrapped the lemon pie. He picked the pie up and began to eat it, like a feral animal. He ate the pie with gusto, almost with an angry joy. He savored every bite of crust, every mouthful of the creamy center, and the homemade whipped cream. It was a large pie, and it began to break in his hands.

He pictured himself as a mental patient in the state hospital or as a student at the state university. In Roque's mind, there was no real difference between a mental hospital and a university. In a sense, they were both mental institutions. One tried to instill a sense of knowledge about the world. It tried to teach you how to interact with it, how to recognize real choices. The other tried to show you the folly of failed paths, the need for order to have a sense of accomplishment, the dignity of advancing through life. But which institution tried to do what? Trouble was, it was almost impossible to distinguish the mentally ill and their needs in the state hospital from the mentally challenged in the state university.

If you played a shell game, Roque thought, and substituted the mental hospital for the state university, hardly anyone would notice the difference. Not the inmates/patients/students. Not the institutional grounds keepers, cafeteria workers, and maintenance crews. Not the professors/shrinks/counselors. Steady as she goes.

At the right moment, as the pie began to implode upon itself, Roque lifted it up, dumped it on his head, and smeared the mess all over his hair, all over his face, as if it were a bowl of oatmeal and he a small child again. He licked his fingers, grabbed some paper towels, wet them, and cleaned up the goo as best he could. Then he went to the bathroom, stripped, and showered.

He put on clean underwear and socks and selected a reasonably new shirt and a clean pair of pants. As a gesture to his Chicano heritage, he put on a good-looking pair of boots he had purchased in Juárez years ago. When he felt ready, everything set, he walked to the chest of drawers and took out the single shot Ruger he kept there. He placed the gun on his wire spool coffee table. Although he didn't believe in empty romantic gestures, he put Beethoven's *Fifth Symphony* on his barely functional record player. Gesture or not, he liked the music. After listening a while, he found Beethoven too heavy. An old lament, almost an alabado came to him and he sang softly to himself:

Mañana me voy,
Mañana me voy
El consuelo que llevo
Es que se acordarán de mí.

Yes, he thought. Tomorrow I go, tomorrow I leave this place. What comforts me is that I will be remembered. But who will remember me? He thought of his parents, long dead. He thought of his children, his ex-wives and girlfriends, and he settled for the cliché they would be better off without him.

And yet one more time he wanted to read a poem from *An Early Martyr*. He opened the book at random and devoured every poem. He followed the advice of one of the poems and put his suicidal thoughts aside, at least for a while. What was it about this book that kept hearkening back to the WCW *Autobiography*?

Slowly, with great reluctance, Roque gave in to his need to satisfy his intellectual curiosity. He rummaged through his books and found the WCW *Autobiography*. He dove into it, flipping pages, checking chapter headings, skimming the paragraphs, digging through the text like a determined badger.

And there it was. William Carlos Williams writing about his efforts to publish his first book of poems. He and his friends created a press, the Alcestis Press. Williams chose *An Early Martyr* as the title. Then came the words that went off like aesthetic dynamite deep inside Roque's psyche. Williams described how the book was dedicated to John Coffee, the town drunk, and how the book was limited to 165 copies, each signed by the author. Roque froze. He read and reread these lines.

Roque could see himself, could feel himself moving as in a very slow motion picture, or as in certain kinds of *mota* experiences, as he closed the *Autobiography*, lifted it ever so carefully, and put it back on the bookshelf. He inhaled, swiveled on his left heel, and it was as if the Milky Way turned in its sidereal motion with him. Step by deliberate step, he walked back to his coffee table and reached for *An Early Martyr*. His arms were not really his own now but Waldos, those curious robot extensions of human arms designed to manipulate radioactive materials from behind protective lead and thick glass. He opened the back cover. Nothing there. The robot arm flipped two more of the back pages, and suddenly there it was. The limited edition of 165 copies (Duca di Modena). The Strathmore permanent all-rag paper for the rest of the edition. The publisher, the press, and the date, September, 1935. And there in all its glory was the signature in black ink: William Carlos Williams.

Roque did not believe in signs and omens, yet he thought he sensed the presence of the good and gentle doctor, this healer who was as honest in his craft with words as he was with his medical care. Roque made his way back to the refrigerator, ignored the wizened apple, and, miracle of miracles, the bottle of Bud was still there. He popped the top and sat down at the table, transfixed by his good fortune. "I am the fucking owner of a fucking first edition book of poems autographed by William Carlos Williams." Roque, who knew the book market fairly well, was not innocent of the money value of this book. It was worth thousands of dollars and would only increase in value. Now he had something more than a set of ambiguous memories to leave to his two children in California. Quietly, as if parting with an old friend, Roque unloaded the Ruger and put it away in the drawer. He took a swig from his flask, capped it, and returned to his coffee table.

Roque knew that Coles had committed some kind of tremendous error in judgment by letting this gem slip through his hands. But Roque had not purchased the book for its monetary value. No, he bought it out of love, pure and simple. In its appearance, in the craftsmanship of its assembly, this book was a work of art. He savored every page. Even the Bud tasted better than it had a right to.

Roque wanted to see Jocelyn. Share the good news with her. But it was very late now. Better to respect her privacy. We might have coffee in the morning, he thought. Who knows where things could go.

Sleep, however, was impossible. Roque stepped out into the Canyon Road night of air perfumed by burning cedar. He jumped on his Ducati and went roaring up Canyon Road, past Camino

Escondido, past Gormley Lane and Camino del Monte Sol. He loved the narrow, climbing road and the cool wind whistling through his shoulder length hair. The Ducati was strong. The ultimate speed and maneuver machine. He passed the turnoff to Cristo Rey and soon found himself riding slightly northeast on the bumpy dirt of upper Canyon Road.

As he angled up the dirt road, he remembered why he had bought this Ducati more than a year ago. He had read that a notorious Italian bandit, a real-life Roman Robin Hood, used a Ducati to make spectacular getaways from the police. In broad daylight. In the heart of Rome. Now he came to the end of the road, near a reservoir, the Sangre de Cristo Mountains looming above him.

Although he loved it, the Ducati had its Achilles heel. When Roque wheeled it around, the electrical system took one shock too many and went completely out. He could kick start it, but he would have to ride in the dark or walk the fairly heavy bike back down the road for several miles. Roque wasn't concerned. The night was lovely with the constellations clearly visible above. The city now below him jeweled the foot of the mountains and reflected the stars, the moon, the planets, and the galaxies. Here, the world looked like it had been created about an hour ago.

The cool night wind, and the occasional howl of dogs and coyotes penetrated every pore of Roque's body. He stood there above the city for what seemed like hours. Immersed in himself and in the world, he let out a piercing *grito* for himself, for this never to be repeated moment: "Ahuah!" Calmly, before sunrise, he walked his Ducati down from the mountain slope.

Every once in a while, Roque would stop to rest. He would take out his small flask of Jack D.

and make a toast. "Here's one for Jocelyn," he said out loud to the knowing moon. At his last stop, he made his final toast. "And one for John Coffee," he said to the shadows of dawn. He found the paved section of lower Canyon Road and moved on down to his apartment in the growing light.

Mrs. Rael

Demetria Martínez

(2000)

Following is an excerpt from *Mexican Rubies*, a novel set in Santa Fe. Mrs. Rael is the owner of Rael's Remedios on the Santa Fe Plaza; one of her workers is Emma, twenty-five, who is having an affair with a married man, a local reporter named Mark.

Not a day passes that I don't give thanks to my Lord and Savior that I had my husbands when I was young; now I'm free to enjoy the rest of my life. And in a house, mind you, that I love as fiercely as I have loved any man.

Adobe walls like ripply muscles rough and cool to the touch. Wood doors that swell with the rains. The smells of cominos and horses and cigar kisses: It's that lived in, loved in aroma of a house where six children and god knows who else—sat down to chile and beans; or, if worse came to worse, Hamburger Helper. I never liked to cook, never will. But those sit-down meals—with whatever husband I had at the time saying grace—were worth every rock that accidentally didn't get cleaned out of the beans. Every chipped cup in my cabinet, every scorch on the wooden table is a story in itself. This is a house made of stories. Which is why I can't throw anything out. I would weaken the very foundation upon which I stand.

This is the house of secrets, too. That door there—hidden behind an India bedspread with a spray of green elephants—connects Rael's Remedios storage room with my laundry room. That door with its arthritic hinges has outlived Pinochet, Papa Doc, Somoza and I don't know how many Central American dictators. I have lost count of the refugees who have gone back and forth through that door. Some people keep track of the years by children or love affairs. Others speak of their twenties, thirties, forties and so on. Me? For better or worse the dictators of the hemisphere help me to keep track of time. It seems all my children were born on the eclipse of a coup or a revolution.

It all began with an extra mattress in the shop's back room, among canisters of corn and restaurant-sized cans of posole that all those years my kids thought I'd made from scratch. My parish priest who I didn't even think read the newspapers called me up one day and told me—he didn't ask me, he told me—to make room; he would be showing up at midnight with a woman who'd seen her family burned alive by death squads, funded by none other than the United States of America. What could I say? I'd prayed more than my share of rosaries for the world. But what if it turned out God was more in need of spare mattresses?

The woman's name was América, accent over the *e*. You have probably seen her on television, queenly and robust in her Mayan dress, making senators squirm as she speaks out on behalf of the wretched of the earth. Oh, but when she came to me. She was a tiny sparrow with clipped wings. We never said a word. I boiled up a touch of oshá and spoon fed her pinto bean juice. I read psalms to her in Spanish until she dozed on the mattress that I'd wrapped up like a Christmas present in pretty, starched sheets.

It wasn't long before my boys were shuffling international guests from house to shop through the cloaked door. I kept watch, along with India, my Sikh assistant from Española, for drive-bys by immigration. If you can believe it, I even bought a police scanner for the boys so they could track la migra. I made them rehearse what they would say if agents came to the front door. We put a used fax machine in the back room for amnesty international letters. I figure if you can't make the Lord's work as interesting and educational as working for the CIA, then don't be surprised if your kids end up on the wrong side of history.

So you can see why I don't have the heart to renovate my house. Or, God forbid, sell it. Not that I don't have to put up a fight with it now and again. Cracked stucco. Curling linoleum. But in the end nothing that can't be solved with a bucket of mud—or cans of posole to force the linoleum to stay put. Sure I love to complain about what a mess the house is; what woman doesn't? So the kids joke that I should sell out and buy a smaller place in one of those so-called gated communities. I can see it now. Adobe Acre Estates. Santa Fe style, whatever that is. Blinding white walls. Wood floors polished down to a chemical gloss. Throw rugs so clean you're afraid to do anything on them except that Zen stuff everyone is into nowadays. *New Yorker* magazines in wicker baskets in the bathroom. And kitchens so vast and scrubbed you could perform autopsies in them.

Sometimes I think those houses will blow away, brown paper bags scuttling along an arroyo. They're too new; they have no history to weigh them down.

This business about a woman needing a room of her own? Don't believe it. Pardon me but she needs the whole damn house. In her name. Otherwise

PART IX

Arte y Tradición

EXPRESSIVE CULTURE

Epilogue:
Recapitulación Breve
Pedro Ribera Ortega
(1973)

Christmas comes but once a year, it is true, but the spirit of la Noche Buena permeates and endures strongly in our lives the year round. It is not only a pious commemoration of Christ's birth, but rather it is a fervent renewal of faith and hope in Almighty God and in our fellow man. It is a challenge to accept the reality of life itself. Just as spring is a promise of summer, and soon enough the leaf-coloring autumn moves in to announce the inevitability of winter, so la Navidad prepares us for the rhythm of life and the whole year through.

This book has been written, certainly not to impress anyone, but rather to contribute something which is missing in southwestern fast-day living. Ours is an age of progress, in all fields of endeavor and many times in our zealous attempt to be "modern," we miss the trees for the forest. The colorful Indian and Spanish heritage which is a rich legacy to the multi-faceted United States can and will disappear if we continue to become ever more indifferent. This generation is young enough to learn, and old enough to know better with regard to the vanishing sense of tradition. Let us save what is worth keeping, carefully eliminating, as it were, the chaff from the wheat.

The sequence of this book is somewhat logical. Respecting the time element involved, the story of each chapter follows through chronologically. December 12th is the great feast day of La Virgen de Guadalupe. To anyone who has ever had the honor of visiting the basilica of Tepeyac, on the outskirts of Mexico City, where the tilma image of Our Lady of Guadalupe is so devoutly venerated, there can be no denying the haunting simplicity of the fervent piety of the countless pilgrims. To an intelligent Catholic New Mexican—not necessarily a Spanish-speaking devotee—there can be no doubt as to what the fantastic and yet so marvelous apparitions of Our Lady on Tepeyac hill were meant to be to all the Americas.

Divine Providence chose a site which would effectively serve as a focal center of the New World. To the north, all the way to present-day Alaska; to the south, through Central America and all through the breadth and length of South America, the Guadalupan message would have a meaning! We have only to read literally the actual words of la Virgen Guadalupana to appreciate the transcendental nature of the marvelous apparitions.

"Know and take heed, thou, the least of my sons, that I am Holy Mary, ever Virgin Mother of the true God, for whom we live, the Creator of the world, maker of heaven and earth. I urgently desire that a temple should be built to me here, to bear witness to my love and to my compassion. For I am a merciful Mother to thee and to all thy fellow people in these lands, who love me and trust me and who invoke my help . . ."

And to make doubly sure that the conquistadores and the padres would have no reason to disqualify the Marian apparitions, Our Lady chose for herself an Arabic-Spanish name: Guadalupe. This was a Marian title that inspired great veneration in faraway Spain. Only a few years previously, an intrepid Admiral called Cristóbal Colón had vowed a pilgrimage to the famous medieval shrine of Our Lady of Guadalupe in the land called Estremadura, in central Spain. To the surprised neophyte Juan Diego the beautiful Lady's name probably sounded like Tequatlaxopeuh or Tequatlanopeuh (she who originated at the summit of the rocks). But Juan's dying uncle, Bernardino, received from Our Lady herself the official title: Santa María de Guadalupe.

The Mother of Christ visited Tepeyac hill for a definite reason: to assure both the natives and the conquistadores that she was about to "forge a new country" (for the Mexicans still call Our Lady of Guadalupe, la Virgen que forjó una patria!), where both cultures could live side by side in the spirit and love of Jesus Christ. So, when on the eve of December 12th—la víspera de la fiesta—we see luminarias and farolitos burning brightly, we begin to put on, as it were, the joyous Christmas spirit.

The civic-minded Sociedad Folklórica in Santa Fe finally took it upon themselves to preserve the fast-disappearing observance of Las Posadas. Annually, at historic San Miguel Mission—at what is known as "the Oldest Church in the United States!"—this tradition-minded feminine group portrays the seeking of shelter by Mary and Joseph. Visitors in the area for the holidays are graciously invited to share in this unique tableau. Not only are the singing and the dialogue between los peregrinos (those portraying the Holy Family, on the outside of the church) and los mesoneros (those who portray the innkeeper and his family, on the inside) very authentic, but the props are just as good. Los misterios, the folk-art images of Mary and Joseph used in Santa Fe, are interesting Mexican handicrafts, having come up to Santa Fe from that quaint colonial town in the interior of Old Mexico called San Miguel de Allende.

The third chapter entitled FAROLITOS ARE NOT LUMINARIAS! Is certainly not meant to be controversial, not to create antagonism among southwestern writers who don't know any better. The best reason which I—as a Spanish-speaking nativo, a descendent of established New Mexican families—can give for it is an appeal to the truth behind our cherished Christmas traditions. In the spirit of genuine creativity and ever-desirous of promoting what is worthwhile in our Indo-Hispanic culture, the historic distinctions and explanations were made. Generally speaking, most of our non-Spanish-speaking amigos don't mind being corrected when they innocently attempt to enjoy and utilize many of our quaint customs.

Down south of the border, especially in the interior of Old Mexico, in the charming placitas and pueblecitos, the common people have developed a double-play of good manners and good grammar, which we progressive Americanos might do well to emulate. Whenever a turista shows regard and respect for things Mexican, the tourist will soon find himself being corrected of grammatical errors and idiomatic phrases in his halting attempt to speak their beautiful language. But the Mexican commoner has such a refined and innate sense of dignity and courtesy that he disarms the ordinary visitor, and he soon finds himself learning more and more Spanish. In this same way, perhaps our insistence on the background of many of our Christmas customs will help somewhat to correct so much innocent mis-information, especially in magazine and newspaper interpretations.

The Old Santa Fe Association, still held together by the militant civic-mindedness of venerable Ina Sizer Cassidy, is to be congratulated for their year-round struggle to retain and promote the atmosphere and charm of Old Santa Fe. At Christmas-time the Association sponsors the city-wide contest for holiday lighting "in the old way." Anyone entering his home in this unique contest of civic beauty has much competition to contend with, so successful has the OSFA been in its Christmas lighting campaign. Farolitos shedding their mellow light on adobe roofs, walls and walks; luminarias, the burning criss-cross structures of pitch wood; nacimientos set up within the hoses and yet visible from the outside; all of this forms the important ingredients of the traditional Christmas lighting and decoration.

With regard to the supposedly traditional number of luminarias to be lighted on Christmas Eve, let me say that I tried to keep an open mind while doing the necessary research for this book. Despite the simple fact that, as a Latino, I, too, like to wear my heart on my sleeve, or as the happy-go-lucky Mexicans say no hay reglas fijas (there are no fixed rules), permit me to be coldly objective in both Old and New Mexico.

The temperamental urge of the Spanish-speaking people to be doing something at the first impulse, come Christmas-time and this penchant for individualidad comes strongly to the fore. The particular devotion of each person decides on the specific number. For example, someone in a particular neighborhood might feel like preparing and lighting three luminarias, one each for Jesus, Mary and Joseph, or for the honor and glory of the Blessed Trinity. Another vecino might want to liven up the neighborhood by lighting twelve luminarias in front of his home, one for each of the twelve apostles. Still another compadre might decide to prepare two tall luminarias, extra large, one to honor el Niño Jesús and another to repay San Antonio for some extraordinary favor granted him during the past year.

So, to be perfectly honest with my readers, there is no specific number that is required by custom. It is up to the particular devotion of the individual to decide the right number needed. The Spanish-speaking remember with individualistic gusto the old saying: Cada uno hace lo que le da la gana! Everybody has the right to do what he thinks best! And in many cases, the availability of suitable wood helps in making a decision; as does the financial means of one's neighbor. What is really

de rigor, what is really necessary to promote the Christmas spirit all around us, is to prepare at least your first luminaria this year; and once you savor the warmth and light of the burning bonfire on la Noche Buena, in the festive mood of Christ's coming, permit yourself the treat of lighting up as many luminarias as your heart desires, next year. From then on, you won't have any trouble figuring out how many hogueras, bonfires, are really necessary.

With farolitos, it is the simple matter of the more the merrier. These quaint mellow lights add life to the earth-hugging adobe homes, walls and walks. Ordinary paper sacks are available at practically any food store. There are some stores or shops that specialize in ornamented paper bags. If you are the ingenious festive home decorator, perhaps silhouettes or cut-outs can spruce up some of your farolitos. Old die-hard traditionalists insist on un-ornamented paper bags and candles. But being an individualist at heart, I don't mind advocating that you act like the proverbial proud and stubborn Spaniard who insists that cada castellano en su castillo! is the best policy. Each man should be the boss of his own home!

Visitors to the City Different—as Santa Fe en-joys to be called—should not miss touring the streets of the town to enjoy the colorful festive lighting of thousands of farolitos and countless luminarias in their primitive simplicity. Usually the local newspaper will announce the specific homes which have been entered in the lighting contest. The Old Santa Fe Association sends its panel of judges to different sections of Santa Fe at specific hours on Christmas Eve. The Power and Light Company and the *New Mexican* also sponsor a contest of electrical lighting and/or a combination of both the traditional and modern lighting methods. And they, too, announce the route to be observed by their panel of judges. Handsome money awards are bestowed on the winners of the various festive lighting contests, which rewards have proven to be an incentive for more and better Christmas lighting in all parts of Santa Fe.

Lightly falling snow, covering everything in sight with a soft mantle of white, burning luminarias and mellow-light farolitos, all this is the best possible prelude to la Misa del Gallo, the midnight services in the Catholic churches and chapels on la Noche Buena. Many people have compared Santa Fe and the surrounding villages and countryside to biblical Palestine. Undoubtedly the warm adobe architecture, the peace and quiet that settles over the land on Christmas Eve, all tend to strengthen the comparison between Santa Fe and the land where Christ was born. But whatever charm our ancient town has, on this Night of Nights, everyone is most welcome to divine services in the Catholic churches. The midnight masses throughout the city beckon all devout worshippers, urging everyone to renew again their faith in the fruitful coming of the long-awaited Messiah.

A few years ago many nativos, especially our grandparents' generation, feared that *Los Pastores*, as a Christmas custom, would soon disappear. Only here and there in scattered placitas would some local impresario take the time required to patiently train a troupe in the archaic Spanish of some local version of *El Coloquio de los Pastores*. And these ensayos, these long rehearsals often stared in early October in order to be ready for the Christmas season. The verbose speeches of the main characters often require extra rehearsals, but still the enthusiasm of the local directors never waned.

I remember how one particular troupe from Rowe, New Mexico, folks who knew my grandparents' family well, came into Santa Fe one Christmas Eve. In those days, some twenty years ago, the troupe would put on their interesting costumes and ride on the back of a large truck through the city, announcing where and when *Los Pastores* would be presented. My grandparents really thought that this was the last time they would ever be presented and so on la Noche Buena, en la sala de la Unión Protectiva, a hall at the corner of Acequia Madre and Camino de Monte Sol, we enjoyed our first time "The Colloquy of the Shepherds." This was truly an unforgettable experience!

Fortunately, for northern New Mexico there are still some directores, who despite the unenviable, thankless hard task of training a troupe, realize that this medieval Christmas drama still has cultural value. I am referring in particular to several teachers of the Española High School, whose renaissance of *Los Pastores* merits them a gold medal for their sincere love for things New Mexican. For several years now, the high school students of Española have enjoyed themselves no end in tackling a difficult dramatic job: that of seriously preparing themselves for a worthwhile production of Old World drama.

What made the greatest impression on me, as just an interested observer, is not only that the Española High School has dared to attempt to put on *El Coloquio de los Pastores*, but more importantly their attitude toward the dramatic presentation itself, and how they have improved the script in keeping with the tradition of the medieval Christmas plays as presented entirely in Spanish, and the enthusiastic teacher-directors succeeded in their endeavor to combine the folk elements with the best of modern dramatic techniques.

One bold innovation of this particular troupe was the costuming. Up to then, the local impresario depended on the ingenuity of the troupe itself, and there were no set regulations as to effective costuming. The Española High School troupe compromised between traditional New Mexican folk costumes and modern conceptions of biblical clothing, and the result enhanced the production a hundred-fold. The version used by this young and talented school-group was one which the enthusiastic folklorist Aurora Lucero Lea had compiled and edited many years ago, and the music was based on the work of Alejandro Flores, a well-known old-timer in the native music field.

Up and down Río Arriba and into Santa Fe County, the Española High School troupe traveled to put on their version of *Los Pastores*. Their schedule was one which even professional troupes might have envied. In 1960 they graciously gave of their holiday vacation time and thought nothing of it, permitting their directors to schedule many extra performances. Perhaps their most elaborate and authentic presentations were those that were put on in El Santuario de Chimayó and also in the quaint Spanish-colonial atmosphere of the adobe church way up in the high country of Trampas. Both of these presentations were preceded by a candlelight procession into the venerable precincts of these fascinating churches.

Actually, once you have seen any one of the countless versions of *Los Pastores*, you will never feel the same again at Christmas-time. Something in *El Coloquio de los Pastores* will become a part of you from then on. It might be the melody of one of shepherds' lullabies, or some dramatic scene of battle between San Miguel Arcángel and the wily Lucifer (the classic battle between GOOD and EVIL); or you might remember some stubborn rebuttal from the inordinately lazy Bartolo, or the sage advice from one or other of the shepherds; but there will be something that will take hold of your memory and imagination, and this remembrance will become part of the Christmas-spirit, never to be forgotten.

The Southwest in general, and the capital city of Santa Fe in particular, has never forgotten that this "Land of Enchantment" of ours was aptly called, centuries ago, the "new Kingdom of St. Francis." All around us, especially at Christmas time, we can sense and savor and enjoy the spirit of simplicity and the humble but proudly-shouldered poverty that characterized the immortal Precursor of the Renaissance, San Francisco de Asís, that cheerful poor man whose saintly earthly life was but an imitation of Christ's.

In the colorful pueblos at Christmas-time the spirit of San Francisco is quite evident in the yuletide celebration of the nativity of the Christ Child. The simple, but majestic, venerable mission churches serve effectively as authentic manger-scenes for the visual representation of the lowly birth of el Niño Jesús. This is an atmosphere which will undoubtedly have gladdened the heart of the man who originated the classic Nativity scene in faraway Italian Greccio. And like "il Poverelo" joyfully singing the Canticle of the Creatures to express his innermost appreciation of "nature and nature's God," the Pueblo Indians today still continue to dance out their prayerful worship. Complementing the traditional Christian liturgical midnight services—la Misa del Gallo—the puebleños further add their own indigenous flavor in the colorful and graceful dances of the buffalo, the deer, and the majestic dance of the eagle.

The Christmas spirit reaches it peak in the solemn joyful Misa de Medianoche, the midnight services celebrated throughout the snow-carpeted land. And from the historic Cathedral in Santa Fe, just as from countless village chapels and Indian mission churches, the faithful wend their way to happy homes to enjoy and partake of the specially prepared fiesta fare. The native New Mexican specialties of the holiday season blend in perfectly with the so-called typical American yuletide foods. Tamales, enchiladas, steaming bowls of posole, sopaipillas, capirotada, all of these viands, platillos selectos de fiesta, emphasize the uniqueness of a southwestern Christmas feastday dinner. An old Mexican toast beautifully describes this holiday feeling: Salud, pesetas y amor, y mucho tiempo para gozarlas! Health, money and love, and may God give you a long life to enjoy them!

Visitors to Old Santa Fe inevitably travel around the historic plaza, pausing to enjoy the many Christmas decorations and the thousands of farolitos that outline the main buildings. La Fonda Hotel "at the end of the Santa Fe Trail" expresses delightfully the true meaning of the Christmas season with its magnificent outside tableau of St. Francis and the Christ Child, while inside in the peaceful patio is displayed a truly distinctive manger scene.

But unfortunately, many of our visitors unconsciously miss el alma y el corazón de Santa Fe, that soul and heart which epitomizes the real Christmas spirit of our venerable town. I am referring to La Conquistadora, the historic statue of America's oldest Madonna, formally known in English as "Our Lady of the Conquest." There in the north chapel of St. Francis Cathedral can be seen the most treasured heirloom of Christianity in the Indo-Hispanic Southwest.

For almost three-and-a-half centuries this historic representation of Christ's Mother has presided over the joys and sorrows, the good days and the bad times, the hopes and tribulations of the people of Santa Fe and New Mexico and of the Southwest. At Christmas-time La Conquistadora is regally dressed in colorful gold robes and magnificent crown, and in her hands is placed an ancient Niño Jesús-the Christ Child where from this venerable santuario in the Cathedral, the "Lady Conqueress" exemplifies the ideals and the hopes of Christian

New Mexico at its very best. A Christmas visit to Old Santa Fe is not complete without a gracious call on "La Conquistadora, Queen and Patroness of the ancient Kingdom of New Mexico and its Villa of Santa Fe."

Bernardo Miera y Pacheco, Celso Gallegos, Eliseo Rodríguez
Mystery, Mastery, and Identity in Hispano Art in Santa Fe
Carmella Padilla
(2009)

Each morning, as the sun rises over the Sangre de Cristos to illuminate the city of Santa Fe, sunbeams pour through the clerestory of Cristo Rey Catholic Church on Canyon Road and bathe its spectacular stone altar screen in pure, pearly light. Made in 1761, the altarpiece is at the heart of Santa Fe's four-hundred-year-old Hispano art, history, and culture. At daybreak, especially, the piece is a radiant testament to the mastery of its maker; its architectural elegance and fine relief-carved façade reveal the practiced hand of a veteran stoneworker, while its spiritual design and subject matter suggest an artist of profound faith. It is a singular example of craftsmanship and innovation from a pivotal stage in the city's creative history. Even after centuries of worship and wear, it remains an icon of originality in the annals of Hispano art in Santa Fe.

Until recently, however, the origins of the altar screen, and particularly, the identity of the artist who painstakingly chiseled the work from pristine white stone, were awash in mystery. As the only known altar screen in Santa Fe—and New Mexico—built entirely of stone, its construction history and unexpected source material long puzzled art historians and others who admired its polychrome exterior and mammoth proportions. By the late nineteenth century, art historians and writers were questioning the particulars of its production. The opinion of most was that the work was not "local"—or made by an artist who was native to, or lived in, Santa Fe. The idea that it was built by craftsmen from the colonial Mexican town of Zacatecas was one popular theory. Others speculated it was one of many religious artworks imported to Santa Fe from Spain or Mexico via the Camino Real. Eighteenth-century documents confirmed the altar stone was quarried in Jacona, just north of Santa Fe. Yet scholars could not be swayed that the artist could be local.

Today, thanks to years of independent research by such Spanish colonial historians as E. Boyd, Norman Neuerberg, Donna Pierce, Felipe Mirabal, Robin Farwell Gavin, Charles Carrillo, and Marie Romero Cash, most scholars agree the piece originated in colonial Santa Fe. Most scholars now also attribute its design and execution to one man: Bernardo Miera y Pacheco, New Mexico's earliest identifiable santero, or saint maker, who lived in Santa Fe from about 1755 until his death in 1785.

The story of the stone altar screen is a fascinating Santa Fe art history mystery. It is also part of a greater cultural narrative of Hispano art in the city that spans four centuries and features recurring themes of artistic mystery, mastery, and identity. What makes Miera y Pacheco's story perhaps most compelling is the question it inspires of how "local" Hispano art has been defined over time. In a city that today puts a premium on being local, the question has taken shape since the days of Miera y Pacheco, an eighteenth-century Renaissance man who, though not native to Santa Fe, was the first Hispano artist who, in style and name, could be connected to extant works. Despite his immigrant roots, Miera y Pacheco's thirty-year residence as a working Santa Fe artist established a verifiable model for a "local" art.

In Miera y Pacheco's time, local art was closely tied to the international artistic styles and trends of Mexico and Spain, as expressed in artworks imported to Santa Fe. Eventually, Hispano artists adapted these prototypes to suit local materials and tastes, developing a local style of their own. As Hispano art evolved amid the ever-shifting social and economic influences of the nineteenth and twentieth centuries, ideas about local art were revised. The early twentieth century, in particular, cast local Hispano art in the light of preservation and its passionate partner, revival, giving rise to a so-called "traditional" art based on Spanish colonial styles. The traditional art movement is often credited with the cultural flowering of subsequent decades. It is also criticized for establishing rigid stylistic concepts and definitions of Hispano art and culture that shape public perceptions to the present day. For many local artists, this artistic categorization has proved hard to shake.

The stories of artists Celso Gallegos (1864–1943) and Eliseo Rodríguez (1905–) are other important paradigms for considering four hundred years of Hispano art in Santa Fe. Each represents the important artistic movements of his time: for Gallegos, the early twentieth-century Spanish colonial "revival" period; for Rodríguez, the vital federal arts programs of the Depression-era Works Progress Administration. Like Miera y Pacheco, Gallegos's and Rodríguez's artistic achievements took place at critical cultural and economic junctures in the city's past. Likewise, their contributions to the Hispano community's creative development are unmatched. Together, the influence of this talented triad is far-reaching, their experience

Altar screen (polychrome stone), 1761. Believed to be made by Bernardo Miera y Pacheco. Originally located at La Capilla Castrense, Santa Fe Plaza, Santa Fe, New Mexico. Now located at Cristo Rey Church, Santa Fe, New Mexico.

Tres caras, detail of altar screen (polychrome stone), 1761. Believed to be made by Bernardo Miera y Pacheco. Originally located at La Capilla Castrense, Santa Fe Plaza, Santa Fe, New Mexico. Now located at Cristo Rey Church, Santa Fe, New Mexico.

invaluable for all who create and appreciate Hispano art in Santa Fe today.

Bernardo Miera y Pacheco
An Eighteenth-Century Mystery Man

The mystery of the stone altar screen begins on the south side of the Santa Fe Plaza in 1758. That year, Governor Francisco Marín del Valle gave eight thousand pesos and personal property to build La Capilla Castrense, a military chapel to serve the soldiers and families of the Spanish presidio (today's Palace of the Governors). The governor's designation of the chapel's patroness as Our Lady of Light, a representation of the Virgin believed to guard against Indian attacks, was most practical in a province where invasions by Navajo, Comanche, Apache, and Ute tribes were at their peak. An altar screen was commissioned in honor of the hallowed Lady. The job apparently went to Marín del Valle's close friend, Bernardo Miera y Pacheco, who brought his family to Santa Fe shortly after the governor's appointment in 1754.

Miera y Pacheco was born in 1713 in the Spanish Basque province of Santander and raised just outside of Burgos, north of Madrid. According to Donna Pierce and Felipe Mirabal in *The Mystery of the Cristo Rey Altar Screen and Don Bernardo de Miera y Pacheco*, published in 1999, Miera y Pacheco was likely in his twenties when he left Burgos for New Spain, initially arriving in El Paso in 1743. He was a military captain upon reaching Santa Fe, though according to documents of the period, he was much more: a husband and father, a rancher and farmer, and a mathematician and accomplished cartographer. During thirty years in New Mexico, Miera y Pacheco mapped Spain's northern frontier perhaps more than any other mapmaker. One of his earliest maps of the New Mexico province, which Marín del Valle commissioned in 1758, was considered the most complete, detailed, and reliable of its time. Miera y Pacheco was also a man of faith. When Marín del Valle established a cofradia, or confraternity, dedicated to Our Lady of Light, he appointed Miera y Pacheco as secretary and involved him in chapel-building plans.

The appointment made perfect sense: Miera y Pacheco was a skilled artist who departed Spain with extensive knowledge of international artistic trends. According to Pierce and Mirabal, his sweeping grasp of the latest in contemporary art and design, as well as historical and contemporary religious subject matter, suggests he may have apprenticed in Mexico or Spain. One important example of his knowledge was the new late baroque style incorporating rococo motifs that took hold in Spain in the early eighteenth century, when the artist was raised, and that was soon transferred to Mexico. The mid-eighteenth-century Altar of the Kings in the Mexico City Cathedral was the country's largest, most prominent artwork in the new baroque-rococo style, and it surely did not escape Miera y Pacheco's notice as he passed through Mexico City on his way to El Paso. The altar's *estípite* columns, in particular, represented a new expression in Mexican art and the influence of Old World conventions on the budding art communities of New Spain. This style of column—featuring an inverted pyramid-like shaft that is wider at the middle than at its base and top—as well as other late baroque influences are believed to have later been introduced to New

Nuestra Señora de Valvanera (above), Santiago Matamoros (below), detail from altar screen (polychrome stone), 1761. Believed to be made by Bernardo Miera y Pacheco. Originally located at La Capilla Castense, Santa Fe Plaza, Santa Fe, New Mexico. Now located at Cristo Rey Church, Santa Fe, New Mexico.

Mexico by Miera y Pacheco with the La Castrense altar screen.

The early colonial period in New Mexico had seen the construction of grand adobe mission churches modeled after those in Mexico, which reflected Spanish, Muslim, Gothic, and Renaissance styles. By 1630, some fifty mission churches had been erected in Spanish settlements and pueblos throughout the province. These were appointed with gold-leaf altar screens, sculptures and paintings of saints, and other imported religious items. But with the 1680 Pueblo Revolt, nearly all was destroyed. After the Spanish reclamation of New Mexico in 1693, imports continued to be popular, though local artisans used native woods and combined imported and local paints to craft additional devotional objects for church and home. By the late eighteenth century, several area santeros were creating santos (images of saints) in a local version of the baroque style. With the exception of Miera y Pacheco, however, the identities of these eighteenth-century artists are unknown.

For its time, the La Castrense altar screen was one of the most significant art commissions in New Mexico. Miera y Pacheco was clearly up to the task. His materials were bold: in addition to 225 tons of native stone, he employed brilliant imported and local vegetal paints. His design was organized and detailed: three horizontal tiers intersected three vertical bays, all resting on a broad base that sprouted six graceful estípite columns. His carving demonstrated a disciplined hand, with deep-relief representations of both time-honored and newly canonized saints—Santiago, San Juan Nepomuceno, San José, San Ignacio, and San Francisco Solano among them—meticulously wrought in individual panels. The altar top featured an image of Our Lady of Valvanera, patroness of Rioja, Spain, a creative nod to the birthplace of Marín del Valle. Etched

into the arched crownpiece above was a likeness of God the Father. And at center, Miera y Pacheco fashioned a niche to frame an oil painting of Our Lady of Light by Miguel Cabrera, then Mexico City's leading painter.

By 1761, the chapel was complete, with a stone relief carving of Our Lady of Light posted above the front door. The main attraction, however, was inside: standing forty feet high and eighteen feet wide, the altar screen was both an artistic and architectural feat. Two dedication panels on the altar base recorded the date of its completion and recognized the artist's benevolent patrons, Marín del Valle and his wife, doña María Ignacia Martínez de Ugarte. For his part, however, Miera y Pacheco left his masterwork unsigned.

The first documented account of La Castrense came fifteen years later with fray Francisco Atanasio Domínguez's 1776 inspection of Santa Fe churches. Domínguez described the altarpiece's distinctive iconography and other characteristics in detail, even citing the source of the native stone, but he never credited Miera y Pacheco. Domínguez, who was closely acquainted with Miera y Pacheco's art and cartography, frequently mentioned the artist in his report in relation to different artwork, though his comments were largely derogatory regarding the artist's skill. The absence of Miera y Pacheco's name, in the written record and on the altar itself, initiated a whodunit riddle to baffle historians for decades to come.

Meanwhile, Miera y Pacheco died in 1785 and was buried in the chapel floor. The late eighteenth century saw greater stability and wealth in the province, and peace was finally achieved between Spanish colonists and rival Indian tribes; Our Lady of Light had done her job well. In 1821, Mexico won independence from Spain, though the victory was relatively short-lived; by 1846, the United States occupied New Mexico, and the Americanization of the new U.S. territory got under way. When Archbishop Jean Baptiste Lamy arrived on the scene in 1851, La Castrense had been abandoned and fallen into ruins. Lamy soon sold the chapel property; he ordered the altar screen moved up the street to the *parroquia*, or parish church, and donated the Miguel Cabrera painting to the local Sisters of Loretto. With construction of Lamy's celebrated St. Francis Cathedral on the parroquia site, the altar screen was placed in storage, where it stayed for the next eighty years.

By 1939, a local movement was afoot to return the altar screen to public view. In an article in *New Mexico Magazine* that year, writer Ina Sizer Cassidy cited art critics' assessment of the altar screen as "the most extraordinary piece of ecclesiastical art that has been preserved within the boundaries of the United States from Spanish Colonial times." Yet she concluded the piece was "carved by pious Spanish and (Mexican) Indian hands in the best period of Spanish-Mexican Baroque style. . . ." Her writing reflected her times, for everything about the unknown master's work contradicted emerging stereotypes of local Hispano artists as self-taught artisans who crafted crude, handmade saints. For those willing to look closer, however, Miera y Pacheco left a trail of tantalizing clues to support a more open-minded history of Hispano art in Santa Fe.

Researchers finally got their chance in 1940, as Archbishop Rudolph A. Gerken arranged to make the altar screen the centerpiece of Santa Fe's newest church. He hired renowned architect John Gaw Meem to design the grand adobe Cristo Rey around Miera y Pacheco's forgotten work. The altarpiece was well preserved, though instead of Miguel Cabrera's painting of Our Lady of Light, the carved stone Virgin from the La Castrense façade was substituted as a rather ill-fitting filler for the central niche. Meem perfectly positioned the clerestory to illuminate the altar at first light. The new exposure brought new attention to the masterpiece, reviving questions whose time for answers had come. As scholars in coming decades studied the work, the answers slowly fell into place.

Miera y Pacheco's depiction of Our Lady of Valvanera in honor of Marín del Valle's homeland provided a starting point. Such dedications were uncommon in New Mexico, a clue to the artist's fluency in the artistic practices of Spain. An understanding of the once-popular late baroque style also came through in the artist's ornate baroque styling: stocky body proportions, upward-gazing poses, heavy drapery, and decorative cherubs and grapes. Perhaps most important was the altar screen's trilevel design, arched crownpiece, and estípite columns, which all were directly connected by scholars to prominent altar screens in Miera y Pacheco's childhood home. For example, the gilded altar screens of La Compañía Church and the Chapel of Santa Tecla in Burgos, Spain, highlight the exact same elements. The former was a built in 1725, when Miera y Pacheco was eleven years old; the latter in 1731, when he was seventeen, old enough to have perhaps apprenticed on the piece. Though completely different in style, but no less important, is the fifteenth-century altar of Burgos's Church of San Nicolás de Bari—where the central carved-and-painted altar screen is made of stone. According to Donna Pierce, who established this connection in Burgos in 1995, the technique of manufacture of this unique altarpiece, which was well established in the Burgos of Miera y Pacheco's youth, may have partly inspired the La Castrense altar screen.

While most scholars now point to the artist as the likely creator of the beloved altar screen, much remains unknown about Miera y Pacheco. The only known physical description comes from a 1779 muster roll for the Santa Fe presidio, which describes him as "five feet tall and sixty-five years of age" with "salt-and-pepper-colored hair and eyebrows, blue eyes, rosy white skin, a straight nose, and a full gray beard." As an artist, he can be definitively connected to about a dozen extant works, including a number of devotional pieces commissioned by Pueblo Indians, from whom he learned valuable artistic techniques that he adapted to his work. Around 1776, he created a wood-and-polychrome altar screen at Zuni Pueblo that featured elegant estípite columns, another connection to his earlier work. In 1780, he made what is perhaps the largest colonial New Mexican retablo (painting on wood) in New Mexico today, an image of San Rafael that doña Apolonia de Sandoval, a prominent Santa Fe citizen, commissioned. Currently in the collection of the Spanish Colonial Arts Society in Santa Fe, it is the only known retablo dated by Miera y Pacheco. Again, he left this notable work unsigned.

Until a definitive biography of Miera y Pacheco is written, many who admire his great stonework may never know his name. As recently as 1990, an *Albuquerque Journal* article still held that Governor Marín del Valle and his wife "made a trip to Mexico, visited churches and engaged the services of Mexican artisans to come to Santa Fe to construct and carve the (Cristo Rey) altar piece." Miera y Pacheco may not have been much for signatures, but he left the most enlightening diary of his life at the altar of his adopted home.

Celso Gallegos

An Uncompromising Contemporary Vision

By the time the story of the La Castrense altar screen began to unwind in twentieth-century Santa Fe, new threads had been spun into the tapestry of local Hispano art. Mexico's 1821 independence from Spain brought the Spanish colonial period to

Celso Gallegos, the "Wood Carver of Santa Fe" by Ina Sizer Cassidy, Santa Fe, New Mexico. Undated. Courtesy Palace of the Governors Photo Archives (NMHM/DCA), Negative no. 009891.

a close with a flow of eastern American immigrants to the city along the new Santa Fe Trail. The 1846 U.S. occupation of New Mexico inspired more dramatic changes in the local culture and economy, particularly with the railroad's arrival in the capital city in 1880. Inexpensive plaster statues, chromolithograph prints, and other mass-produced religious and domestic goods were now readily available by train. The influx impacted production of religious and utilitarian works by area Hispano artists, though contrary to still-prevalent myth, local art forms did not completely disappear.

The railway also carried adventurous Americans eager to explore the unfamiliar landscapes and cultures of the West. By the time New Mexico achieved statehood in 1912, a creative "colony" of immigrant artists, writers, and other aesthetes had claimed Santa Fe as home. By decade's end, many had joined efforts to boost the city's profile as a tourist destination through a variety of cultural, economic, and architectural pursuits. Nationally, it was a time of historical revivals; native, or "primitive," arts and crafts were all the rage. In Santa Fe, plans to promote aesthetic connections to the city's Spanish colonial past spawned a Hispano art "revival" that would influence the work of local artists for decades to come.

The Spanish Colonial Arts Society was born in Santa Fe in 1925. Cofounders artist Frank Applegate and writer Mary Austin envisioned the society as a way to help Hispano and Hispana artists create a cottage industry of local art forms that had waned with the coming of the railroad. Artists would be encouraged to create new santos, weavings, furniture, and other religious and utilitarian goods based on "traditional" Spanish colonial-New Mexican models the society col-

San Jorge y el Dragón (St. George and the Dragon), pine varnish, by Celso Gallegos, Agua Fria, New Mexico, circa 1930–39. Bequest of Alan and Ann Vedder. Collection of Spanish Colonial Arts Society, Inc. Courtesy Museum of Spanish Colonial Art.

lected. By publicly promoting colonial Hispano art, the society hoped to encourage its production and preservation.

In 1926, the society launched the first Spanish Market exhibition and sale in downtown Santa Fe. Featuring fifteen artists, it was a small but successful show. For artist Celso Gallegos, whose wood carvings proved most popular with exhibit-goers and earned him first prize, the market world was far from his home village of Agua Fría, six miles west of Santa Fe. A carpenter by trade, Gallegos was a poor but prolific carver of highly original religious and secular works whose talent was little known beyond his village before he was tapped to show at Spanish Market. In the market spotlight, his reputation as an unschooled artistic genius was quickly fixed among a growing group of Hispano arts patrons. At sixty-two, it was Gallegos's first public exhibition, and when Applegate handed over the sixty dollars patrons had paid for his work, the artist wept. Yet whatever commercial meaning patrons ascribed to Gallegos's "traditional" art was vastly different than his traditional life.

Gallegos had spent his life on the land where he was born in 1864 to José Jacinto Gallegos and Florentina Domínguez Gallegos. They lived next door to the San Isidro Church, which was built on donated family land and where his parents were deeply involved. His father was church *sacristán*, or caretaker, who assisted visiting priests, maintained the church, and rang the bells before mass. His mother was church *rezadora*, or reader of prayers, whose recitation of traditional prayers and hymns was central to various church rituals. Gallegos married Adelaida Montoya shortly before the turn of the century. She died after birthing their only daughter, and the child was subsequently raised by a relative.

Gallegos never remarried, but with his parents' death, he assumed both of their volunteer positions at church. He was held in high respect as an intensely spiritual man who spent much of his days in meditation, often praying in his small woodshed as he carved. He also tended a small farm in the nearby community of Cieneguitas. Every sunrise, he steered his burro and buggy to the farm; at noon, he guided them home along the dusty Agua Fría road, once part of the Camino Real.

Gallegos's journey to Santa Fe's art circles was surely less predictable than his daily schedule. Exactly when he began carving is unknown. Yet his unpainted style quickly stood out as an unself-conscious and wholly original approach to the prototypical polychrome santos of nineteenth-century New Mexico. Among the artistic models the society promoted to Spanish Market artists were works by nineteenth-century santeros who came after Miera y Pacheco. These known and unknown early New Mexico masters—Rafael Aragón, Pedro Antonio Fresquís, José Benito Ortega, and the Laguna Santero among them—had developed a localized style of bultos (sculptures of saints), retablos (religious paintings on wood), and other devotional art. Spanish Market artists were encouraged to imitate their techniques and iconography in hopes that they might grow into masters themselves.

If mastery was a mold, however, Gallegos was an ill fit. As in his faith, he poured his entire spirit into his art, originally making santos as offerings to his church. Unlike the routine of his religion, however, carving was an utterly free-spirited expression of his faith, his community, and his keen humor. Gallegos carved knotty pieces of pine, scrap wood, and assorted materials with a pocketknife, following their natural shapes and textures. His figures often had wildly imperfect proportions; a twisted or hunched torso, foreshortened legs and arms, and weblike hands were stylistic trademarks. The size of his work was also unprescribed, ranging from a bulky, apelike Christ on a cross, to San Antonio in miniature, to delicate wooden finger rings and rosaries. His frequent variations on a theme inspired diverse, imaginative works: San Isidro may be depicted as a bulto, a relief-carved retablo, or a panel fashioned from cut-out forms. One of his favorite subjects, the horse, may be shown in profile or with human attributes; in one delightful cut-out retablo, two seated horses appear to engage in conversation over a few beers. His subject might even be carved in stone; like Bernardo Miera y Pacheco, Gallegos was the only known artist of his time to work in the medium.

Gallegos's spontaneous style extended to chests, cemetery markers, walking canes, even hand-embroidered burlap. His front yard was inhabited by whimsical horses, birds, and other animals, while the front room of his old adobe hosted a giant carved caricature of a cigarette-smoking bride. To his neighbors, Gallegos was a kind and rather eccentric old man. To Hispano arts patrons, he was a "folk artist," even though some viewed his style as too crude to be commercial.

The Spanish Market was held sporadically at first, though Gallegos was a regular participant. From 1930 to 1933, the society's year-round Spanish Arts shop in Sena Plaza also showcased Gallegos's work. The private Native Market store on Palace Avenue provided him additional exposure and income from 1934 to 1940. Meanwhile, the local *El Pasatiempo* newspaper proclaimed Gallegos "one of the best known and beloved of the native craftsmen, and one of the most skilled." In 1932, his work was featured in a prestigious American folk art exhibit in Chicago. By the late 1930s, New York collectors were driving to Agua

Fría to meet the San Isidro Santero, as Gallegos had come to be known.

A sign in Gallegos's yard said "La Curiosidad," a term for curio shop. Literally speaking, it meant "curiosity." Given his humble history, Gallegos surely felt his sudden notoriety was curious indeed. He was well into his sixties when the society came along, his hands arthritic from years spent carving for no one but himself and his God. Success clearly benefited his life with important financial support and perhaps, a greater sense of creative pride. Nonetheless, Gallegos continued to farm and tend to the daily affairs of his church. Despite some pressure to conform to new definitions of traditional Hispano art as perfect copies of old works, Gallegos refused to be pigeonholed by the modern marketplace. He unrestrained style never changed.

Gallegos's uncompromising contemporary vision inspired his art until his death in 1943 at age seventy-nine. His work had by then been collected by individuals and museums nationwide, including the Spanish Colonial Arts Society, which today holds the largest collection of his work. In 1953, the Palace of the Governors held a memorial exhibition accompanied by an article in *El Palacio* magazine by renowned curator and Gallegos's friend, E. Boyd. In the article, "Celso Gallegos: A Truly Spontaneous Primitive Artist," Boyd placed Gallegos among the "better known American folk artists in the Atlantic states." It was high praise that also revealed how descriptions of local Hispano art as "traditional," "folk," and "primitive" were by then deeply ingrained. Not long after, a new priest at San Isidro Church threw decades of Gallegos's artworks away, judging them too crude for the modern eye. The priest's modern eye was clearly blind to the fact that Gallegos had been the first to bridge the gap between traditional and contemporary Hispano art in Santa Fe.

Eliseo Rodríguez

El Sexto Pintor

The rise of the early twentieth-century Hispano arts movement provided extraordinary opportunities for Santa Fe-area artists. Even as efforts to standardize traditional Hispano art were under way, visionaries like Celso Gallegos managed to maintain their artistic identity and ideals. Indeed, early in the movement, artists had some flexibility to interpret traditional art forms in new ways. In the coming decades, however, traditional Hispano art often became mired in misunderstood history and patronizing academic viewpoints that, instead

Eliseo Rodríguez, December 1958, Santa Fe, New Mexico. Courtesy Rodríguez family.

of pushing local Hispano artists forward, stalled them in their tracks.

In the 1930s, artist Eliseo Rodríguez had a rare opportunity to resurrect a colonial art form that had flourished in eighteenth- and nineteenth-century New Mexico, then waned into obscurity. The art of straw appliqué was a localized version of Spanish, Mexican, and European marquetry work that was not among the Spanish Colonial Arts Society's early priorities for revival. Rodríguez's charge to resuscitate the work was handed down by local leaders of the Federal Art Project (FAP), a national Depression-era relief program of the Works Progress Administration (WPA) that Rodriguez joined in 1936 for seventy-eight dollars a week. Like the society, the local FAP provided programs to support production of traditional Spanish colonial art by Hispano artists. As society activities came to a halt in 1934 following the deaths of cofounders Mary Austin and Frank Applegate, the FAP played a critical role in helping maintain the local Hispano arts economy.

Rodriguez was a promising young painter originally hired by the FAP to portray New Mexican land-scapes, culture, and history in paint-ings, murals, and mosaics. Mostly, he painted familiar images from in and around his Santa Fe home—still lifes

with Mexican ceramics, the aspens in autumn, the Santuario de Chimayó, saints, and biblical scenes. In addition to oils-on-canvas, he made reverse paintings on glass and late in his FAP tenure, silk screens. Some of his paintings were shown in WPA traveling exhibitions, though today, most of his FAP works are unidentified.

Despite the burdens of the Depression, it was the job of a lifetime for Rodríguez, who had dreamed since childhood of a painting career. But as his creative focus shifted, at the suggestion of state FAP director Russell Vernon Hunter, Rodríguez's

Autumn Little Tesuque, circa 1950, oil on canvas, 33½ x 27½ inches by Eliseo Rodríguez, Santa Fe, New Mexico. Collection of Yolanda and Lalo Griego. Photo by Blair Clark.

fine-art dream took a back seat to a lost "folk art." Historical models were few, but Rodríguez quickly worked out the puzzle of how to inlay straw on wood. He just as quickly became bored at mimicking the floral and geometric motifs that were central to straw appliqué design. Experience led him to approach the medium as a painter; patiently applying glittery golden sticks of straw to wood, Rodríguez integrated figurative imagery into the medium to express narrative stories and themes. His complex, richly shaded "paintings in straw" were a thoroughly modern breakthrough in a traditional medium. Rodríguez not only resurrected straw appliqué, he made it his own.

His ingenuity led to a prosperous art career that extended far past the FAP. By the time of his death in 2009 at ninety-three, Rodríguez was one of the most respected and influential Hispano artists in Santa Fe. In conjunction with longtime work as a furniture maker and teacher and other art-related employment, sales of straw appliqué helped Rodriguez and his wife Paula build a family of seven children and a thirteen-room adobe house. Paula learned straw appliqué at her husband's side, becoming a noted artist in her own right, while many of their children and grandchildren work in the medium today. The couple took straw appliqué from infancy to maturity, showing for decades at Spanish Market, where the art is now a mainstay. Their works have been collected, exhibited, and honored in Santa Fe and worldwide.

For Rodríguez, success was bittersweet. While he had continued to paint, his exposure at Spanish Market and other traditional arts venues led him to be generally labeled as an unschooled folk artist. Even as art historians and collectors praised the painterly qualities of his straw work, most never imagined Rodríguez ever picked up a paintbrush, much less was formally trained. The

irony, as scholar Tey Marianna Nunn wrote in *Eliseo Rodríguez: El Sexto Pintor* in 2001, was that "only because of Rodríguez's formal art training did straw appliqué—which commonly had been considered a 'handicraft'—become an intricate, involved, and entirely different art form. . . ."

Rodríguez was eight when he found his creative muse in the eastside hills of Santa Fe where, every morning, he and his father took the family's goats and sheep to graze. As the rising sun splashed red-gold streaks across Atalaya Hill, Rodríguez memorized the colors, patterns, and textures so that he could draw them later in the day. Born on Canyon Road in 1915 to Juan Manuel and Tomasita Rodríguez, the boy's family had moved to the nearby San Acacio foothills in 1923 as development encroached on Canyon Road. A group of influential eastern American artists had begun building homes in the neighborhood in the early 1920s. Drawn to the rural character and multicultural romance of Santa Fe, these artists found creative inspiration and recognition in depicting the city's landscapes and the cultural traditions of local Hispano and Pueblo communities. Their work helped establish an identity for the city as an exotic cultural destination. The downtown Pueblo Revival-style art gallery of the Museum of New Mexico (today the New Mexico Museum of Art), which opened in 1917, was partly envisioned as a venue for exhibiting the work of these new resident artists.

For a budding young artist like Rodríguez, it was ideal: the prestigious Santa Fe art colony practically lived in his backyard. Among those in residence were painters Józef Bakos, Fremont Ellis, Walter Mruk, Willard Nash, and Will Shuster—better known as Los Cinco Pintores—who often exhibited en masse at the downtown museum. The men built side-by-side houses on Camino del Monte Sol, around the corner from Rodríguez's

Still Life: NM Crucifix, circa 1952, oil on canvas, 33½ x 28 inches, by Eliseo Rodríguez, Santa Fe, New Mexico. Collection of Rodríguez family. Photo by Blair Clark.

home. Rodríguez quickly made himself known to each artist, hiring himself out to work in their gardens and at other odd jobs. He also made it clear he wished to be a painter.

The painters critiqued Rodríguez's drawings, offering creative tips and painting supplies to encourage his work. At fifteen, Rodríguez received a scholarship to the downtown Santa Fe Art School funded by another generous employer, the renowned western writer T. T. Flynn. The school's sole Hispano student, he attended painting classes for three years, working on paper and canvas in ink, charcoal, pastel, watercolor, and oil. From modernism, realism, and impressionism to expressionism, cubism, and abstractionism, he displayed a versatility that became the hallmark of his work. The Cinco Pintores remarked upon his promise as a painter, as did such renowned artist friends as John Sloan, Sheldon Parsons, and William Penhallow Henderson.

At twenty, Rodríguez married Paula Gutiérrez of Rowe. Children and the Depression soon followed. Before long, straw appliqué was the cen-

terpiece of Rodríguez's creative life. Painting was relegated to the middle of the night.

Years passed. But from the 1930s to the 1990s, Rodríguez never stopped painting. He produced hundreds of still lifes, landscapes, portraits, religious scenes, and other classic New Mexican themes. When World War II took him to the South Pacific for three years, he kept his skills fresh by painting portraits from photos of his fellow soldiers' loved ones. With the exception of seven paintings shown in group exhibitions at the downtown fine arts museum from the 1930s to the 1950s, however, most of Rodríguez's paintings would never be publicly seen. In a September 1952 *El Palacio* article on the "Thirty-Ninth Annual Exhibition of New Mexico Artists"—in which Rodríguez exhibited alongside Emil Bistram, Randall Davey, Fremont Ellis, Gene Kloss, Olive Rush, and other important Santa Fe artists—Rodríguez's work is called "characteristically New Mexican" and "strong in color and design." His parallel career in straw appliqué was soaring, but Rodríguez the painter is described in the article as "lesser-known."

Nonetheless, as the only local Hispano painter to participate in those early museum shows, Rodríguez broke important new ground that was essential to the continued development of Hispano art in Santa Fe. Despite disappointment, Rodríguez's strong artistic identity transcended the often-vague distinctions between "fine art" and "folk art." He understood that his example would go a long way in motivating local Hispanos to stay true to their muse. He never underestimated his contributions to traditional art, nor did he discount the positive contributions of the traditional art movement for many in Santa Fe. He held firm, though, in his belief that, one day, local Hispano artists would also be acknowledged and acclaimed as fine artists.

In 1985, Rodríguez's painting career was recognized as he became the only native Santa Fe Hispano artist to receive a plaque on the downtown museum's fine-art walk of fame—alongside the names of the Cinco Pintores and other early mentors. And in 2001, at eighty-five, he celebrated his first one-man show of paintings at the museum. *Eliseo Rodríguez: El Sexto Pintor* gave Rodríguez long-overdue recognition as one of the most enduring painters in the Southwest. More important, for many who were just discovering the depth and dedication of his talent, the exhibit provided a new definition for Hispano art in Santa Fe.

As the careers of Bernardo Miera y Pacheco, Celso Gallegos, and Eliseo Rodríguez demonstrate, the cultural, economic, and social circumstances that have driven the development of Hispano art through the centuries are fraught with benefits and bias. While some may argue that cultural bias has made local Hispano art resistant to change, others praise the commercial benefits that allow local artists opportunities to move ahead. The Spanish Market now boasts hundreds of traditional artists, including men and women of all ages, some of national and even international renown. A thriving "contemporary" Hispano art market features countless more, known and unknown, working in a range of media. And more than ever, collectors and museums are bringing local Hispano art into the public eye.

The fortunes and failures of Hispano art in Santa Fe can be difficult to judge when viewed in the light of four centuries, however. As a city that holds art and history in high esteem, the promotion of some kind of local Hispano art has been a potent source of ethnic pride for generations of artists who find fulfillment in tracing their work to that of their forebears. Some artists find inflexibility in narrowly defined views of local art, but others see legitimacy in the longevity of artistic traditions. Whether the advancement of a local Hispano art has proved right or wrong will likely never be reconciled. Nor will the question of how to define local Hispano art for our time. What is clear is that the pioneering expressions of Miera y Pacheco, Gallegos, and Rodríguez are central to the cultural life and identity of modern-day Santa Fe. Their artistry is for the ages. ☀

Credits

The editors are grateful to the authors and publishers for their permission to print their contributions. We have made every reasonable effort to identify and locate copyrights for every item we have included in our anthology. In particular we would like to acknowledge the prior publication of the following items.

Alarcón, Francisco X. "Barrio de Analco," first published in *Saludos, Poemas de Nuevo México: Poems of New Mexico*, edited by Jeanie C. Williams and Victor di Suvero (Tesuque, New Mexico: Pennywhistle Press, 1995). Reprinted by permission of the author.

Archuleta, Tommy. "¿Dónde Vivo Yo?" first published in *La Herencia del Norte* (Winter 2007). Reprinted by permission of the author.

Baca, Jimmy Santiago. "Bells," first published in *Black Mesa Poems* (New York: New Directions Press, 1989). Reprinted by permission of the author.

Chávez, Fray Angélico. "Doña Tules, Her Fame and Her Funeral," first published in *El Palacio* (August 1950). Reprinted by permission of the Chávez estate.

———. "The Colonel and the Santo," first published in *From An Altar Screen: Tales from New Mexico* (New York: Farrar, Straus and Cudahy, 1957). Reprinted by permission of the Chávez estate.

Córdova, G. Benito. "The Spider & The Pants" from *Big Dreams and Dark Secrets in Chimayó* (Albuquerque: University of New Mexico Press, 2006). Reprinted by permission of the University of New Mexico Press.

Cuesta, Fr. Benedicto. "Santa Fe—Coplas Para El Tiempo Santo," first published in *El Paisano: Nuevo México Vida y Dilema / New Mexico Life and Dilemma* (Santa Fe: Sunstone Press, 1976). Reprinted by permission of author.

Gonzales Thomas, Anita. "Before the War," first published in *Turn Left at the Sleeping Dog: Scripting the Santa Fe Legend,* edited by John Pen La Farge (Albuquerque: University of New Mexico Press, 2001). Reprinted by permission of the University of New Mexico Press.

Himmerich y Valencia, Robert. "What Goes Around Comes Around," first published in *A New Mexico Scrapbook: 23 New Mexicans Remember Growing Up*, compiled and edited by Michael Miller (Huntsville, Ala.: Honeysuckle Imprint, c. 1991). Reprinted by permission of the author.

Jaramillo, Cleofas. "A Night of Horror," first published in 1955 and reprinted in *Romance of A Little Village Girl*, introduction by Tey Diana Rebolledo (Albuquerque: University of New Mexico Press, 2000). Reprinted by permission of the University of New Mexico Press.

Mares, E. A. "Once A Man Knew His Name," first published in *Voces: An Anthology of Nuevo Mexicano Writers*, edited by Rudolfo Anaya (Albuquerque: University of New Mexico Press, 1987). Reprinted by permission of the author.

Mora, Pat. "Ode to Santa Fe," first published in *Adobe Odes* (Tucson: University of Arizona Press, 2006). Reprinted by permission of the University of Arizona Press.

Ortega, Pedro Ribera. "Epilogue: Recapitulación Breve," from *Christmas in Old Santa Fe* (Santa Fe: Sunstone Press, 1973). Reprinted by permission of Sunstone Press.

Romero, Levi. "Juxtaposition," first published in *A Poetry of Remembrance: New and Rejected Works* (Albuquerque: University of New Mexico Press, 2009). Reprinted by permission of the University of New Mexico Press.

Romero, Orlando. "When Cultures Meet," from *Remembering San Gabriel del Yunge Oweenge: Papers From the October 20, 1984, Conference Held at San Juan Pueblo, New Mexico* (Santa Fe: Sunstone Press, 1987). Reprinted by permission of the author.

Romero Cash, Marie. "Sum-Sum-Summertime," from *Tortilla Chronicles: Growing Up in Santa Fe* (Albuquerque: University of New Mexico Press, 2007). Reprinted by permission of the University of New Mexico Press.

Ulibarrí, Sabine. "Mi abuela cobraba interés," from *Xenomorph Magazine* (Xeno Corp.) (Winter 1988). Reprinted by permission of the author.

Vialpando, Robert Lara. "Los duraznos de mi casa," from *Juan and Juanita in the Land of Enchantment* (New York: Vantage Press, 1979). Reprinted by permission of Mrs. Leticia Vialpando (Mrs. Robert L. Vialpando).

Younis, Vincent. "Shine Boys: A Story About Santa Fe," from *Shine Boys: A Story About Santa Fe* (Taos: Blinking Yellow Books, 1995). Reprinted by permission of the Younis family.

Contributors

J. Chris Abeyta is a Chicano poet, writer, musician, actor, and community educator born and raised in Santa Fe. He is a father and grandfather, with his roots in the same adobe house built in the 1850s. Over the years, his work has appeared on local radio, newspapers, and television. Since 1973 his band, Lumbre del Sol, has delighted audiences at dances and concerts all around Santa Fe with a bilingual mix of nativo lyrics, rock, and salsa. His involvement in presenting and teaching these works in the community reflects who he is, de la gente. Chris has received many awards for his cultural and social activism.

Francisco X. Alarcón is a member of the PEN New Mexico Advisory Board, a Chicano poet, and educator. He teaches at the University of California, Davis, and is the author of ten collections of poetry including *No Golden Gate for Us, Snake Poems: An Aztec Invocation, De Amor Oscuro/Of Dark Love,* and *Body in Flames. Laughing Tomatoes and Other Spring Poems/Jitomates risueños y otros poemas de primavera* is a bilingual collection of poems for children. He is the recipient of many literary awards, including the American Book Award 1993, the 1993 PEN Oakland Josephine Miles Award, and the 1984 Chicano Literary Prize.

Jesús María Hilario Alarid (1834–1917) was born in Galisteo, a village in the vicinity of Santa Fe. He became the village teacher at Galisteo and taught reading and writing in the lower grades. He was also an accomplished musician and cultivated the traditional verse forms employed by the *bardo,* or poet-balladeer. Beginning in the late 1880s he became closely identified with several newspapers in and around Santa Fe, submitting his letters, communiqués, and poetry to *El Boletín Popular* (Santa Fe), *El Independiente* (Las Vegas), and the *Santa Fe Gazette.* His writing includes personal descriptions and firsthand accounts of the manners and customs that prevailed in communities in north central New Mexico in the Territorial period.

Tommy Archuleta is a young Santa Fe nativo who graduated from the renowned College of Santa Fe Creative Writing Program. He articulates an expansive vision of culture, history, and place in his poems, which are appearing in a growing number of reviews and anthologies. His work has been accessible to all in the pages of local publications *La Herencia del Norte,* but his poetics addresses all four horizons. Tommy has received awards and recognition for his work and was a participant in the New York State Summer Writers Institute at Skidmore College.

He was a Mimi Bresler Smith and Patricia Robertson Amusa-Shonubi Fellow there.

Jimmy Santiago Baca was born in 1952 in Santa Fe, then abandoned as a small child. He was raised in orphanages, on the streets, and for six years in prison, where he began writing poems. He was encouraged early on by Denise Levertov, who accepted his poems for *Mother Jones* magazine. *Immigrants in Our Own Land* was Baca's first collection. In 1987, his semiautobiographical novel in verse, *Martin and Meditations on the South Valley*, was published by the famed City Lights Books and received the American Book Award. A self-styled "poet of the people," Baca has conducted countless writing workshops with children and adults. Other collections include *C-Train and Thirteen Mexicans: Dream Boy's Story* (Grove Press, 2002), *Healing Earthquakes* (2001), *Set This Book on Fire* (1999), *In the Way of the Sun* (1997), *Black Mesa Poems* (1995), *Poems Taken from My Yard* (1986), and *What's Happening* (1982).

Fray Alonso de Benavides (1578–1635) was born in the Portuguese Azores, ordained a Franciscan friar in 1603, and came to Santa Fe in 1626 to assume the post of custos, or leader, of the New Mexico missions. In three years he established at least ten conventos, or mission centers, before returning to Mexico, then Spain, to advocate for more resources. For this purpose he wrote the famous 1630 *Memorial* to the religious and secular authorities. In a kind of atlas, his colorful and detailed reports describe communities, agriculture, mineral resources, and of course miracles and conversions of thousands of natives. Father Benavides was the first to write of the spiritual journeys of Sor María de Ágreda, the Spanish nun whose bilocations to New Mexico created a sensation. Benavides died at sea in 1635, en route to his assignment in Portuguese Goa.

Bonafé (c. 1860–c. 1920), "Good Faith," is a pseudonym for the anonymous Santa Fe correspondent to the Las Vegas, New Mexico, newspaper *El Independiente*. His candid reports kept readers in Las Vegas informed of comings and goings in the capital some sixty miles to the southwest. Acting as a kind of cultural reporter, Bonafé documented the details of social events, public meet-ings, and the ever-changing political scene. In his writings, Bonafé often expressed his chagrin at the acute Americanization that had taken hold of Santa Fe in the 1890s.

Eusebio Chacón (1870–1948) The scion of an early pioneering family in southern Colorado, Chacón is considered the first Neomexicano novelist. A native of Trinidad, Colorado, Chacón was educated at the Jesuit College of Las Vegas, New Mexico, and received a law degree from Notre Dame University in 1889. As poet, novelist, and essayist, Chacón submitted his works to Spanish-language newspapers in New Mexico and southern Colorado throughout his life. Here we offer New Mexico's own foundational novel *Tras la tormenta, la calma* (*The Calm after the Storm*) set in Santa Fe. Dolores is a beautiful mestiza who is the living allegory for New Mexico and its travails. The novella was published in Santa Fe in 1892 together with a fantastic tale entitled *El hijo de la tempestad* (*Son of the Storm*).

Felipe Maximiliano Chacón (1873–1949) Journalist and poet, Chacón was born in Santa Fe to Urbano Chacón and Lucia Ward. A first cousin to Eusebio Chacón, Felipe was educated at St. Michael's College in the capital and spent his life editing Spanish-language newspapers in Las Vegas, Santa Fe, Bernalillo, and Albuquerque. In 1924, while he was the editor of *La Bandera Americana* in Albuquerque, Felipe published *Obras de Felipe Maximiliano Chacón: Prosa y Poesía* (*Works of Felipe Maximiliano Chacón: Prose and Poetry*), the first and only collection of poetry and prose to have been published by a native New Mexican at that time. Chacón spent the last part of his life in El Paso, Texas. At his death in 1949 he was buried at Mount Calvary Cemetery in Albuquerque.

José Rafael Sotero Chacón (1833–1925) was born in Santa Fe when New Mexico was still under the Mexican flag. At age eleven, he attended military school in Chihuahua. In 1846 he was called back to Santa Fe to defend the capital from the impending invasion of the Army of the West under Gen. Stephen Watts Kearny. Several years later he joined the U.S. Army and fought in the 1855 Ute campaign, after which he became a trader. When the news of the Civil War came, Chacón mustered a company of relatives and friends and reported to Fort Union to become a captain under the command of Kit Carson. He fought many battles, and he and his company helped turn back the Confederate Army in 1862. He wrote the most complete Hispano memoir of the nineteenth century.

Fray Angélico Chávez (1910–96) was born in Wagon Mound, New Mexico, and baptized Manuel Ezequiel. In 1912 his family moved to San Diego, California. The missions he was exposed to there inspired him to follow in the footsteps of fray Junípero Serra. At age fourteen he was admitted to St. Francis Seminary in Mount Healthy, Ohio. In 1971 Chávez left the priesthood following a crisis of faith. He continued to use Fray Angélico Chávez as the nom de plume even after separating himself from the Franciscan Order. He was a consummate humanist, historian, artist, and writer. His acclaimed poetry and short stories are often embedded in historical themes. His genealogical and archival expertise has resolved many historical problems and shed new light on the Spanish colonial period. His best-known books include *La Conquistadora: The Autobiography of an Ancient Statue* and *The Origins of New Mexico Families in the Spanish Colonial Period in Two Parts: The Seventeenth (1598–1693) and Eighteenth (1693–1821) Centuries.*

G. Benito Córdova is an anthropologist, cultural historian, and novelist who was among the first scholars in New Mexico to write about genízaro culture, history, and identity. Genízaros, or detribalized, Hispanicized Indians, comprised a third of the population of New Mexico by 1776. Córdova was born in Abiquiú, a genízaro village, about which he wrote *Abiquiú and Don Cacahuate: a folk history of a New Mexican village* (1973). In 1992 he was a curator of American Encounters, a Smithsonian Columbian Quincentenary exhibition featuring New Mexico that was seen by hundreds of thousands of visitors. Later he wrote *The 3 1/2 Cultures of Española* (1990), a cultural inquisition informed by his work in the public schools. His novel is titled *Big Dreams and Dark Secrets in Chimayó* (2006), a picaresque saga richly populated by figures from folk stories and indigenous mythology.

Benedicto Cuesta (1923–2006) was an educator, journalist, scholar, and priest who lived and served rural parishes in northern New Mexico for more than twenty years. Born in Spain and educated at the Universities of Salamanca and Notre Dame, Father Cuesta lived in Mexico and South America before falling in love with New Mexico in the 1970s. For years he taught Hispanic culture and language courses at New Mexico Highlands University and worked on many cultural projects, including radio programs. He documented many New Mexican folk traditions that he traced back to their Iberian roots. *El Paisano: Nuevo México, Vida y Dilema* (1976) is a compendium of personal reflections, poetry, and sketches of New Mexican traditions and culture.

José "Joselín" Escobar (c. 1870–c. 1910) was a poet and journalist born in Zacatecas and educated in Mexico who fled the dictatorship of Porfirio Díaz and came to the United States around 1891. He spent the decade of the 1890s working with the fledgling newspapers that were springing up in Spanish-speaking communities across the Southwest. Escobar was hired in 1896 by the prominent Colorado politician Casimiro Barela to edit and manage *Las Dos Repúblicas*. We have chosen to reproduce the extant portions of his epic poem "Popé" that chronicles the Pueblo Revolt through the eyes of the commanding figure of the Taos Indian, Popé. Escobar came to be known popularly as *El cantor de Popé* (The Singer of Popé). The last notice of Escobar was as editor of the El Paso newspaper *Las Dos Américas* in the fall of 1898.

Gloria Armenta Gonzales spent her early years on a ranch in northeastern New Mexico, which gave her a unique, almost geological, view of culture and place. At home in Santa Fe, Gonzales writes eloquently about her sense of grief and loss for the cultural and political changes of her beloved city. Through art and story, she works through anger to reconciliation. Her poems on love, family, spirituality, womanhood, and nature have been published in two key anthologies of New Mexico women writers, *Nuestras Mujeres* and *Las Mujeres*

Hablan, and in the journals of *Puerto del Sol* and the Colorado Mile High Poetry Society. Gonzales published collections include *A View from My Porch* and *Another View from My Porch*.

Robert Himmerich y Valencia is a former history professor at the University of New Mexico and a past editor of the *New Mexico Historical Review*. With an MA and PhD in Mexican and Latin American history, his book, *The Encomenderos of New Spain 1521–1555*, charts the rise and decline of the institution of the encomienda. He lives in Santa Fe but commutes to his farm in Peña Blanca, where he grows oats, pinto beans, and blue corn. He retired from the U.S. Marine Corps in 1973 after twenty-three years of service with combat tours in both Korea and Vietnam.

Alberto "Al Hurricane" Sánchez was born Alberto Nelson Sánchez in 1936 in Dixon, New Mexico. He is also known as El Padrino, the Godfather of Nuevomexicano music. His Italian mother nicknamed him Hurricane for knocking everything down in his path but calmed the storm by introducing him to music. By age three he was singing and by five was playing the guitar. At twelve, he performed at the wishing well in Old Town in Albuquerque. Al Hurricane is a legendary guitar stylist and has accompanied such greats as Fats Domino, Marvin Gaye, Chuck Berry, and Chubby Checker all around the world. His love of New Mexico and its music has always brought him home to his fans. Although his specialty is the *canción*, or lyrical song, sung to the big band arrangements that typify the Albuquerque style, Al is also a fine composer of traditional corrido ballads. He wrote "Corrido de la Prisión de Santa Fe" with his brothers Amador "Tiny Morrie" and Gabriel "Baby Gaby" Sánchez. Among his many awards is the New Mexico Governor's Award for music.

Cleofas Jaramillo (1878–1956) is famous for her poignant writing about the Nuevomexicano culture of the past, its decline, and adaptation to American customs and culture. In *Shadows of the Past, Romance of a Little Village Girl* and *The Genuine New Mexico Tasty Recipes*, she remembers and idealizes another New Mexico before the coming of the Anglos. She also writes to teach the newcomers to fully appreciate New Mexico by learning its history and tasting its cuisine. Jaramillo was active in cultural preservation, not only through her writing but also by founding Santa Fe's Sociedad Folklórica. Her relationship with the art colony and writer Mary Austin motivated her mission to interpret her culture for others through the English language. As a young widow, she became a shrewd and independent businesswoman. Her strength was brought to bear with a heartrending and horrific crime. The murder of her young daughter Angelina shocked all of Santa Fe in 1931.

Alfredo Celedón Luján is a norteño, or northern New Mexican, raised in Nambé. A career educator and coach, he has taught generations of students at Monte del Sol Charter School, Pojoaque Valley Schools, Santa Fe Preparatory School, and the Native American Preparatory School. His writing on Nuevomexicano culture has been published in the *New Mexico Humanities Review*, *Puerto Del Sol*, *La Herencia del Norte*, the *Southwest Review*, and numerous professional journals for teachers of writing and English. Luján is also a National Endowment for the Humanities Fellow.

E. A. Mares is a Nuevomexicano poet, essayist, playwright, translator, and historian who is one of the founding members of La Academia de la Nueva Raza, New Mexico's first Chicano think tank. He is a University of New Mexico professor emeritus of English and creative writing. His writing includes many firsts— the very first critical treatment of the myth of Aztlán, *coyotismo* and cultural hybridity, and the role of the picaro in the cultural history of New Mexico. Perhaps his greatest contribution is the restoration of Padre Antonio José Martínez of Taos. Through historical research and Chautauqua presentations, Mares reinstated the padre as one of the cultural heroes of New Mexico. Mares's poems are widely anthologized in journals and anthologies. Books include *Unicorn Poem*, *The Unicorn Poem & Flowers and Songs of Sorrow*, and *There are Four Wounds, Miguel*.

Demetria Martínez is an acclaimed poet, journalist, and novelist who earned fame and admiration during the notorious conspiracy trials of the 1980s waged against the sanctuary movement and environmental activists. She won the Western States Book Award for her first novel, *Mother Tongue* (1994). The background of the story is based on her work as an investigative journalist writing articles for the *National Catholic Reporter* on the refugees displaced from Central America by Ronald Reagan's wars. In 1997 she was charged with conspiring against the U.S. government and aiding the entry of Salvadorans into the country. Verses from her own poetry were used against her in the prosecution. She was acquitted in 1988. Martínez's poetry is widely published and anthologized. Her books include *Confessions of a Berlitz Tape Chicana*, *The Devil's Workshop*, and *Breathing Between the Lines*.

Valerie Martínez is the first Santafeña to be declared poet laureate of her native Santa Fe (2008–10). A graduate of Vassar and the University of Arizona, her poetry, essays, and translations are widely published and anthologized. Her prize-winning collections of poems include *Absence, Luminescent* (1999), *World to World* (2004), and *A Flock of Scarlet Doves* (2005). Her theater piece, "Heart of the Goddess," is set in a sixteenth-century Aztec village and contemporary America and has been staged in several venues. She is also a member of the of the community based Littleglobe Inc., whose *Memorylines Santa Fe: Voces de Nuestros Jornadas* is a new opera commissioned by the Santa Fe Opera and the Lensic Theater. She has taught creative writing at the University of Arizona, Ursinus College, New Mexico Highlands University, University of New Mexico, in the rural schools of Swaziland, and the College of Santa Fe.

Pat Mora is a widely published and anthologized poet who has won many awards for her many volumes. She has the Kellogg National Leadership Fellowship Award, the National Endowment for the Arts Award, the Southwest Book Award, and the Aztlán Literature Award. Mora was born in El Paso, Texas, but currently resides in Santa Fe, New Mexico. She writes on many topics, including poetry, children's books, and non-fiction writing. Some of her books include *Confetti: Poems for Children*, *Aunt Carmen's Book of Practical Saints*, and *Agua Santa*.

Pedro Ribera Ortega (1931–2003) was a devoted cultural activist and the editor of *El Nuevo Mexicano*, the last of the local Spanish-language newspapers in Santa Fe, which stopped publication in 1958. Rivera Ortega, inspired by Fray Angélico Chávez's historical documentation of the Madonna in Santa Fe's Cathedral, was an enthusiastic supporter of Chávéz's proposal to revive the statute's honor guard, La Cofradía de la Conquistadora, in 1956 and was a lifelong member. Rivera Ortega contributed a number of columns to the local press on Santa Fe customs and traditions, publishing *Christmas in Old Santa Fe* (1973) and *La Conquistadora: America's Oldest Madonna* (1975). He was also a founding member of Los Caballeros de Vargas, a group that organizes fiesta events and the annual re-creation of don Diego de Vargas's entry into Santa Fe in 1692 following the Pueblo Revolt.

Carmella Padilla is a renowned freelance writer and cultural journalist who has written extensively and incisively about the dynamics of Hispano art and culture in northern New Mexico. Her publications are national in scope and include the *Wall Street Journal*, the *Dallas Morning News*, and *Latina*, *Hispanic*, *Vista*, *Travel Holiday*, *El Palacio*, and *New Mexico* magazines. With an extensive and inside knowledge of santero and religious art, she edited the *Spanish Market Magazine* from 1992 to 1999 and was a coauthor of *Spanish New Mexico: The Spanish Colonial Arts Society Collection* (1996). Padilla's first book, *The Chile Chronicles: Tales of a New Mexico Harvest* (1998), was awarded the Historical Society of New Mexico's Ralph Emerson Twitchell Award for a significant contribution to the field of history. Her interests also extend to popular culture, as evident in *Low 'n' Slow: Lowriding in New Mexico* (2003), a definitive treatment of a colorful subject. Awards and honors follow her everywhere she goes.

Lydia Armenta Rivera is a proud native Santafeña born in 1938 on Canyon Road. Since she was raised in close proximity to both grandmother and great-grandmother, her privileged view and memories of traditional Santa Fe are very rich. Her *bisabuela* was a beloved curandera and nurse practitioner who also wrote poetry, and she is working on a biography of her. Lydia was a nun for four years, married and raised a family, and enjoyed a career as a teacher of French and theater, and as a school counselor. She was a regular contributor to *La Herencia del Norte* in its first five critical years, and enlivened its pages with her memories of *nuestra villa*.

Leo Romero has been writing poetry, stories, and tending books and blue bottles for many years in Santa Fe. Born in the mountain village of Chacón, he grew up in Las Vegas. He is best known for his fanciful portrayal of village characters in northern New Mexico, which critics and reviewers have linked to the contemporary Latin American currents of magic realism. Central in his cast of characters is Celso, a classic picaro, or philosopher-rogue figure, with roots that stretch from the mountains of New Mexico into sixteenth-century Spain. His poetry appears in many journals and anthologies. Among his books of poetry are *Agua Negra, Celso, During the Growing Season*, and *Going Home Indian*. *Rita and Los Angeles* is his short-story collection.

Levi Romero is from the Embudo Valley of northern New Mexico, a bilingual poet whose language is immersed in the regional *manito* dialect of that region with its seventeenth-century archaisms and melodic registers. His work has been published throughout the United States, Mexico, and Spain. Romero has presented in such diverse venues as City Lights in San Francisco, the Smithsonian, and the ladies lingerie section at the Wal-Mart in Taos. His writing is a narrative tapestry of formal poetics woven through a palette of Nuevomexicano colloquialisms, sensorial perceptions, and the poetic richness of vernacular language. His poem, "A de dónde yo soy," was published by Scholastic as part of nationwide educational project. He recently taught creative writing at the University of New Mexico and is currently a research scholar at its School of Architecture and Regional Planning. Romero is a member of the Macondo Writers Workshop. Books of his poetry include *A Poetry of Remembrance: New and Rejected Works* and *In the Gathering Silence*.

Orlando Romero created a sensation in the early days of the boom of Chicano literature with his novel, *Nambé Year One* (1976). With a longtime career as director of the History Library in the Palace of the Governors, and years of facilitating the research of others, he has been a constant player in the cultural process and politics of Santa Fe. His venues for cultural journalism have included the weekly *Santa Fe Reporter* and many other journals. Besides the novel, his most substantial book project has been the massive *Adobe: Building and Living with Earth*, in collaboration with David Larkin. His family history goes back to 1598. He lives in Nambé.

Marie Romero Cash is a celebrated Santa Fe artist and *santera* renowned for her carvings and paintings of the saints in the eighteenth- and nineteenth-century New Mexico style. Her religious art can be found in numerous churches in both the United States and Mexico. She has written *Living Shrines: Devotional Spaces in Northern New Mexico Homes* and *Santos: Enduring Images of Northern New Mexican Village Churches*. Her poignant memoir, *The Tortilla Chronicles: Growing Up in Santa Fe*, documents life in 1950s Santa Fe and provides a fascinating glimpse into the daily life of a Nuevomexicano family. Her parents helped revive the artisan trade of tinsmithing and inspired her to become an artist. Her writing is an antidote to the tourist narratives that saturate the City Different with romantic exoticism and American exceptionalism, Southwest style.

Enrique H. Salazar (1858–1915) A journalist and essayist, Salazar established *La Voz del Pueblo* in Santa Fe in 1889. After moving to Las Vegas, Salazar sold *La Voz* in 1890 but continued in newspaper work with *El Independiente*, a newspaper he founded in 1894 and that he published until 1910. A graduate of St. Michael's College, Salazar learned the printing trade from W. H. Manderfield at the offices of the *Santa Fe New Mexican*. Throughout his career in journalism, Salazar opened every installment of his newspapers with masterful editorial essays that covered a wide range of topics of interest to Spanish-speaking New Mexicans. Salazar wrote on questions of history, education, labor, literacy, maintenance of language and culture, land grants, and other subjects. In the piece we reproduce here, "New Mexico in 1950," Salazar, writing in 1908 when New Mexico was still a territory, plays the role of futurist and social prognosticator to present his predictions, albeit tongue in cheek, of what the future might bring for New Mexico's natives and their capital, Santa Fe.

Anita Gonzales Thomas (1908–99) had deep roots in Santa Fe as a member of the Delgado, Gonzales, and Baca clans. Her mother Elizabeth was Gov. Clyde Tingley's secretary of state in the 1930s and gave her daughter a strong sense of community and cultural pride. A seasoned authority on local history and Nuevomexicano folk traditions, she collaborated with researchers and activists on numerous cultural, museum, and community projects. She was a member of Santa Fe's Sociedad Folklórica and active on many boards and advisory groups. Although she rarely published any of her own writing, many have written about her.

Sabine Ulibarrí (1919–2003) Uli, as his friends and students called him, was a poet, teacher, writer, critic, and statesman born in Tierra Amarilla, the northern village he immortalized in his bilingual stories. Ulibarrí served in World War II with the U.S. Army Air Corps and was decorated with the Distinguished Flying Cross and the Air Medal. He received his doctorate in Spanish literature from UCLA and taught for years at the University of New Mexico. Ulibarrí is renowned for his clever use of language in crafting his stories and for exploring the poetics of rural New Mexican Spanish. His stories are considered some of the earliest roots of modern Chicano literature. His books, *Mi Abuela Fumaba Puros (My Grandmother Smoked Cigars)* (1977) and *Tierra Amarilla* (1971), are considered as quintessential examples, classics in their own day, which have inspired countless young writers and educators.

Roberto Lara Vialpando (1907–96) was a well-known educator and professor of modern languages and literature and coauthor, with José T. López, and Edgardo Núñez, of one of the very first literary histories of New Mexican literature. He was also an activist intensely involved with the cultural life of his community of Alcalde, New Mexico. He was instrumental in recovering texts, choreography, and performance traditions of folk and ritual dramas such as Los Comanches and the matachines dance drama performed in Alcalde to this day. In the 1920s and 1930s, he earned his BA from Indiana Central University; an MA from the University of Utah; and a PhD from the Universidad Interamericana, Saltillo, Mexico. After serving with the U.S. Army Medical Corps during World War II, he went back to school. In addition to his college classes, he taught elementary and high school classes; served as a high school principal for many years; and was former director of the Spanish Department for the Santa Fe schools.

Vincent Younis was born in Santa Fe in 1951, a member of a renowned four-generation family of artisan tinsmiths, or *hojalateros*. A wanderer at heart, he dropped out of school at age seventeen and explored the United States for many years before returning to the west side of Santa Fe. He is a writer, visual artist, woodworker, and musician. *His Shine Boys: A Story About Santa Fe* (1995) is a rough and richly textured street-level memoir about a Hispano childhood in Santa Fe. Cultural and class relations are painfully clear in the eyes of a child.

About the Editors and Photographer

Rosalie C. Otero was born and raised in Taos and served a brief stint as a most beautiful Fiesta Queen! To a Taoseña, Santa Fe has always been a rival city in many respects. In comparison to any of New Mexico's other cities, however, our beloved capital is more sophisticated, wealthier, more flamboyant, and the central hub of political and social activity. Santa Fe was where Taoseños went for special events, many, like the city's fiestas, that blended the historical and the modern. It was also the place to see the latest movies and scrutinize the most modern styles. A student of Rudolfo Anaya, Otero has published short fiction that addresses these contradictory and sometimes hilarious issues in reviews and anthologies. She has also published critical essays on ethnicity, conflict, and art. At the University of New Mexico, she directs one of the pioneer university honors programs in the nation. She has written many articles on the philosophy and practice of university honors and has enabled hundreds of her students to realize their *sueños*.

A. Gabriel Meléndez is a teacher, researcher, and cultural historian. For him Santa Fe has been the intersection of countless dreams and evocations. "It is a place," says Meléndez, "where I lived many previous lives. In one of these, I was a brujo with the power to fly across the mesas and over the Sangre de Cristos. I spent my time playing monte in Santa Fe saloons and visiting with an *amante* in Chacón. In another, I was a church mouse, *siempre por los rincones*." Meléndez has published fiction and poetry in various anthologies and collections. His first book *So All is Not Lost: The Poetics of Print in Nuevomexicano Communities* (1997) was reissued by the University of Arizona Press in 2005 as *Spanish-language Newspapers in New Mexico*. It documents the history of the Spanish-language press and its role in fostering literacy and creativity in communities across the Southwest. Meléndez is professor of American studies at the University of New Mexico.

Enrique R. Lamadrid spent his early years at the "teacherage" behind Allison James School where his parents taught, the last row of houses on the northern edge of Santa Fe in the early 1950s. The advantage (or disadvantage) of that location was that he could see and hear Zozobra burning from his bedroom. Needless to say, he spent his first few Santa Fe Fiestas under the bed. Professor of Spanish, now chair of the Spanish and Portuguese Department, and former director of Chicano Hispano Mexicano studies at the University of New Mexico, Lamadrid is a literary folklorist known for his documentation of festival and musical traditions and his writing on the cultural history of New Mexico. His collaborations with photographer Miguel A. Gandert include *Pilgrimage to Chimayó, Nuevo México Profundo: Rituals of an Indo-Hispano Homeland*, and *Hermanitos Comanchitos: Indo-Hispano Ritual of Captivity and Redemption*, honored by the American Folklore Society with the Chicago Prize for ethnographic writing. He is also a recipient of the Américo Paredes Prize from the American Folklore Society for his cultural activism and work with festivals and museums.

Miguel A. Gandert was born in Española, New Mexico, and raised in Santa Fe, where he first picked up a camera to work on his junior high school yearbook. After studying photography at the University of New Mexico, Gandert emerged as one of the premier documentary photographers of greater Mexico. He learned how to dance with his camera in the many traditional feast days he has visited. His vision of cultural process and traditional ritual has changed the way people think about mestizaje and the complexities of cultural identity. Gandert's national and international exhibitions include venues such as the Whitney Museum of American Art, the Smithsonian, the Museum of Fine Arts in Santa Fe, and the Museo Nacional de Arte in Bolivia. The Beinecke Rare Book and Manuscript Collection at Yale archives his work. His award-winning exhibit and book, *Nuevo México Profundo: Rituals of an Indo-Hispano Homeland* (2000), was featured at the inaugural exhibit of the National Hispanic Culture Center in Albuquerque.